P9-DCZ-898

GO TO: Page 281 for Usage Glossary
Page 299 for Terms Glossary
Page 323 for Index
Page 354 for Online Research Basics

Quick Access Boxes

FOR DAVID,
WHO MAKES IT ALL GREAT FUN

SIMON & SCHUSTER

Reference for Writers
Second Edition

Lynn Quitman Troyka

Prentice Hall
Upper Saddle River,
New Jersey 07458

Library of Congress Cataloging-in-Publication Data

Troyka, Lynn Quitman
    Simon & Schuster quick access reference for writers / Lynn Quitman
Troyka.—2nd ed.
        p.   cm.
    Includes index.
    ISBN 0-13-096596-0
    1. English language—Rhetoric—Handbooks, manuals, etc.
    2. English language—Grammar—Handbooks, manuals, etc.   3. Report
writing—Handbooks, manuals, etc.   I. Simon and Schuster, Inc.
    II. Title.
    PE1408.T6964   1997
    808'.042—dc21   97-14280
                                                                         CIP

Editorial Director: Charlyce Jones Owen
Development Editor: Joyce Perkins
Director of Production and Manufacturing: Barbara Kittle
Senior Managing Editor: Bonnie Biller
Senior Production Editor: Shelly Kupperman
Manufacturing Manager: Nick Sklitsis
Prepress and Manufacturing Buyer: Mary Ann Gloriande
Creative Design Director: Leslie Osher
Art Director / Interior Design: Carole Anson
Supervisor of Production Services: Lori Clinton
Handwriting Art: Mirella Signoretto
Cover and Tab Design: Ximena P. Tamvakopoulos
Marketing Director: Gina Sluss
Marketing Manager: Rob Mejia

This book was set in 10/12 Palatino by Prentice Hall Production Services and printed and bound by Banta, Inc. The cover was printed by Banta, Inc.

Page 21: Excerpt from "Safe Lifting Techniques" by John Warde, *The New York Times*, March 11, 1990. Copyright © 1990 by The New York Times Co. Reprinted by permission.

Page 36: Excerpt from "Sports Only Exercise Our Eyes" from *The Best of Sydney J. Harris.* Copyright © 1975 by Sydney J. Harris. Reprinted by permission of Houghton Mifflin Company. All rights reserved.

Page 117: Dictionary entry for *contrary* reprinted with permission of Macmillan Reference USA, a Simon & Schuster Macmillan Company, from *Webster's New World College Dictionary*, Third Edition Copyright © 1997 by Simon & Schuster Inc.

© 1998, 1995 by Lynn Quitman Troyka
Published by Prentice-Hall, Inc.
Simon & Schuster/A Viacom Company
Upper Saddle River, NJ 07458

Printed in the United States of America

10   9   8   7   6   5   4

ISBN 0-13-096596-0

Prentice-Hall International (UK) Limited, *London*
Prentice-Hall of Australia Pty. Limited, *Sydney*
Prentice-Hall Canada Inc., *Toronto*
Prentice-Hall Hispanoamericana, S.A., *Mexico*
Prentice-Hall of India Private Limited, *New Delhi*
Prentice-Hall of Japan, Inc., *Tokyo*
Simon & Schuster Asian Pte. Ltd., *Singapore*
Editora Prentice-Hall do Brasil, Ltda., *Rio de Janeiro*

Contents

H HOW TO USE YOUR QUICK ACCESS

W WRITING PROCESS

T THINKING AND READING CRITICALLY

G GRAMMAR BASICS

C CORRECT SENTENCES

E EFFECTIVE SENTENCES AND WORDS

P PUNCTUATION

R RESEARCH WRITING

M MLA DOCUMENTATION

A APA, CM, CBE DOCUMENTATION

⊢ FOCUS ON ESL

Preface

Welcome to the second edition of the *Simon & Schuster Quick Access Reference for Writers*. It has a jaunty nickname, the result of the first edition's becoming so popular and widely used. The nickname is *Quick Access*. (Some people have even shortened it to two letters: *QA*). This nickname pleases me greatly because the words *quick access* precisely capture my intent as I was writing the book for you.

My goal is to help you as a writer find information you need fast and easily. Each element in *Quick Access* works toward that goal. Also, I hope you hear in this book, as in my comprehensive *Simon & Schuster Handbook for Writers,* a supportive voice that expresses how strongly I respect and admire students. *Quick Access* gives you answers for questions about writing that students ask most often.

Here's a preview of *Quick Access*

Quick Access to Contents

Open the front cover for the Divider Directory, a listing of the book's twelve parts. • *New for this edition:* You can see the entire Divider Directory immediately upon opening the front cover. This makes it easy to glance over the contents of all twelve major parts of your book. • Also, when you open the back fold-out cover, the Capsule Contents displays the book's contents in greater detail so you can scan it by looking over one large sheet. The standard table of contents begins on page vii.

Quick Access to Each Major Part

Quick Access's twelve dividers correspond to its twelve major parts. • *New for this edition:* Four new parts give easier access to ESL issues and add much more about basic grammar; an entirely new part on reading, thinking, and synthesizing; and an entirely new part on how to use *Quick Access* successfully. Also, to help you find your way quickly, a letter tied to each part's content identifies the part (for example, W for Writing Process, G for Grammar Basics) and is very visible on the dividers—front, back, and tab. •

Quick Access to Every Chapter and Its Sections

Each part's chapters and sections are listed on the back of that part's divider, so that you can locate what you want instantly. • *New for this edition:* The letter identifying a part combines with a number to identify each chapter in that part. For example, **C** Correct Sentences has as its first chapter C1 Sentence Fragments, and its second chapter is C2 Comma Splices and Fused Sentences. Each section in a chapter has an identifying letter-number-letter code. For example, the first section in C1 is C1.a, and the second section is C1.b. For more about using codes for quick access to information, see **H** How to Use Your Quick Access. •

Quick Access to Every Page

The spiral binding allows *Quick Access* to open flat, fold over flat, and stay open at any page. • *New for this edition:* Each divider tab lists inclusive page numbers for that part, so that locating information by page numbers is now as easy as locating information by codes. •

Quick Access to Every Element on Each Page

• *New for this edition:* At the upper outside corner of each page, a "data cluster" contains all location information. In the blue block, you can find the codes for the sections on each page. Beside the blue block, you can find titles—on left pages the letter and title of the part, and on right pages the letter-number and title of the chapter. Under the titles, you can find the page number. • In the "access area" at the edge of each page, you can find the code for each section starting on the page; blue flags with the numbers of QA Boxes; and large exclamation points to alert you to Alerts—special reminders so that you do not forget smaller, related details in context.

Quick Access to QA Boxes

QA Boxes summarize and distill important information, giving quick answers and clear models. A list of all 64 QA Boxes appears on the first two pages after the Divider Directory.

Quick Access to Learning About *Quick Access*

• *New for this edition:* The book's first part, **H** How to Use Your *Quick Access*, explains how to use this book, with 10 pages to familiarize you with strategies for finding information. To cement your learning, exercises, and activities give you valuable practice. •

Quick Access to MLA, APA, CM, and CBE Documentation

Thorough coverage of four major styles of documentation includes MLA, APA, CM, and CBE styles. At divider **M** MLA Documentation, *Quick Access* has 24 in-text citations and 71 Works Cited models. At divider **A** APA, CM, CBE Documentation, Quick Access has 18 in-text citations and 54 References models in APA style; 54 bibliographic note models for Chicago Manual (CM) style; and 27 References models for Council of Biology Editors (CBE) style. Detailed instructions for laying out the information needed to tell your reader about your sources appear in QA Boxes, one for each of the four documentation styles.

Quick Access to ESL Information
• *New for this edition:* ESL information is easy to find because it now has its own divider. • **F** Focus on ESL is based on the highly praised ESL chapters in the fourth edition of my *Simon & Schuster Handbook for Writers*.

Quick Access to Help with Usage Rules and with Grammatical Terms
The extensive Usage Glossary lists words and terms to use and to avoid, with many examples of preferred usage. The Terms Glossary provides definitions of all terms shown in small capital letters—for example, GERUND—throughout *Quick Access*.

I hope that while you are using this book you will realize that you, the student, were in my mind's eye as I wrote and revised. The controlling conviction behind *Quick Access* is that knowledge empowers students, for it frees us all to enjoy the pleasures of language and to fulfill, with energy and joy, our potentials as writers.

Acknowledgments
I am deeply grateful to students, colleagues, friends, and family who give generously of their suggestions and warmth. Each person shares in my writing by transforming my intensely personal activity into occasions of interaction.

All students and colleagues whom I have had the pleasure of acknowledging in three editions of the *Simon & Schuster Handbook for Writers* influenced me very directly as I made the choices necessary for this briefer *Simon & Schuster Quick Access Reference for Writers*. In addition, I heartily thank the members of the *Southeast Regional Editorial Advisory Board for Prentice Hall and Lynn Troyka:* Peggy Jolly, University of Alabama, Birmingham; Steve Prewitt, David Lipscomb University; Maryanne Reis, Elizabethtown Community College; Mike Thro, Tidewater Community College, Virginia Beach; and Sally Young, University of Tennessee, Chattanooga. Similarly, I am grateful to the members of the Southwest Regional Editorial Advisory Board for Prentice Hall and Lynn Troyka: Jon Bentley, Technical–Vocational Institute; Kathryn Fitzgerald, University of Utah, Salt Lake City; Maggie Smith, University of Texas, El Paso; Martha Smith, Brookhaven College; and Donnie Yeilding, Central Texas College.

Others who influenced my thinking about what to include in a brief book and how to make the information optimally accessible include Alan Baxter, Technical Careers Institute, New York City; Tommy J. Boley, University of Texas, El Paso; Ann Boyle, Wake Forest University; Richard Burt, Oakland Community College; Philip

Cooksey, Rose State College; Thomas K. Dean, Cardinal Stritch College; Betty Dietz, De Anza College; Robert M. Esch, University of Texas, El Paso; Martha French, Fairmont State College; Judith E. Funston, State University of New York, College at Potsdam; Raymond C. Hayes, Wingate College; Will Hochman, University of Southern Colorado, Pueblo; Julia Innis, Ohio University; B. W. Keene, University of Tennessee, Martin; Barbara McClure, Santa Rosa Junior College; Eileen Moeller, Syracuse University; Cheryl Mott, Delgado Community College; David Mulry, New Mexico Highlands University; Elizabeth Mahn Nollen, West Chester University; Beverly Wilson Palmer, Pomona College; Margaret M. Panos, University of Massachusetts, Dartmouth; J. Michael Pilz, Bucks County Community College; Maureen Potts, University of Texas, El Paso; Paul W. Ranieri, Ball State University; Laura Renick-Butera, DeVry Technical Institute, Woodbridge; Paul W. Rogalus, Plymouth State College; Donna Selby, Towson State University; Beverly J. Slaughter, Brevard Community College; Alison Smith, University of Illinois, Urbana-Champaign; Neal Snidow, Butte College; J. Maurice Thomas, Wingate College; Linda Warwick, Portland Community College; James D. Williams, University of North Carolina, Chapel Hill; and Carole Yee, New Mexico Institute of Mining and Technology.

At Prentice Hall/Simon & Schuster, many people helped me to fulfill my vision for *Quick Access*. Above all, Joyce F. Perkins, who served as development editor for my *Simon & Schuster Handbook for Writers*, first, third, and fourth editions, is central to *Quick Access* because she immersed herself in every page with detailed, astute attention. Joyce Perkins brings to her project far more than her years of developing college English texts; as all authors who have worked with her know, she brings an incredibly keen eye for what's essential in delivering useful information, in writing with clarity and grace, and in nurturing the creativity of a writer. Gina Sluss, Director of Marketing for Humanities and Social Sciences, and Rob Mejia, Marketing Manager for English, served informally but crucially as part of the editorial team.

When the focus switched to book production, Shelly Kupperman, Senior Production Editor, Bonnie Biller, Senior Managing Editor, and Lori Clinton, Supervisor of Production Services, brought their intensity, perfectionism, and bracing skill to each aspect of the project. Leslie Osher, Creative Design Director, and especially Carole Anson, Art Director, are responsible for the best design yet. Ximena Tamvakopoulos, artist and designer, created the charming designs for covers and dividers. Also in important roles were Phil Miller, President, Humanities and Social Sciences, and Barbara Kittle, Director of Production and Manufacturing.

My family and friends nourish my spirit and enrich my days. Ida Morea, my Administrative Assistant and friend, daily enhances my work with her lovely warmth, conscientiousness, and excellence. With love, I salute Susan Bartlestone; Kristen Black, along with Dan, Lindsey, and Ryan Black; Rita and Hy Cohen; Alan, Lynne, Adam, and Joshua Furman; Elaine Gilden Dushoff; Elliott Goldhush; Warren Herendeen; Edith Klausner, my sister; Myra Kogen; Jo Ann Lavery; Lisa Lavery; Ida Morea, Jerrold Nudelman; my mother, Belle F. Quitman and the late Sidney L. Quitman, my father; Betty Renshaw; Magdalena Rogalskaja; Shirley and Don Stearns; Marilyn and Ernest Sternglass; Muriel Wolfe; and Gideon and Tzila Zwas. Most of all, my husband and sweetheart, David Troyka, blesses my life with his strength, good sense, laughter, and love.

Lynn Quitman Troyka
New York, 1998

About the Author

Lynn Quitman Troyka earned her Ph.D. at New York University and taught for many years at the City University of New York (CUNY), including Queensborough Community College, the Center for Advanced Studies in Education at the Graduate School, and in the graduate program in Language and Literacy at City College. She served also as Senior Research Associate in the Instructional Resource Center, CUNY.

Dr. Troyka is an author in composition/rhetoric for the *Encyclopedia of English Studies and Language Arts*, Scholastic, 1993, and in basic writing for the *Encyclopedia of Rhetoric*, 1994. Former editor of the Journal of Basic Writing (1985–88), she has published in journals such as *College Composition and Communication*, *College English*, and *Writing Program Administration* and in books from Southern Illinois Press, Random House, the National Council of Teachers of English (NCTE), and Heineman/Boynton/Cook. She has lectured at hundreds of colleges and universities and at national and international meetings.

Dr. Troyka is the author of the *Simon & Schuster Handbook for Writers*, Fourth Edition, Prentice Hall, 1996; the *Simon & Schuster Concise Handbook*, Prentice Hall, 1992; and *Structured Reading*, Fourth Edition, Prentice Hall, 1995. She is co-author (with Richard Lloyd-Jones, John Gerber, et al.) of *A Checklist and Guide for Reviewing Departments of English*, Modern Language Association (MLA); and of *Steps in Composition*, Sixth Edition (with Jerrold Nudelman), Prentice Hall, 1994.

Dr. Troyka currently serves as Chair of the Two-Year College Association (TYCA) of the NCTE. She is a past chair of the Conference on College Composition (CCCC), of the College Section of NCTE, and of the Writing Division of MLA. She was named Rhetorician of the Year in 1993, was given the Nell Ann Pickett Award for Service in 1995 by CCCC and TYCA, and chaired the 1995--96 Task Force on the Future of CCCC.

"All this information," says Dr. Troyka, "tells what I've done, not who I am. I am a teacher. Teaching is my life's work, and I love it."

How to Use Your *Quick Access*

Usage
Glossary

H1

! Alert

Terms Glossary

Index

!

QA BOX

tutorial

H HOW TO USE YOUR *QUICK ACCESS*

H1 What's in This Book

I wrote this book, *Quick Access*, to help you with writing: writing essays and research papers for your college courses, writing essay exams, writing anything you expect others to read.

The words *Quick Access* precisely capture my intent as I was writing the book for you. I want you as a writer to find whatever information you need fast and easily. I know you can use the book successfully because I have built into it so many ways for you to find information.

To help you become familiar with the way *Quick Access* works, I explain and illustrate here the major features that make your book easy to use. At the end of this part you will find questions and answers to get you moving around in *Quick Access*, looking for the kinds of information you likely will need in your own writing.

Using dividers to help you get information   H1.a

Quick Access has 12 dividers to separate major parts. The dividers tell you where to look for information. A part's page numbers are given on the tab of its divider. The descriptions below can help you get to the right divider.

- **H   How to Use Your *Quick Access*** (first divider) You are here now. Look here for answers to your questions about how to find information in your handbook and for guided practice in using the book.

- **W   Writing Process** (second divider) Look here for answers to your questions about writing essays and essay exams successfully.

- **T   Thinking and Reading Critically** (third divider) Look here for answers to your questions about effective processes for reading and thinking.

- **G   Grammar Basics** (fourth divider) Look here for answers to your questions about English grammar (parts of speech, especially verbs and pronouns, and sentence structures).

- **C   Correct Sentences** (fifth divider) Look here for answers to your questions about sentence errors (sentence fragments, comma splices, and much more).

- **E   Effective Sentences and Words** (sixth divider) Look here for answers to your questions about ways to develop your own writing style.

- **P** **Punctuation** (seventh divider) Look here for answers to your questions about using punctuation.
- **S** **Spelling and Mechanics** (eighth divider) Look here for answers to your questions about spelling and about the use of hyphens, capital letters, italics (underlining), abbreviations, and words or figures for numbers.
- **R** **Research Writing** (ninth divider) Look here for answers to your questions about library research and other kinds of research, about using source material, about writing and revising a research paper, and about avoiding plagiarism.
- **M** **MLA Documentation** (tenth divider) Look here for answers to your questions about documenting sources in Modern Language Association (MLA) style. Also, you can find out how to mention sources in the body of your paper as well as how to list your sources at the end of your paper. You can also find out how to format your paper in MLA style.
- **A** **APA, CM, CBE Documentation** (eleventh divider) Look here for answers to your questions about documenting sources in American Psychological Association (APA) style, Chicago Manual (CM) style, or Council of Biology Editors (CBE) style. You can also find out how to format your paper in APA style.
- **F** **Focus on ESL** (twelfth divider) Look here for answers to questions of special interest to you if your first language is not English.

H1.b Using lists to help you get information

- **Book's Contents on Divider Directory** On the inside front cover and the first page of the book, the Divider Directory lists each part and the chapters in that part. Read down each column to see the parts covered by each divider. For example, at the top of the farthest left column on the inside front cover, you can see **H** How to Use Your Quick Access and its chapters; **W** Writing Process and its chapters in the middle; **T** Thinking and Reading Critically and its chapters at the bottom.
- **Contents on the Back of Each Divider** The detailed contents of the part are listed on the back of its divider.
- **Capsule Contents** Inside the back cover, including the fold-out, is the Capsule Contents, which shows the book's complete contents with shortened titles that you can scan very quickly.
- **Index** The Index contains an alphabetical list of all the subjects in *Quick Access*. Use it to find the subject that you

want information about and the numbers of the pages where it is discussed. The Index begins on page 323.

- **QA Box List**   On the two pages immediately following the Divider Directory is the QA Box list of all QA Boxes in alphabetical order, with QA Box numbers and page numbers. QA Boxes give you especially important information or summaries of longer topics.

- **Response Symbols**   On the outside of the back cover foldout, a list of Response Symbols contains abbreviations your instructor may write on your papers. The Response Symbols list explains each abbreviation and refers you to a section where you can find a detailed discussion of the topic.

- **Table of Contents**   In the first few pages of *Quick Access* is a table of contents typically found in all books. It is the most detailed listing of *Quick Access*'s contents.

- **Terms Glossary**   The Terms Glossary contains an alphabetical list of words related to English grammar and to writing. When a word in this book is printed in small capital letters (for example, VERB or APPOSITIVE), you can find its definition in the Terms Glossary. It begins on page 299.

- **Usage Glossary**   The Usage Glossary contains an alphabetical list of commonly confused words, homonyms (such as *their, there, they're*), and words and phrases that can cause usage problems. It begins on page 281.

Using codes to find information   H1.c

In the diagram on page xxxv, you can see examples of the codes described here.

- **Codes with Letters and Numbers**   H, W, T, G, C, E, P, S, R, M, A, F are each a code for one part and one divider, as explained in **H1.a**. When one of these letters is followed by a number (for example, G1 or M3 or F6), the combination is a code for one chapter in a part. A letter-number-letter combination (for example G1.c or M3.b or F6.a) is a code for a main section within a chapter. When you find the topic you're looking for in any of the lists described in **H1.b**, use its code or its page number to get to the place you want.

- **Data Cluster**   In the upper outside corner of each page is a cluster of data to help you locate information. Letter-number codes are in white in the blue box. Sometimes in this box, an arrow pointing left appears in front of a code. The arrow means that the section begins on an earlier page. Next to the blue box is an identifying title, in blue type, on the top line. Below this title, the page number is given in black type.

■ **Access Area** Down the outer edge of each page, outside the vertical row of dots, more codes help you locate information: section numbers (for example, G1.c or M3.b or F6.a); QA Box numbers—white in blue flags; exclamation points signaling Alerts—pointers about matters of style, usage, grammar, punctuation, mechanics, and related issues.

H1.d Using special features to help you understand

In the diagram on the opposite page, you can see examples of the special features described here.

■ **Examples** Use examples to see typical writing problems and effective solutions. Some examples show simple editing changes in handwriting. Other examples use No/Yes versions to show more complex problems and solutions.

■ **Bracketed Explanations Following Examples** Use the bracketed explanations that accompany most examples for more information about the problem and the choice of a particular solution.

■ **Cross-References** Use cross-references to find additional information related to the topic.

■ **Defined Terms** Use the Terms Glossary toward the back of *Quick Access* to find the definition of any term printed in small capital letters (for example, NONRESTRICTIVE CLAUSE).

H1.e Understanding editing and proofreading marks

When you look at examples with editing changes, you may see some unfamiliar marks. Here is a list of editing and proofreading marks, some of which occur in the examples in *Quick Access*. You can also use these marks when you are editing and proofreading your own papers.

Mark	Function	Example
℮	delete	take this ~~this~~ out
⌗	begin a new paragraph	This is the end. ⌗ This is a new beginning.
∿	transpose letters	transpoes/letters
∿	transpose words	words/transpose
∧	insert	caret A signals an addition
#	add space	addspace
◡	close up space	clo se up space

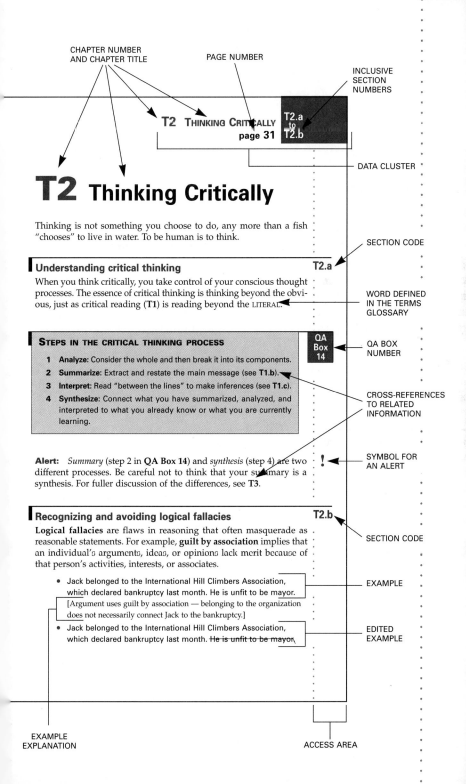

CHAPTER NUMBER
AND CHAPTER TITLE

PAGE NUMBER

INCLUSIVE
SECTION
NUMBERS

T2 THINKING CRITICALLY
page 31

T2.a
to
T2.b

DATA CLUSTER

T2 Thinking Critically

Thinking is not something you choose to do, any more than a fish "chooses" to live in water. To be human is to think.

SECTION CODE

Understanding critical thinking   T2.a

When you think critically, you take control of your conscious thought processes. The essence of critical thinking is thinking beyond the obvious, just as critical reading (**T1**) is reading beyond the LITERAL.

WORD DEFINED
IN THE TERMS
GLOSSARY

STEPS IN THE CRITICAL THINKING PROCESS

QA
Box
14

QA BOX
NUMBER

1 **Analyze:** Consider the whole and then break it into its components.
2 **Summarize:** Extract and restate the main message (see **T1.b**).
3 **Interpret:** Read "between the lines" to make inferences (see **T1.c**).
4 **Synthesize:** Connect what you have summarized, analyzed, and interpreted to what you already know or what you are currently learning.

CROSS-REFERENCES
TO RELATED
INFORMATION

Alert: *Summary* (step 2 in **QA Box 14**) and *synthesis* (step 4) are two different processes. Be careful not to think that your summary is a synthesis. For fuller discussion of the differences, see **T3**.

!

SYMBOL FOR
AN ALERT

Recognizing and avoiding logical fallacies   T2.b

Logical fallacies are flaws in reasoning that often masquerade as reasonable statements. For example, **guilt by association** implies that an individual's arguments, ideas, or opinions lack merit because of that person's activities, interests, or associates.

SECTION CODE

- Jack belonged to the International Hill Climbers Association, which declared bankruptcy last month. He is unfit to be mayor.
  [Argument uses guilt by association — belonging to the organization does not necessarily connect Jack to the bankruptcy.]

EXAMPLE

- Jack belonged to the International Hill Climbers Association, which declared bankruptcy last month. ~~He is unfit to be mayor~~.

EDITED
EXAMPLE

EXAMPLE
EXPLANATION

ACCESS AREA

H2 Hands-On Practice Using Your *Quick Access*

H2.a Learning where to look for what you want to know ▌

Using the Divider Directory and dividers, answer these questions.

1 What pages is **E** Effective Sentences on? (Give inclusive page numbers for part E.)

2 How many chapters are found in **S** Spelling and Mechanics?

3 In the Index, you discover that information you want is on page 210. Which divider should you turn to?

4 You need some ideas for writing an effective concluding paragraph for your essay. Which divider should you turn to?

5 Your instructor is discussing MLA style for documenting sources. Which divider should you turn to?

Using the content lists, QA Box list, Response Symbols, the Usage Glossary, Terms Glossary, and Index, answer these questions.

6 You want to check whether *your* or *you're* is correct in a particular sentence. Which lists can lead you to the answer? Which list gets you to the answer fastest?

7 Which list helps you find a summary of comma rules and examples of comma use?

8 Your instructor has written // in the margin of your paper. Which list do you need? What does the symbol // stand for? Where does the list send you? When you get there, how many pages of information does this topic have?

9 You see the term CORRELATIVE CONJUNCTION, printed in small capital letters, in a discussion. If you do not know its meaning, what list should you consult?

10 You have just been assigned a research project. Which lists lead you to advice about how to schedule your research project?

Using the data clusters in the top outside of pages, answer these questions.

11 Section C2.b discusses correcting comma splices and fused sentences. On what pages is this information?

12 What does the arrow in front of T1.b on page 32 tell you?

13 What is the title of the chapter with material on pages 42 and 43? How do you know?

14 In the Usage Glossary, what code appears in the color block of the data cluster? the Terms Glossary? the Index?

15 You're looking for section G2.f and get to page 60. Now what?

Solving problems   H2.b

Using *Quick Access*, solve these problems writers typically have.

A You are assigned an essay and need help thinking of ideas. You wonder whether you might even have writer's block. Where can you find information in *Quick Access* to help solve these problems?

B An instructor has written *v* beside the word *freezed* in a paper. What does *v* mean? How did you find out? Where did you find the solution? What is the solution?

C You have noticed that sometimes the first letter after a colon is capitalized and sometimes it is not. What does *Quick Access* advise you to do? Where did you find the advice?

D Are the words *advise* and *advice* used correctly in item **C**, above ? Where did you find the answer?

E A writer who has a tendency to write sentence fragments wants help finding them before she turns an essay in. Where can she find help in *Quick Access*? Based on the advice in *Quick Access*, what three things should she look for in her sentences?

Learning to use documentation models   H2.c

Referring to the MLA models for a Works Cited list in section M2.b, arrange information for each of the following sources correctly for a Works Cited list in MLA style. For a Works Cited list, arrange the entries, unnumbered, in alphabetical order.

An article by Judith Martin in *Newsday* (January 27, 1991) on pages 9 and 11 in the second section of this newspaper. The title of the article is "Here's Looking at You."

A book by the same Judith Martin who wrote the article described above. The book's title is *A Friend of Your Own*. It was published in 1993 by Polen Publishers, Ltd. The place of publication is Springfield (Illinois), and the book has 388 pages.

Your face-to-face interview of Alan Womack on October 19, 1997, from 9:00–11:00 a.m. at the Dwight Memorial Library in Texarkana, Texas. You taped the interview.

An essay entitled "Social Bodies" by Ted Polhemus. You found it in a book of essays by several different authors. The title of the book is *The Body as a Medium of Expression*, and it was edited by Ted Polhemus and Jonathan Benthall. The book has 840 pages. The essay you used is on pages 13 to 35. The book was published by E. P. Dutton & Company in 1975, a publisher headquartered in New York City.

An article from an online magazine called *'Zine*, which does not have a print version. The title of the article is "No Body There," and the author's name is Javeen Ryan-Bloch. You got to the article through AOL (America Online), and you printed it out on 24 June 1998. The "issue" of *'Zine* was identified at the beginning as June 21–28, 1998. *'Zine* does not number pages.

H2.d Answers

Here are answers for the 15 questions in H2.a. Although I have tried to think of all possibilities, you may have found others.

1. Pages 105-124. Look on the tab of divider **E**.
2. Six chapters. Look on the back of divider **S**.
3. Divider **M**. Look at inclusive page numbers on the tab of each divider until you find the page range that 210 falls within.
4. The descriptions of dividers in section **H1.a** above tell you that this question about essay writing is likely answered in **W**. Turning to the back of divider **W**, you can find W4, a chapter about writing paragraphs, and W4.g, a section about writing concluding paragraphs.
5. Divider **M** MLA Documentation.
6. *Your, you're* is listed in the Index and in the Usage Glossary. (You can also find these words in QA Box 42, a list of homonyms and other confusing words.)
7. The word *summary* is a clue here. QA Boxes contain many summaries of important information. Checking the QA Box list, you can see that QA Box 41 shows comma patterns.
8. In the Response Symbols list you can see that / / indicates faulty parallelism. The cross-reference sends you to section E3.a for a discussion of parallelism on pages 112–114.
9. Go to the Terms Glossary for a definition of correlative conjunctions and a cross-reference to G1.h for a fuller discussion. (*Correlative conjunctions* is also in the Index.)
10. The Capsule Contents, the full Contents in the front of *Quick Access*, and the content list on the back of divider **R** all show section R1.a, Scheduling for research writing. Also, the QA Box list on page ii shows that QA Box 48 is a research writing schedule.
11. Section C2.b is on pages 93, 94, and 95.

12   The arrow means that section T1.b is continued from page 31.

13   The title of the chapter on these pages is Thinking Critically. The chapter title and the chapter number appear (sometimes in shortened form) above the page number on right-hand pages. On page 43, the title is T2 Thinking Critically.

14   In the Usage Glossary, *Usage* is printed in white in the color block. In the Terms Glossary, *Terms* is in the color block. In the Index, *Index* is in the color block.

15   The arrow before G2.f in the color block on page 60 tells you to turn to page 59. On page 59, the code G2.f in the access area shows you where this section begins.

Answers to problems A–E appear below.

A   **W** Writing Process is the divider for these kinds of writing problems. Any of the content lists show you that W1 is about getting started. In the Index, an entry *Ideas for writing* tells you that many strategies are covered and gives you page numbers for them. Also in the Index, the entry *Writer's block, overcoming*, tells you where this topic is discussed.

B   Look at the Response Symbols list. In this case, you find that *v* signals a verb form error, and the cross-reference sends you to section G3.a. The second item mentions that regular verbs end in *-d* or *-ed* and that irregular verbs vary. It refers you to a list of irregular verbs, where you can see that the right verb form for *freeze* is *froze*, not *freezed*. If your essay is marked with symbols and abbreviations not in the Response Symbols list, consult your instructor about their meaning.

C   Of the many ways you can get to this answer, the Index is quickest. It has listings under *Capitalization* and under *Colon(s)* for pages 141 and 165. There you find out to use a lowercase letter when the words following a colon are not a complete sentence and that you have a choice to capitalize or not when a complete sentence follows a colon. You are also reminded there to be consistent, whichever choice you make.

D   Yes, *advise* and *advice* are used correctly. The Usage Glossary and QA Box 42 both tell the meanings and functions of *advise* and *advice*. (The words are also listed in the Index.)

E   Any of the content listings and the Index show that this writer should use the test for sentence completeness in C1.a. The writer should probably put a Post-it ® on QA Box 36, so that she can refer quickly to its guidance in looking for fragments where a subject is missing, a verb is missing, or a clause starting with a subordinating word is capitalized and punctuated as though it were a complete sentence.

The Works Cited list based on the source information in H2.c appears below.

Works Cited

Martin, Judith. "Here's Looking at You." <u>Newsday</u>
27 Jan. 1991, sec. 2: 9+.

---. <u>A Friend of Your Own</u>. Springfield, IL:
Polen,1993.

Polhemus, Ted. "Social Bodies." The Body as a
<u>Medium of Expression</u>. Ed. Jonathan
Benthall and Ted Polhemus. New York: Dutton,
1975. 13—35.

Ryan-Bloch, Javeen. "No Body There." June 21—28,
1998:   <u>'Zine</u>. Online. AOL. 24 June 1998.

Womack, Alan. Personal interview. 19 Oct. 1997.

Writing Process

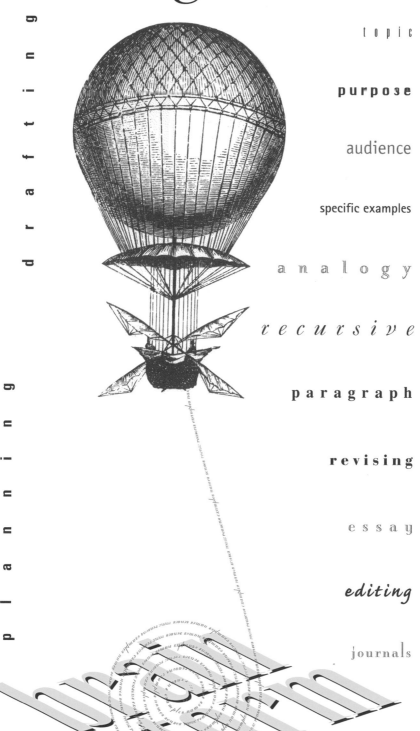

planning   drafting

topic

purpose

audience

specific examples

analogy

recursive

paragraph

revising

essay

editing

journals

W | Writing Process
pages 1-30

W WRITING PROCESS

W1 Getting Started

Making preliminary decisions W1.a

When you start a new writing project, you face many decisions even before you sit at a keyboard or pick up a pen. Then as you begin to write, you might need to revise some of these decisions. To get started how can you most efficiently sort out all you need to think about? Focus separately on decisions about TOPIC, PURPOSE, AUDIENCE, and the specific writing situation. Then try to fit the groups of decisions together, adjusting them to create a whole. **QA Box 1** summarizes the questions to ask yourself as you make preliminary decisions about what you will write.

PRELIMINARY DECISIONS FOR WRITING

QA Box 1

WHAT IS MY TOPIC?
If you have a topic, does it need to be narrowed (see **W1.d**), expanded, or left as is? If you need to pick your own topic, see **W1.e** for help in finding ideas.

WHAT IS MY PURPOSE?
Is your overall writing purpose to give information to readers or to persuade them about a debatable subject? What writing strategies might help you fulfill your purpose? You can narrate, describe, explain how to do something, illustrate with examples, define, compare and contrast, analyze and classify, use an analogy, discuss causes and effects; see **W4.f**.

WHO IS MY AUDIENCE?
Do you want to reach a general audience (as represented by the "general reading public") or an expert audience (as represented by readers who share specialized knowledge)? To reach your readers, what should you consider about their backgrounds: age? gender? level of education? roles in life? beliefs? extent of knowledge and attitudes toward the topic?

WHAT ARE THE SPECIFIC REQUIREMENTS OF MY WRITING SITUATION?
When are DRAFTS due? How long is the paper supposed to be? Are you expected to draw on only your current knowledge and personal experience as you write, or can you also read or conduct other research about your topic?

W1.b Understanding the writing process

Many people assume that a real writer can magically write a finished product, word by perfect word. Experienced writers know that **writing** is a **process**, a series of activities that start the moment they begin thinking about a topic and end when they complete a final draft.

QA Box 2

AN OVERVIEW OF THE WRITING PROCESS

Planning means gathering ideas and thinking about a focus.
Shaping means considering ways to organize your material.
Drafting means writing your ideas in sentences and paragraphs.
Revising means evaluating your draft and then rewriting it by adding, cutting, replacing, moving, and often totally recasting material.
Editing means checking the technical correctness of your grammar, spelling, punctuation, and mechanics.
Proofreading means reading your final copy for typing errors or hand-writing legibility.

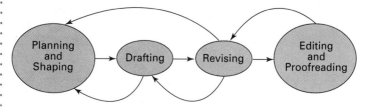

Planning and Shaping → Drafting → Revising → Editing and Proofreading

Visualizing the writing process

To understand this process, remember that writing is a recursive activity. As the circles and arrows show, planning is not over when drafting begins, drafting is not over when the major activity shifts to revising, and so on. As you work with the writing process, observe what works best for you. Do not be impatient with yourself and do not get discouraged. Writing takes time—it never happens magically for anyone. Below you can see how the first paragraph of **W1.b** was reworked into final form.

- ~~Section W1.a discusses early decisions. This section~~

~~explains the process of writing:~~ Many people assume that a real writer can _^*magically* write a finished product, ~~easily,~~ *word by perfect word.*

Experienced writers know ~~better than~~ that_(;) writing is a

process, ~~that involves~~ a series of activities that start *the moment they begin* ~~when the writers start~~ thinking *about a topic* and end ~~with~~ *when they complete* a final draft.

—Draft and revision of the first parabraph in W1.b by Lynn Quitman Troyka

Choosing a writing topic

When choosing your own topic, do not assume that all subjects are suitable for academic writing. For example, the old reliable essay about a summer vacation is not safe territory unless you have something extraordinary to report. Your essays need to dive into issues and concepts, and they should demonstrate that you can use specific, concrete details to support any generalizations you make.

Narrowing a topic

One challenge in dealing with topics comes when you choose or are assigned a very broad subject. You have to narrow the subject by breaking it into subdivisions. Most very broad subjects can be broken down in hundreds of ways, but you need not think of all of them. When one seems possible, think it through at the start so that you can decide whether you can develop it well in writing. What separates most good writing from bad is the writer's ability to move back and forth between general statements and specific details (see **W4.d**).

For example, if the subject is marriage, you might narrow it to what makes marriages successful. But you cannot depend merely on generalizations such as "In successful marriages husbands and wives learn to accept each other's faults." You need to explain why accepting faults is important, and you need to give concrete illustrations of what you are talking about.

Uncovering ideas for writing

If you sometimes worry that you have nothing to write about, remember that most people know far more than they give themselves credit for. Your challenge is to uncover what is in your mind but seems not to be.

No one technique for finding ideas works for all writers in all situations. Relax and experiment. If one method does not provide enough useful material, try another.

Keeping a Journal

Writing in a journal allows you to have an informal "conversation on paper" with yourself. You can draw on your observations, your dreams, your reading.

Keeping a journal helps in three ways. First, writing every day gives you the habit of productivity. The more you write, the more you get used to the feeling of words pouring out of you onto paper, and the easier it becomes to write in all situations.

Second, writing to yourself helps you think through ideas that need time to develop. Writing is a way of discovering, of allowing thoughts to emerge as the physical act of writing moves along. Third, your journal becomes a source of ideas for topics (see **W1.c**).

Freewriting

Freewriting means writing down whatever comes to mind about whatever topic surfaces, without stopping to worry about whether ideas are good or spelling is correct. **Focused freewriting** means starting with a set topic: a favorite word or sentence from your journal, a quotation you like, or perhaps a topic assigned for a course.

When you freewrite, do nothing to interrupt the flow. Do not censor any thoughts or flashes of insight. Do not review or cross out. Some days your freewriting might seem mindless, but other days it can reveal interesting ideas to you.

! **Computer Tip:** If you use a word processor, you can avoid the temptation to criticize your freewriting by dimming the screen so that you cannot see the words on it. Thus your ideas are recorded, but you cannot see them until you brighten the screen again.

Brainstorming

Brainstorming means listing everything you can think of about a topic. Let your mind range freely, generating quantities of ideas before analyzing them.

Brainstorming is done in two steps. First, make a list. Then try to find patterns in the list and ways to group the ideas. Discard items that do not fit into any group. Groups with the most items are likely to be ones you can write about most successfully.

Here is some brainstorming done by a student, Carol Moreno, whose essay on women lifting weights appears in **W5.c**. Moreno grouped the items marked with an asterisk and used them in her third paragraph.

```
safety with free weights (barbells)*
do not bend at the waist*
do not hold your breath
use leg strength to straighten up*
do not allow a twist*
concentrate on each move
```

Asking and Answering Questions

Here are exploratory questions to stimulate your thinking if you run out of ideas:

- What is it?
- What is it the same as?
- How is it different?
- Why or how does it happen?

- How is it done?
- What causes it or results from it?
- What does it look, smell, sound, feel, taste like?

Also journalists try to uncover comprehensive information about a topic by asking Who? What? When? Why? Where? How? The answers can reveal various perspectives. For example, Carol Moreno, whose essay appears in **W5.c**, asked these questions, Who was in my first weight-lifting class? What reasons did other women have for taking the class? Why did I get interested in weight lifting? When did I realize that weight lifting wasn't just an activity for guys? How do I feel about weight lifting now?

Clustering

Clustering, also called **mapping**, is a visual form of brainstorming. Start with your subject circled in the middle of a sheet of unlined paper. Then, moving from the center, draw lines that end with circles, and label each circle with the name of a major division of your subject. Then move out from each circle to subdivisions by associating to further ideas and related details. Here is part of Carol Moreno's clustering. Moreno developed these ideas for the fifth paragraph of her essay (see **W5.c**).

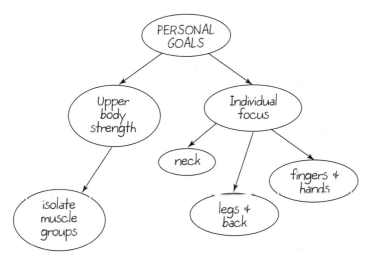

Clustering that became Carol Moreno's paragraph 5

Planning a thesis statement   W1.f

A **thesis statement** is the central message of an essay. Compose your thesis statement with care so that it accurately reflects the content of your essay. As you are writing, if you find a mismatch between your thesis statement and your essay's content, revise to coordinate them better.

To compose a thesis statement, first make an **assertion**, a simple statement that mentions your topic and your position regarding it. The exact wording of an assertion rarely finds its way into the essay, but the assertion serves as a focus as you progress toward a fully developed thesis statement.

For her essay about women lifting weights (see **W5.c**), Carol Moreno used this progression from basic assertion to final thesis statement.

- I think women can pump iron like men. [This assertion is a start.]

- If she is trained well, any woman can "pump iron" well, just like a man. [This preliminary thesis is more developed because it mentions training, but the word *well* is used twice and is vague, and the word *any* is inaccurate.]

- In spite of most people thinking only men can "pump iron," women can also do it successfully with the right training. [This draft is better because it is becoming more specific, but "most people thinking only men" is not an aspect of the topic Moreno intends to explore. Also the concept of building strength, a major aspect of Moreno's final draft, is missing.]

- With the right training, women can also "pump iron" successfully to build strength. [This is the final version of Moreno's thesis statement. *Also* is a transitional word connecting the thesis statement to the sentence that comes before it in Moreno's introductory paragraph.]

The final version fulfills requirements described in **QA Box 3**.

QA Box 3

BASIC REQUIREMENTS FOR A THESIS STATEMENT

1. It states the essay's subject, but it is not a repeat of the essay's title.
2. It reflects the essay's PURPOSE (see **W1.a**), but it does not announce its intention simply with "The purpose of this essay is. . . ."
3. It includes a focus—words that convey the writer's point of view.
4. It makes a general statement—one that leads to a set of main ideas and supporting details. It is not merely a statement of fact that leads nowhere.
5. It uses specific language and avoids vague words.
6. It may give the major subdivisions of the topic.

W1.g Outlining

Some writers always use outlines; others prefer not to. Writers who outline do so at various points in the WRITING PROCESS: before DRAFTING, to flesh out, pull together, and arrange material; or while REVISING, to check the logic and flow of a draft's organization. Outlines often clearly reveal flaws—missing information, undesirable repetitions, digressions from an essay's thesis.

An **informal outline**, which can be particularly useful when main ideas are still evolving, does not have to follow all the formal conventions of outlining. Consider an informal outline as a working plan that lays out the major chunks of an essay's content. Here is part of an informal outline for an essay with this thesis statement: *Chances are good that most adults will need to know how to live alone, briefly or longer, at some time in their lives.*

Sample Informal Outline

```
Circumstances that force living alone
        Grown children leave
        College, graduate school
        Jobs in other cities
        Some marriages don't last forever
        One spouse might die
```

A **formal outline** follows the conventions of content and format that display material in such a way that relationships among ideas are clear and content is orderly. A formal outline can be a **topic outline**, with each item a word or phrase; conversely, it can be a **sentence outline**, with each item a complete sentence. Never mix the two styles in a formal outline. The example in **QA Box 4** shows part of a sentence outline.

CONVENTIONS OF FORMAL OUTLINES

QA Box 4

FORMAL OUTLINE FORM

Thesis Statement:

I. First main idea

  A. First subordinate idea

      1. First reason or example

      2. Second reason or example

          a. First supporting detail

          b. Second supporting detail

  B. Second subordinate idea

II. Second main idea

SAMPLE OF A FORMAL SENTENCE OUTLINE

Thesis Statement: Common noise pollution, which causes many problems in society, can be reduced.

I. Noise pollution comes from many sources.

  A. Noise pollution occurs in many large cities.

      1. Traffic rumbles.

Continued on next page

➤ QA Box 4, continued from previous page

> 2. Construction work blasts.
>   a. Dynamite destroys old buildings and bedrock.
>   b. Pile drivers and riveters pound new buildings into place.
> B. Noise pollution occurs in the workplace.
>   1. Machines boom and whine in factories.
>   2. Telephones, computers, and other equipment create constant low-level noise.
> II. Noise pollution causes many problems.
>
> **GUIDELINES**
>
> - Each level must have at least two subdivisions; no I without a II, no A without a B, and so on. If a level has only one subdivision, either eliminate it or expand the material to at least two subdivisions.
>
> - Make sure all subdivisions are at the same level (a main idea cannot be paired with a supporting detail).
>
> - Make all entries on the same level grammatically parallel (as in *Traffic rumbles* and *Construction work blasts*).

W2 Drafting

W2.a Writing a first draft

A first draft is preliminary. It is not meant to be perfect; it is meant to give you something to revise. These approaches can help you write a first draft.

- Put aside all your notes from uncovering ideas (see **W1.e**) and writing a THESIS STATEMENT (see **W1.f**). Write a DISCOVERY DRAFT by being open to finding ideas and making connections that spring to mind as you write.

- Keep your notes from uncovering ideas (**W1.e**) and writing a thesis statement (**W1.f**) at hand and write a structured first draft by working through all your material.

- Use a combination of approaches. When you know the shape of your material, write according to that structure. When you do not know what to say next, switch to writing a discovery draft.

The direction of drafting is forward: Keep pressing ahead. If you wonder about the spelling of a word or a point in grammar, underline the material to check it later—and keep moving ahead. If you cannot think of an exact word, use a SYNONYM and mark it to change later— and move on. If you are worried about your sentence style or the order in which you present details within a paragraph, write *Style?* or *Order?* in the margin and return to it later to revise—and press forward. If you begin to run dry, reread what you have written—but only to propel yourself to further writing, not to distract you into rewriting.

For the final draft of a student essay, see **W5.c**. For earlier drafts of selected parts, see **W3.d** and **W3.f**.

Overcoming writer's block   W2.b

If you get blocked while drafting, try the strategies listed in **QA Box 5**, which experienced writers often use to get started.

WAYS TO OVERCOME WRITER'S BLOCK   QA Box 5

AVOID STARING AT A BLANK PAGE.
Relax and move your hand across the page or keyboard while you think about your TOPIC.

VISUALIZE YOURSELF WRITING.
Imagine yourself where you usually write, with the materials you need, busy at work.

PICTURE AN IMAGE OR SCENE OR IMAGINE A SOUND THAT RELATES TO YOUR TOPIC.
Start writing by describing what you see or hear.

WRITE YOUR MATERIAL IN THE FORM OF A LETTER TO A FRIEND.
Relax and chat on paper to someone with whom you feel comfortable. Also try writing the letter as if you were someone else.

START IN THE MIDDLE.
Write from the center of your essay out, instead of from beginning to end.

Drafting on a computer   W2.c

As you draft, if you have questions or want to elaborate on something but need to keep moving ahead, insert a symbol that will alert you to "talk to yourself" and revise later. (Your word-processing program can search for these symbols, making them easy to find later.) Resist any urge to consider a rough draft the final version merely because it looks neat when you print it out.

W2.d Writing answers for essay exams

Writing answers for essay exams requires you to synthesize and apply your knowledge, thereby showing what you know in a clear, direct, well-organized way. Because writing essay exams is usually time-limited, you will likely spend most of your time drafting answers, with lesser allotments to PLANNING, organizing, and REVISING. Here are some strategies to help you read and answer essay exam topic prompts effectively.

STRATEGIES FOR WRITING ESSAY EXAMS

1 Do not start writing immediately.

2 Read the test completely. If you have a choice, select topics you know the most about, and decide how much time to spend on each.

3 Reread each topic prompt you plan to respond to, underlining any cue words that say what you must do in your answer. Look for words such as *analyze, classify, criticize, compare, define, discuss, explain,* and *give reasons.* Also underline key words that tell you what subject and ideas you are to write about. Suppose you read "Criticize the architectural function of the modern football stadium." The cue word is *criticize,* which tells you to write about positive and negative aspects. The key words are *architectural function* and *modern football stadium,* which state the subject and ideas to write about.

4 Use the WRITING PROCESS as much as possible within the constraint of the time limit. Allot time for planning and revising. For a one-hour, one-essay test, for example, take about 10 minutes to jot down the major ideas and to plan their arrangement, and save about 10 minutes to reread, revise, and edit.

W3 Revising, Editing, and Proofreading

Revising, which means "seeing again," involves taking a DRAFT from its first to its final version by evaluating, adding, cutting, replacing, and moving material, and then editing and proofreading.

W3.a Knowing how to revise

To revise, you evaluate your DRAFT and decide where improvements are needed. Then you make the changes and evaluate them, both alone and in the context of the surrounding material. This process continues until you are satisfied that the essay is in a final draft.

STEPS FOR REVISING

1 Shift mentally from suspending judgment (your attitude during idea gathering and drafting) to making judgments.
2 Read your draft critically to evaluate it. Be systematic, guided by the questions in the Revision Checklists (**QA Box 6**) or by material supplied by your instructor.
3 Decide whether to write an entirely new draft or to revise the one you have. Do not be overly harsh. Many early drafts provide sufficient raw material for the revision process to get underway.

Using the organizing power of your thesis statement and essay title   W3.b

If your THESIS STATEMENT does not match what your essay says (see **QA Box 3**), revise either the thesis statement or the essay—or both. Use the thesis statement's controlling role to bring it and the essay in line with each other.

An essay's title can also play an important organizing role, so do not wait until the last minute and merely tack a title on. Draft a title early and, as you revise, check that it continues to relate to the content of your evolving essay.

A **direct title** tells exactly what the essay will be about: for example, *Women Can Pump Iron, Too.* An **indirect title** hints at an essay's topic: LEMONADE, NOT LEMONS. The indirect approach can intrigue a reader as long as the connection is not too obscure.

Alert: A title stands alone. Do not open an essay by referring to the title as though its words are in the essay's first sentence. **!**

Revising on a computer   W3.c

A computer makes the activities of revision easy to do. For example, you can add anything from a word to a paragraph, and if you are unsure about the best location for the new material, you can type it and then move it to more than one place to try out the different locations. See where it works best, and then delete the extras.

Because the computer makes rearranging relatively painless, you may create many versions of your DRAFT until you are satisfied with the order. Try reordering your body paragraphs, splitting or joining some existing paragraphs, and moving your last paragraph to the first position. You may be surprised. However, resist the temptation to revise endlessly. The key to revision is evaluation and reworking, not mere rearranging.

Delete cautiously. If you think you want to drop material, move it to the end of your document. You may want to return the material to your draft later. If not, you can always delete it when you edit (see **W3.h**).

W3.d Using revision checklists

A revision checklist can help focus your attention as you evaluate your writing. **QA Box 6** provides comprehensive checklists. Do not let them overwhelm you; adapt them to your own needs.

QA Box 6

REVISION CHECKLISTS

If you cannot answer each question "yes," you need to revise. References in parentheses tell you where you will find useful information.

THE WHOLE ESSAY AND PARAGRAPHS

1. Is your essay topic suitable and sufficiently narrow? (**W1.c, W1.d**)

2. Does your thesis statement communicate topic, focus, and purpose? (**W1.f, QA Box 3**)

3. Does your essay reflect awareness of your readers? (**QA Box 1**)

4. Is your essay arranged effectively? (**W1.g**)

5. Have you cut material that goes off the topic? (**W3.b**)

6. Does your introduction relate to the rest of your essay? (**W4.a**)

7. Do your body paragraphs express main ideas in topic sentences as needed? (**W4.c**) Are your main ideas clearly related to your thesis statement? (**W1.f**)

8. Are your body paragraphs developed with specific, concrete support for each main idea? (**W4.d**)

9. Do your paragraphs maintain coherence, using transitions and other techniques as necessary? (**W4.e**)

10. Does your conclusion provide a sense of completion? (**W4.g**)

SENTENCES AND WORDS

1. Are your sentences concise? (**E1**)

2. Do your sentences show clear relationships among ideas? (**E2**)

3. Do you use effective parallelism, and does your writing style reflect variety and emphasis? (**E3**)

4. Have you eliminated sentence fragments? (**C1**) Have you eliminated comma splices and fused sentences? (**C2**)

5. Have you eliminated confusing shifts? (**C3.a–d**) Have you eliminated mixed and incomplete sentences? (**C3.e–f**)

Continued on next page

> QA Box 6, continued from previous page

---

6 Have you eliminated misplaced and dangling modifiers? (**C4**)

7 Have you used exact words? (**E4.a–b**)

8 Is your language appropriate and your usage correct? (**E4.d**, **Usage Glossary**)

9 Have you avoided sexist language? (**E5**)

Here is part of a revised first draft of a paragraph in a paper on women lifting weights (for the final draft, see the fourth paragraph of the student essay in **W5.c**). The student writer, Carol Moreno, decided as she reread her first draft that the paragraph did not have enough specific, concrete details (see **QA Box 9**).

My topic sentence needs work

- After safety comes our needs for physical strength. A

  well-planned, progressive weight training program. ~~You~~
  begins   *a person*
  ~~begin~~ with whatever weight ~~you~~ can lift comfortably and
                  adds to the base weight as she gets stronger.
  then gradually ~~add~~ What builds muscle strength is the
                       the lifter does,
  number of "reps" ~~we do~~ not necessarily an increase in the
       resistance from adding
  amount of ~~added~~ weight. In my class, we ranged from 18
                       pudgy,   couch potato
  to 43, scrawny to ~~fat~~, and ~~lazy~~ to superstar, and we
                                                      I'm
  ?Start each developed a program that was (OK) for us. Some *being*
  sentence   *lazy*
  here?   women didn't listen to our instructor who urged us   *here*
  Not sure
                  try
  not to ~~do~~ more reps or weight than our programs called
            our first workouts
  for, even if ~~it~~ seemed too easy. This turned out to be
                                 the next morning
  good advice because those of us who didn't listen woke up
                                                           ^
  feeling as though our bodies had been twisted by evil forces.

Knowing how to edit   W3.e

Editing means finding and fixing any errors in grammar, spelling, punctuation, capitals, numbers, italics, and abbreviations.

Edit after you have finished revising (see **W3.a–d**). When you edit, resist any impulse to hurry. Editing takes concentration—and often the time to look up rules and conventions in this book.

W3.f Using an editing checklist

- As you edit, be systematic. Use the Editing Checklist in **QA Box 7**, adapting it to your personal needs.

QA Box 7

EDITING CHECKLIST

If you cannot answer each question "yes," you need to edit. References in parentheses tell you where you will find useful information.

1 Is the grammar correct? (**G1–G8**)

2 Are the sentences correct? (**C1–C4**)

3 Are commas used correctly? (**P2, P3**)

4 Are all other punctuation marks used correctly? (**P1, P4–8**)

5 Are capital letters, italics (or underlining), abbreviations, numbers, and hyphens used correctly? (**S2–S6**)

6 Is the spelling correct? (**S1**)

Here is part of an edited draft paragraph for Carol Moreno's essay; you can find the complete final draft in **W5.c**.

> - When my grandmother fell and broke her hip last summer, I wanted to help take care of her. Because she was bedridden, she needed to be lifted at times, but I was shocked to discover that I could not lift her without my mothers or brothers help. My grandmother does not weigh much, but she was to much for me. My pride was hurt, and even more important, I began to worry about my plans to be a nurse specializing in the care of elderly people. What if I was to weak to help my patients get around? When I realized that I could satisfy one of my Physical Education requirements by taking a weight-lifting course for women, I decided to try it. Many people picture only big macho men wanting to lift weights, but times have changed. With the right training, women can also "pump iron" successfully to build strength.

Knowing how to proofread W3.g

Proofreading involves a careful, line-by-line reading of a final, clean version of your essay before you hand it in. Neatly correct any errors you find. If a page has numerous errors, retype (or recopy) it. No matter how hard you have worked on the process of writing your paper, if your final copy is inaccurate or messy, you will not reach your readers successfully. Here are some useful techniques:

PROOFREADING TIPS

- Proofread with a ruler so that you can focus on one line at a time.
- Start at the end of a paragraph or an essay and read backward word by word to avoid being distracted by the content.
- Read your final draft aloud so that you see and hear errors; look for omitted letters and words as well as repeated words.

Using a computer to edit and proofread W3.h

To help you proofread and edit, use the block command to highlight a section, so that you can work in small segments and reduce the tendency to read too quickly to detect errors.

You might try making your own "spell-and-style checker" by keeping a file of the mistakes you have made in the past. You can then call up the file and search your DRAFT to check. If you use a spell-check, proofread your paper anyway for words that are misused rather than misspelled, and words that cannot be identified by a spell-check because the errors are real words (for example, *form* for *from*).

W4 Rhetorical Strategies for Paragraphs

Rhetorical strategies in writing are techniques for presenting ideas so that a writer's intended message is delivered with impact and clarity. As you will see from the explanations and examples in this chapter, all rhetorical strategies reflect the typical patterns of thought that humans use quite naturally. As you try out these strategies, especially as they keep you aware of sequencing and arranging sentences, you can apply them to composing your paragraphs, and, in some situations, whole essays.

A **paragraph** is a group of sentences that work together to develop a unit of thought. Paragraphing permits writers to divide material into manageable parts and to arrange the parts into a unified whole. An academic essay usually consists of an introductory paragraph, a group of body paragraphs, and a concluding paragraph.

W4.a Writing introductory paragraphs

An effective introductory paragraph prepares the reader for what lies ahead, so it must relate clearly to the rest of the essay. The paragraph consists of one or more introductory devices that serve to stimulate a reader's interest (see **QA Box 8**). Also, student writers are often required to include a THESIS STATEMENT in the introductory paragraph (see **W1.f**). Experienced writers, depending on their writing purpose, might choose not to use this signal to an essay's content. When a thesis statement is used, most instructors prefer it to appear in the last sentence or two of the introductory paragraph, as in paragraph 1.

1 "Alone one is never lonely," May Sarton says in her essay "The Rewards of Living a Solitary Life." Most people, however, are terrified of living alone. They are used to living with others—children with parents, roommates with roommates, friends with friends, husbands with wives. When the statistics catch up with them, therefore, they are rarely prepared. Chances are high that most adult men and women will need to know how to live alone, briefly or longer, at some time in their lives.

—Tara Foster, student

QA Box 8

INTRODUCTORY PARAGRAPHS

DEVICES TO TRY

- Providing relevant background information
- Relating a brief, interesting story or anecdote
- Giving a pertinent statistic or statistics
- Asking a provocative question or questions
- Using an appropriate quotation
- Making an analogy
- Defining a term used throughout the essay
- Identifying the situation

STRATEGIES TO AVOID

- Making obvious statements that refer to what the essay is about or will accomplish, such as "I am going to discuss the causes of falling oil prices"
- Apologizing, as in "I am not sure I'm right, but this is my opinion"
- Using overworked expressions, such as "Haste really does make waste, as I recently discovered" or "Love is grand"

Writing effective body paragraphs — W4.b

Body paragraphs typically state a main idea and present logical support for that idea. Effective body paragraphs usually share three characteristics:

- *Unity*: All the sentences relate clearly to a main idea and to each other (see **W4.c**).
- *Development*: Specific, logical examples and details support the main idea (see **W4.d**).
- *Coherence*: Sentences relate to each other in content, in grammatical structure, and in word choice (see **W4.e**).

Writing and using topic sentences — W4.c

A **topic sentence** contains the main idea of a paragraph, focusing and controlling what the paragraph can include.

Starting with a Topic Sentence

When a topic sentence starts a paragraph, readers immediately know what general subject will be discussed.

> 2 The cockroach lore that has been daunting us for years is mostly true. Roaches can live for twenty days without food, fourteen days without water; they can flatten their bodies and crawl through a crack thinner than a dime; they can eat huge doses of carcinogens and still die of old age. They can even survive "as much radiation as an oak tree can," says William Bell, the University of Kansas entomologist whose cockroaches appeared in the movie *The Day After*. They'll eat almost anything—regular food, leather, glue, hair, paper, even the starch in book bindings. (The New York Public Library has quite a cockroach problem.) They sense the slightest breeze, and they can react and start running in .05 seconds; they can also remain motionless for days. And if all this isn't creepy enough, they can fly too.
>
> —Jane Goodman, "What's Bugging You"

Ending with a Topic Sentence

Putting the topic sentence at the end of the paragraph lets you create a feeling of anticipation in your reader.

> 3 The trouble with the clans and tribes many of us were born into is not that they consist of meddlesome ogres but that they are too far away. In emergencies we rush across continents, and if need be, oceans to their sides, as they do to ours. Maybe we even make a habit of seeing them, once or twice a year, for the sheer pleasure of it. But blood ties seldom dictate our addresses. Our blood kin are

often too remote to ease us from our Tuesdays to our Wednesdays. For this we must rely on our families of friends. If our relatives are not, do not wish to be, or for whatever reasons cannot be our friends, then by some complex alchemy we must try to transform our friends into our relatives. If blood and roots don't do the job, then we must look to water and branches, and sort ourselves into new constellations, new families.

—Jane Howard, "A Peck of Salt"

Implying a Topic Sentence

Paragraphs that make a unified statement without the use of a topic sentence likely consist of additional details supporting an earlier paragraph's topic sentence. Writers must carefully construct such paragraphs so that the main idea is very clear even though it is not explicitly stated.

W4.d Using details to develop body paragraphs

To develop body paragraphs, use specific, concrete details that support the generalization given in the paragraph's TOPIC SENTENCE. What separates most good writing from bad is the writer's ability to move back and forth between generalizations and specific details. "RENNS" is a memory device writers use to check whether their paragraphs are developed with sufficient detail. **QA Box 9** explains RENNS.

QA Box 9

RENNS FOR SPECIFIC, CONCRETE DETAILS

R REASONS

E EXAMPLES

N NAMES

N NUMBERS

S SENSES (SIGHT, SOUND, SMELL, TASTE, TOUCH)

The details do not have to occur in the order of the letters in RENNS, and most paragraphs have only a selection of RENNS. For example, paragraph 4 has three types, as the analysis after it explains.

Whether bad or good, in tune or not, whistling has its practical side. Clifford Pratt is working with a group of speech therapists to develop whistling techniques to help children overcome speech problems through improved breath control and tongue flexibility.

4 People who have a piercing whistle have a clear advantage when it comes to hailing cabs, calling the dog or the children, or indicating approval during a sporting event. And if you want to leave the house and can't remember where you put your keys, there's a key chain on the market now with a beep that can be activated by a whistle: You whistle and the key chain tells you where it is.

—Cassandra Tate, "Whistlers Blow New Life into a Forgotten Art"

Paragraph 4 uses Examples: treatment for children with speech difficulties; convenience for hailing cabs, dogs, and children and for sounding off at sporting events; and a signaling key chain. It uses Names: Clifford Pratt, speech therapists, children (not the general term *people*), and dogs (not the general term *animals*). It uses Senses: the feeling of flexibility, the sound of a whistle and of a beeping key chain, and the roar of a sporting event.

Crafting coherent paragraphs W4.e

A paragraph is coherent when its sentences relate to each other in content, form, and language.

Using Transitional Expressions

Transitional expressions, including CONJUNCTIVE ADVERBS, signal connections from one idea to the next, within and among paragraphs.

CONJUNCTIVE ADVERBS AND TRANSITIONAL EXPRESSIONS AND THE RELATIONSHIPS THEY SIGNAL

QA Box 10

Addition	also, besides, equally important, furthermore, in addition, moreover, too,
Comparison	in the same way, likewise, similarly,
Concession	granted, naturally, of course,
Contrast	at the same time, despite that, however, in contrast, instead, nevertheless, on the contrary, on the other hand, otherwise, still,
Emphasis	certainly, indeed, in fact, of course,
Example or illustration	as an illustration, for example, for instance, namely, specifically, thus,
Result	accordingly, as a result, consequently, hence, then, therefore, thus,
Summary	finally, in conclusion, in short, in summary,
Time sequence	eventually, finally, meanwhile, next, now, subsequently, then, today, tomorrow, yesterday,

---

Do not overuse transitional expressions. Also, make sure each fits the meaning you want to deliver, and vary the expressions you use.

Alert: Within a sentence, a transitional expression is usually set off with commas (see **P2.f**); between INDEPENDENT CLAUSES, a transitional expression is preceded by a semicolon (see **P4.b**).

In paragraph 5, transitional words and phrases are in boldface.

> Jaguars, **for example**, were once found in the United States from southern Louisiana to California. **Today** they are rare north of the Mexican border, with no confirmed sightings since 1971. They
> 5 are rare, **too**, in Mexico, where biologist Carl Koford estimated their population at fewer than a thousand in a 1972 survey. Some biologists think the number is even smaller **today**. **Similarly**, jaguars have disappeared from southern Argentina and Paraguay.
>
> —Jeffrey P. Cohn, "Kings of the Wild"

Using Deliberate Repetition and Parallelism

The **deliberate repetition** of key words can help bring coherence to a paragraph. A key word is usually related to the main idea in the topic sentence or to a major detail in the supporting sentences. To avoid being monotonous, use deliberate repetition sparingly. **Parallelism** also bestows coherence. It involves repeating grammatically equivalent structures several times. The repeated tempos and sounds create connections among sentences and ideas. In paragraph 6, consider the effect of the repeated key word *work*, underlined, and of the repeated parallel structures shown here in boldface type. Other effective parallelism exists too.

> The world of <u>work</u> into which Jacinto and the other seven-year-olds were apprenticed was within sight and sound of the pueblo. **It was <u>work</u>** under blazing suns, in rainstorms, in pitch-black nights. **It was <u>work</u>** that you were always walking to or walking from, <u>work</u> without wages and <u>work</u> without end. **It was <u>work</u>** that gave you a
> 6 bone-tired feeling at the end of the day, so you learned **to swing** a machete, **to tighten** a cinch, and **to walk** without lost motion. Between seven and twelve you learned all this, each lesson driven home when your *jefe* said with a scowl: "*Asi no, hombre; asi.*" And he showed you how.
>
> —Ernesto Galarza, *Barrio Boy*

W4.f Using patterns for body paragraphs

Knowing various patterns for body paragraphs allows you to choose among various ways to help your paragraphs deliver their meanings most effectively. Although the patterns here are shown in isolation, paragraph patterns often overlap in essay writing because many patterns share characteristics. As you write, use paragraph patterns to communicate meaning, not merely to use a particular pattern.

Narration (Telling a Story)

Narrative writing tells about what is happening or what has happened. Narration is usually written in chronological order.

7

We walked down the path to the well-house, attracted by the fragrance of the honeysuckle with which it was covered. Someone was drawing water and my teacher placed my hand under the spout. As the cool stream gushed over one hand she spelled into the other the word *water*, first slowly, then rapidly. I stood still, my whole attention fixed upon the motions of her fingers. Suddenly I felt a misty consciousness as of something forgotten—a thrill of returning thought; and somehow the mystery of language was revealed to me. I knew then that "w-a-t-e-r" meant the wonderful cool something that was flowing over my hand. That living word awakened my soul, gave it light, hope, joy, set it free! There were barriers still, it is true, but barriers that could in time be swept away.

—Helen Keller, *The Story of My Life*

Description (Picturing in Words)

Descriptive writing gives the writer the chance to share sense impressions. Paragraph 8 uses spatial (location) sequence. Other sequences for description include from general to specific and from least to most important.

8

The old store, lighted only by three fifty-watt bulbs, smelled of coal oil and baking bread. In the middle of the rectangular room, where the oak floor sagged a little, stood an iron stove. To the right was a wooden table with an unfinished game of checkers and a stool made from an apple-tree stump. On shelves around the walls sat earthen jugs with corncob stoppers, a few canned goods, and some of the two thousand old clocks and clockworks Thurmond Watts owned. Only one was ticking; the others he just looked at.

—William Least Heat Moon, *Blue Highways*

Process (Giving Instructions or Advice)

Process writing describes a sequence for doing something, from learning to drive to proposing marriage. A process description is usually developed in chronological order and should include all the steps of the process being discussed.

9

Carrying loads of equal weight like paint cans and toolboxes is easier if you carry one in each hand. Keep your shoulders back and down so that the weight is balanced on each side of your body, not suspended in front. With this method, you will be able to lift heavier loads and also to walk and stand erect. Your back will not be strained by being pulled to one side.

—John Warde, "Safe Lifting Techniques"

Example (Giving Illustrations)

Writing developed with **examples** uses illustrations to provide concrete, specific information in support of the main idea. Examples are often arranged from least to most important.

10 One major value of rain forests is biomedical. The plants and animals of rain forests are the source of many compounds used in today's medicines. A drug that helps treat Parkinson's disease is manufactured from a plant that grows only in South American rain forests. Some plants and insects found in rain forests contain chemicals that relieve certain mental disorders. Discoveries, however, have only begun. Scientists say that rain forests contain over a thousand plants that have great anticancer potential. To destroy life forms in these forests is to deprive the human race of further medical advances.

—Gary Lee Houseman, student

Definition (Giving the Meaning)

Writing developed by a **definition** explains a topic by discussing the meaning of a word or a concept in more detail than that in a dictionary definition. An effective written definition uses specifics to explain abstractions.

11 Chemistry is that branch of science which has the task of investigating the materials out of which the universe is made. It is not concerned with the forms into which they may be fashioned. Such objects as chairs, tables, vases, bottles, or wires are of no significance in chemistry; but such substances as glass, wool, iron, sulfur, and clay, as the materials out of which they are made, are what it studies. Chemistry is concerned not only with the composition of such substances, but also with their inner structure.

—John Arrend Timm, *General Chemistry*

Comparison and Contrast (Explaining Likenesses and Differences)

Writing developed by a **comparison** deals with similarities, whereas writing about **contrasts** deals with differences. Two structures are most common: A **point-by-point structure** moves back and forth between the items being compared, as in paragraph 12. A **block structure** discusses one item completely before discussing the next, as in paragraph 13; in it, the sentence *Business is usually a little different* signals the transition between the two parts of this comparison.

12 My husband and I constantly marvel at the fact that our two sons, born of the same parents and only two years apart in age, are such completely opposite human beings. The most obvious differences became apparent at their births. Our first born, Mark, was big and bold—his intense, already wise eyes, broad shoulders, huge and heavy hands, and powerful, chunky legs gave us the impression that he could have walked out of the delivery room on his own. Our second son, Wayne, was delightfully different. Rather than having the football physique that Mark was born with, Wayne came into the world with a long, slim, wiry body more suited to running, jumping,

and contorting. Wayne's eyes, rather than being intense like Mark's, were impish and innocent. When Mark was delivered, he cried only momentarily, then seemed to settle into a state of intense concentration, as if trying to absorb everything he could about the strange, new environment he found himself in. Conversely, Wayne screamed from the moment he first appeared. There was nothing helpless or pathetic about his cry either—he was darn angry!

—Roseanne Labonte, student

13 Games are of limited duration, take place on or in fixed and finite sites and are governed by openly promulgated rules that are enforced on the spot by neutral professionals. Moreover, they are performed by relatively evenly matched teams that are counseled and led through every move by seasoned hands. Scores are kept, and at the end of the game, a winner is declared. Business is usually a little different. In fact, if there is anyone out there who can say that the business is of limited duration, takes place on a fixed site, is governed by openly promulgated rules that are enforced on the spot by neutral professionals, competes only on relatively even terms, and performs in a way that can be measured in runs or points, then that person is either extraordinarily lucky or seriously deluded.

—Warren Bennis, "Time to Hang Up the Old Sports Clichés"

Analysis and Classification (Dividing into Parts and Grouping)

Analysis, also called **division**, divides a subject into its component parts; **classification** groups things together. Paragraph 14 identifies a new type of zoo design and then analyzes why this new kind of design has developed, specifying three reasons for "the landscape revolution."

14 The current revolution in zoo design—the landscape revolution—is driven by three kinds of change that have occurred during this century. First are great leaps in animal ecology, veterinary medicine, landscape design, and exhibit technology, making possible unprecedented realism in zoo exhibits. Second, and perhaps most important, is the progressive disappearance of wilderness—the very subject of zoos—from the earth. Third is knowledge derived from market research and from environmental psychology, making possible a sophisticated focus on the zoo-goer.

—Melissa Greene, "No Rms, Jungle Vu"

Classification groups information according to a shared characteristic. Paragraph 15, for example, discusses three separate groups of sports signals.

15 Many different kinds of signals are used by the coaches. There are flash signals, which are just what the name implies: The coach may flash a hand across his face or chest to indicate a bunt or hit-and-run. There are holding signals, which are held in one position for several seconds. These might be the clenched fist, bent elbow, or both hands on knees. Then there are the block signals. These divide the coach's body into different sections, or blocks. Touching a part of his body, rubbing his shirt, or touching his cap indicates a sign. Different players can be keyed to various parts of the block so the coach is actually giving several signals with the same sign.

—Rockwell Stensrud, "Who's on Third?"

Analogy (Finding Unusual Similarities)

Analogy is a kind of comparison, finding similarities between objects or ideas that are not usually associated with each other. An analogy is particularly effective for explaining something unfamiliar in terms of something familiar.

16   Casual dress, like casual speech, tends to be loose, relaxed, and colorful. It often contains what might be called "slang words": blue jeans, sneakers, baseball caps, aprons, flowered cotton house-dresses, and the like. These garments could not be worn on a formal occasion without causing disapproval, but in ordinary circumstances they pass without remark. "Vulgar words" in dress, on the other hand, give emphasis and get immediate attention in almost any circumstances, just as they do in speech. Only the skillful can employ them without some loss of face, and even then they must be used in the right way. A torn, unbuttoned shirt, or wildly uncombed hair can signify strong emotions: passion, grief, rage, despair. They are most effective if people already think of you as being neatly dressed, just as the curses of well-spoken persons count for more than those of the customarily foul-mouthed.

—Alison Lurie, *The Language of Clothes*

Cause-and-Effect Analysis (Discovering Reasons and Results)

Causes lead to an event or an effect; effects result from causes. Writing developed by a **cause-and-effect** analysis examines outcomes and reasons for outcomes.

17   Because television is so wonderfully available as child amuser and child defuser, capable of rendering a volatile three-year-old harmless at the flick of a switch, parents grow to depend upon it in the course of their daily lives. And as they continue to utilize television day after day, its importance in their children's lives increases. From a simple source of entertainment provided by parents when they need a break from child care, television gradually changes into a powerful and disruptive presence in family life. But despite their increasing resentment of television's intrusions into their family life, and despite their considerable guilt at not being able to control their children's viewing, parents do not take steps to extricate themselves from television's domination. They can no longer cope without it.

—Marie Winn, *The Plug-In Drug*

Writing concluding paragraphs   W4.g

An effective concluding paragraph brings the discussion to an end
that follows logically from the THESIS STATEMENT and its support in the
essay. A conclusion that is merely tacked on to an essay does not
deliver a sense of completion. In contrast, an ending that flows gracefully and sensibly from what has come before enhances an essay. **QA
Box 11** summarizes techniques to use and to avoid in concluding
paragraphs.

CONCLUDING PARAGRAPHS   QA Box 11

DEVICES TO TRY

- Using any device appropriate for introductory paragraphs—see
  QA Box 8—but avoid using the same one in both the
  introduction and the conclusion
- Summarizing the main points of the essay—but avoid a
  summary if the essay is fewer than three pages long
- Asking for awareness, action, or a similar resolution from
  readers
- Looking ahead to the future

STRATEGIES TO AVOID

- Introducing new ideas or facts that belong in the body of the
  essay
- Rewording the introduction
- Announcing what you have done, as in "In this paper, I have
  explained the drop in oil prices"
- Making absolute claims, as in "I have proved that oil prices do
  not affect gasoline prices"
- Apologizing, as in "Even though I am not an expert, I feel my
  position is correct" or "I may not have convinced you, but
  there is good evidence for my position"

Paragraph 18 is a conclusion that poses a challenging question and
ends by asking people to be prepared to face living alone. (For the
introduction to the same essay, see paragraph 1.)

18   People need to ask themselves, "If I had to live alone starting
tomorrow morning, would I know how?" If the answer is "No," they
need to become conscious of what living alone calls for. People
who face up to life usually do not have to hide from it later on.

—Tara Foster, student

W5 Essay Arrangements

An essay delivers its message most effectively when the elements of the essay are arranged for greatest clarity and impact. No one arrangement fits all essays, but all arrangements are based on the ancient concepts of storytelling: Each essay has a beginning, a middle, and an end. (For advice on writing the individual paragraphs of an essay, see **W4**.) This chapter explains arrangements for two typical types of essays and then shows the final draft of a student essay.

W5.a Typical arrangements in essays with an informative purpose

1   *Introductory paragraph*: leads into the topic of the essay, trying to capture the reader's interest (**W4.a**).

2   *Thesis statement*: states the central message of the essay, accurately reflecting the essay's content (**W1.f**). In an academic essay, the thesis statement usually appears at the end of the introductory paragraph.

3   *Background information*: gives basic material that provides a context for the points being made in the essay. Depending on its complexity, this information appears in its own paragraph or is integrated into the introductory paragraph.

4   *Points of discussion*: support the essay's thesis. Each point is a general statement backed up by specific details. This material forms the essay's core, with each point occupying one or two paragraphs, depending on the overall length of the essay. The general statements, as a group, comprise a "mini-outline" of the essay. The specific details bring the generalizations to life with RENNS (see **W4.d**).

5   *Concluding paragraph*: ends the essay smoothly, not abruptly, flowing logically from the rest of the essay (**W4.g**).

W5.b Typical arrangements in essays with a persuasive purpose

1   *Introductory paragraph*: sets the context for the position argued in the essay while trying to arouse the reader's interest (**W4.a**).

2   *Thesis statement*: states the position being argued (**W1.f**). In a short essay, the thesis statement often appears at the end of the introductory paragraph.

3 *Background information*: gives basic information needed for understanding the position being argued. Depending on its complexity, this material is integrated into the introductory paragraph or given in its own paragraph.

4 *Reasons or evidence*: supports the position being argued. This material is the core of the essay. Each reason or type of evidence usually consists of a general statement backed up with specific details or examples. Depending on the length of the essay, one or two paragraphs are devoted to each reason or type of evidence.

5 *Anticipation of likely objections and responses to them*: mentions positions opposed to the one being argued and rebuts them briefly. In classical argument, this refutation appears in its own paragraph, immediately before the concluding paragraph. Alternatively, it comes immediately after the introductory paragraph, as a bridge to the rest of the essay. Another arrangement allows for including the opposing position and a response to it in each body paragraph.

6 *Concluding paragraph*: ends the essay smoothly, not abruptly, flowing logically from the rest of the essay (**W4.g**).

A sample student essay W5.c

> Women Can Pump Iron, Too
>
> When my grandmother fell and broke her hip last summer, I wanted to help take care of her. Because she was bedridden, she needed to be lifted at times, but I was shocked to discover that I could not lift her without my mother's or brother's help. My grandmother does not weigh much, but she was too much for me. My pride was hurt, and even more important, I began to worry about my plans to be a nurse specializing in care of elderly people. What if I were too weak to help my patients get around? When I realized that I could satisfy one of my Physical Education requirements by taking a weight-lifting course for women, I decided to try it. Many people picture only big, macho men wanting to lift weights, but times have changed. With the right training, women can also "pump iron" successfully to build strength.

TITLE

INTRODUCTION

THESIS STATEMENT

Continued on next page

BACKGROUND
INFORMATION

Women who lift weights, I was happy to learn from my course, can easily avoid developing overly masculine muscle mass. Women can rely on their biology to protect them. Women's bodies produce only very small amounts of the hormones that enlarge muscles in men. With normal weight training, women's muscles grow longer rather than bulkier. The result is smoother, firmer muscles, not massive bulges. Also, women benefit most when they combine weight lifting, which is a form of anaerobic exercise, with aerobic exercise. Anaerobic exercise strengthens and builds muscles, but it does not make people breathe harder or their hearts beat faster for sustained periods. In contrast, aerobic exercises like running, walking, and swimming build endurance, but not massive muscles, because they force a person to take in more oxygen, which increases lung capacity, improves circulatory health, and tones the entire body. Encouraged by my instructor, I balanced my weight-lifting workouts by swimming laps twice a week.

SUPPORT:
FIRST ASPECT
OF TRAINING

Striving for strength can end in injury unless weight lifters learn the safe use of free weights and weight machines. Free weights are barbells, the metal bars that round metal weights can be attached to at each end. To be safe, no matter how little the weight, lifters must never raise a barbell by bending at the waist, grabbing the barbell, and then straightening up. Instead, they should squat, grasp the barbell, and then use their leg muscles to straighten into a standing position. To avoid a twist that can lead to serious injury, lifters must use this posture: head erect and facing forward, back and neck aligned. The big advantage of weight machines, which use weighted handles and bars hooked to wires and pulleys, is that lifters must use them sitting down. Therefore, machines like the Nautilus and Universal actually force lifters to keep their bodies properly aligned, which drastically reduces the chance of injury.

Continued on next page

Once a weight lifter understands how to lift safely, she needs a weight-lifting regime personalized to her specific physical needs. Because benefits come from "resistance," which is the stress that lifting any amount of weight puts on a muscle, no one has to be strong to get started. A well-planned, progressive weight-training program begins with whatever weight a person can lift comfortably and gradually adds to the base weight as she gets stronger. What builds muscle strength is the number of repetitions, or "reps," the lifter does, not necessarily an increase in the amount of resistance from adding weight. Our instructor helped the women in the class, who ranged from 18 to 43, scrawny to pudgy, and couch potato to superstar, develop a program that was right for our individual weights, ages, and overall level of conditioning. Everyone's program differed in how much weight to start out with and how many reps to do for each exercise. Our instructor urged us not to try more weight or reps than our programs called for, even if our first workouts seemed too easy. This turned out to be good advice because those of us who did not listen woke up the next day feeling as though our bodies had been twisted by evil forces.

In addition to fitting a program to her physical capabilities, a weight lifter needs to design an individual routine to fit her personal goals. Most students in my group wanted to improve their upper body strength, so we focused on exercises to strengthen arms, shoulders, abdomens, and chests. Each student learned to use specific exercises to isolate certain muscle groups. Because muscles strengthen and grow when they are rested after a workout, our instructor taught us to work alternate muscle groups on different days. For example, a woman might work on her arms and abdomen one day and then her shoulders and chest the next day. Because I had had such trouble lifting my grandmother, I added exercises to strengthen my legs and back. Another student, who had

Continued on next page

SUPPORT:
SECOND ASPECT
OF TRAINING

SUPPORT:
THIRD ASPECT
OF TRAINING

CONCLUSION:
OUTCOME
WITH CALL
TO ACTION

hurt her neck in a car crash, added neck-strengthening exercises. Someone else, planning to be a physical therapist, added finger- and hand-strengthening exercises.

At the end of our 10 weeks of weight training, we had to evaluate our progress. Was I impressed! I felt ready to lift the world. When I started, I could lift only 10 pounds over my head for 3 reps. By the end of the course, I could lift 10 pounds over my head for 20 reps, and I could lift 18 pounds for 3 reps. Also, I could swim laps for 20 sustained minutes instead of the 10 I had barely managed at first. I am so proud of my weight-training accomplishments that I still work out three or four times a week. I am proof that any woman can benefit from "pumping iron." Not only will she become stronger and have more stamina, she will also feel energetic and confident. After all, there is nothing to lose--except maybe some flab.

Thinking and Reading Critically

SYNTHESIS

critical thinking

evaluate

critical reading

SUMMARY

thinking and reading critically

thinking and reading critically

cause

effect

reasoning

T THINKING AND READING CRITICALLY

T1 Reading Critically

Reading is an active process—a dynamic, meaning-making encounter involving the interaction of the page, eye, and brain. When you read, your mind actively makes connections among what you already know, what you are currently learning, and what is new to you.

Understanding the reading process   T1.a

Reading calls for making predictions. As you read, your mind is constantly guessing what is coming next. Once it discovers what comes next, it either confirms or revises its prediction and moves on. For example, if you encountered the chapter title "The Heartbeat," your predictions could range from romance to how the heart pumps blood. As you read on, you would confirm or revise your prediction according to what you found—you would be in the realm of romance if you encountered a paragraph about lovers and roses, and you would be in the realm of physiology if you encountered diagrams of the heart and information about electrical impulses controlling contractions of muscle fibers. Deciding on your purpose for reading before you begin can help your prediction process. Most reading in college is for the purpose of learning new information, appreciating literary works, or reviewing notes on classes or readings. These purposes involve much rereading; one encounter with the material is rarely enough.

The speed at which you can expect to read is determined by your purpose in reading. When you are hunting for a particular fact, you can skim the material until you come to what you want. When you read about a subject you know well, your mind is already familiar with the material, so you can move somewhat rapidly, slowing down when you come to new material. When you are unfamiliar with the subject, your mind needs time to absorb the new material, so you have to proceed slowly.

Engaging in the reading process   T1.b

During the reading process, full meaning emerges as you read on three levels.

STEPS IN THE READING PROCESS

1. Read for *literal meaning*: Read "on" the lines to see what is stated.
2. Read to make *inferences*: Read "between" the lines to see what is implied but not stated.
3. Read to *evaluate*: Read "beyond" the lines to see whether the

writer deals fairly with the reader. Decide whether the writer's reasoning is sound or faulty, the writer's words are accurate or slanted, and the writer's interaction with the reader is fair or manipulative.

Reading on these three levels is discussed in detail in the next three sections. Be careful as a reader not to stop at the literal level. Only when you go to the next two levels is complete understanding possible.

Reading for Literal Meaning

Reading for **literal meaning**, sometimes called reading "on" the line, calls for you to understand what is said. It does not include impressions or opinions about the material. The literal level focuses on the key facts, the line of reasoning in an ARGUMENT, or the central details of plot and character. Also important are the minor details that lend texture to the picture.

Whenever you encounter a complex writing style that makes literal-level reading difficult, break the sentences down into shorter units or reword them into a simpler style. When you find a concept that you need to think through, take the time to come to know the new idea. Although no student has unlimited time for reading and thinking, rushing through material to "cover" it rather than understand it costs more time in the long run.

QA Box 12 offers suggestions that can help you comprehend most efficiently what you are reading.

QA Box 12

WAYS TO HELP YOUR READING COMPREHENSION

- When reading about an unfamiliar subject, associate the new material with what you already know. If necessary, build your store of prior knowledge by reading easier material on the subject in other sources.

- If your mind wanders, be fiercely determined to concentrate, and resist the appeal of other thoughts. Do whatever it takes: Arrange for silence or music, for being alone or in a crowded library's reading room, for reading at your best time of day.

- Allot sufficient time to work with new material. Discipline yourself to balance classes, working, socializing, and participating in family activities with the unavoidable, time-consuming, yet totally engaging demands of reading, learning, and studying. Nothing prevents your success as much as lack of time.

- If you are unfamiliar with any key terms in your reading, take time to list them and their meanings. Try to figure meanings

Continued on next page

➤ *QA Box 12, continued from previous page*

out by using context clues. Many textbooks have a list of important terms and their definitions (often called a "glossary") at the end of each chapter or at the back of the book (as in this handbook). Also, always have a good dictionary at hand. As you accumulate new words, keep a list of them taped inside your textbook so that you can consult the information easily.

Reading to Make Inferences

Reading to make **inferences**, sometimes called reading "between" the lines, means understanding what is implied but not stated. Often you have to infer information, or background, or the author's purpose.

The process of inferring adds texture and invaluable background to facilitate your interpretation of a passage. As you read to make inferences, consult **QA Box 13**.

CHECKLIST FOR MAKING INFERENCES DURING READING

QA Box 13

1　What is implied rather than stated?

2　What words carry important implied meanings, or connotations, as well as their literal meanings, or denotations? (For more about word meanings, see **E4**.)

3　What information does the author assume I already have when I start to read the material?

4　What information about the author's background, principles, and point of view does the author seem to assume I have?

5　What attitudes toward the topic does the author seem to assume I have?

Reading to Evaluate

Evaluative reading, sometimes called reading "beyond" the lines, calls for many skills: recognizing the impact of the author's tone, detecting prejudice, and differentiating fact from opinion. Evaluative reading demands concentration and a willingness to deal with matters that are relative and sometimes ambiguous.

The **tone** emerges from all aspects of the material, from the writer's choice of words to the content of the message. Most readers are wary of a highly emotional tone. An author's tone should be appropriate to the author's purpose and audience. For example, most academic writing should not use language that is either overly informal or overly stiff and formal (see **E4.d**). Most authors use a serious tone, but sometimes they use humor to get their point across; if you read such material exclusively for its literal meaning, you will miss the point.

In writing, **prejudice** is revealed in negative opinions based on beliefs rather than on facts or evidence. Positive language can be used to disguise negative opinions, so it is important to recognize when underlying assumptions are negative: "Poor people like living in crowded conditions because they are used to the surroundings" or "Women are too nurturing to succeed in business." Underlying negative opinions can distort information.

Facts are statements that can be verified by experiment, research, and/or observation, as opposed to **opinions**, which are statements of personal beliefs. Because opinions contain ideas that cannot be verified, they are open to debate.

An author sometimes intentionally blurs the difference between fact and opinion. A discerning reader must be able to tell the difference. One aid in differentiating between fact and opinion is to think beyond the obvious. For example, is "Strenuous exercise is good for your health" a fact? Although the statement has the ring of truth, it may not be true for people with severe arthritis or advanced heart disease.

T1.c Engaging in critical reading

To read critically is to think about what you are reading while you are reading it. To help yourself do so, use specific approaches such as reading systematically and reading actively and closely, explained below. As you use these approaches, adapt them to your personal style of getting the most out of your reading.

Reading Systematically

To read systematically is to use a structured plan for delving into the material. Your goal is to come to know and truly understand the material and—equally important—to be able to discuss it and even write about it clearly.

GUIDELINES FOR READING SYSTEMATICALLY

1 **Preview:** Before you start reading, look ahead. Glance over the pages you intend to read so that your mind can start making predictions (see **T1.a**). Looking ahead prepares your mind for the material. As you look over the pages, ask yourself questions that the material stimulates. Do not expect to answer all the questions at this point; their purpose is merely to focus your thoughts.

To preview a textbook, first get an overview of the whole book by reading the chapter titles (book titles can be misleading). Next, survey the chapter you are assigned by reading all the headings large and small; all boldface words (in darker print); and all visuals and their captions, including photographs, drawings, tables, figures, and charts. If a glossary is at the end of the chapter, scan it for words you do and do not know.

To preview material that has few or no headings, read and ask questions about the book title and chapter titles (if any); about the author's name and any introductory notes about the author, such as those in many books of collected essays; and about pivotal paragraphs, such as the first few paragraphs and (unless you are reading for suspense) the last pages or paragraphs. If a preface or introduction begins a book, be sure to read it or at least skim it early on.

2 **Read:** Read the material actively and closely, as explained in the next section. Seek the full meaning at all levels explained in **T1.b**. Most of all, expect to reread. College-level material can rarely be fully understood and absorbed in one reading. Budget your time so that you can make many passes through the material.

3 **Review:** Go back to the things you looked at when you previewed the material. Ask yourself the same sorts of questions as during your preview, this time answering them as fully as possible. If you cannot do so, reread for the answers. For best success, review in chunks—small sections that you can capture comfortably. Do not try to cover too much at once.

You can stimulate your concentration during this reading by always staying aware of your intention in reviewing. This awareness will help you stay alert. Also, the next day, and again about a week later, repeat your review. As much as time permits, re-review at frequent intervals during a course. The more reinforcement, the better.

Collaborative learning can help you reinforce what you learn from reading. Ask a friend or classmate who knows the material to discuss it with you, even test you. Conversely, offer to teach the material to someone; you will quickly discover whether or not you have mastered it well enough to communicate it.

Reading Actively and Closely

Annotating is the secret to success in reading actively and closely. **Annotating** means writing notes to yourself in a book's margins, underlining or highlighting key passages, and using asterisks and other special marks to focus your attention.

Active reading calls for making annotations that relate to the content and meaning of the material. Summarize major points in the margin. When you review, they will stand out. If you underline or highlight, be sure to jot in the margin key words or phrases that will jog your memory when you need to recall what is important. Extract meaning on the literal, inferential, and evaluative levels (see **T1.b**).

Close reading calls for making annotations that record the connections you make between the material and what you already know or have experienced. Close reading can make you ask questions or form opinions about the material. This is your chance to have a conversation on paper with the author. Let your mind range across ideas you associate with what you are reading. Consider yourself a partner in the making of meaning, a full participant in the exchange of ideas, opinions, and experiences that typify a college education.

The excerpt below shows annotations for both close reading and active reading.

Doesn't matter who wins, but tactics and prowess can be admired.

Although I like to play, and sometimes like to watch, I cannot see what possible difference it makes which team beats which. The tactics are sometimes interesting, and certainly the prowess of the players deserves applause—but most men seem to use commercial sports as a kind of (narcotic) shutting out reality, rather than heightening it.

Sports talk is boring.

There is nothing more boring, in my view, than a prolonged discussion by laymen of yesterday's game. These dreary conversations are a form of (social alcoholism,) enabling them to achieve a (dubious rapport) without ever once having to come to grips with a subject worthy of a grown man's concern.

Other examples include soap operas and sitcoms.

When my son and husband watch together, the rapport is very real.

It is easy to see the (opiate) quality of sports in our society when tens of millions of men will spend a splendid Saturday or Sunday fall afternoon sitting (stupefied) in front of the TV, watching a "big game," when they might be out exercising their own flaccid muscles and stimulating their lethargic corpuscles.

Instead of watching men should exercise.

Annotations for active reading and close reading (close-reading annotations are circled)

If you feel unable to write in a book—even though the practice of annotating texts dates back to the Middle Ages—try keeping a "double-entry notebook." On one side of each sheet of paper write close-reading notes on the content; on the other side, enter active-reading notes detailing the connections you make. Be sure to include information that identifies the passages referred to so that you can easily locate them again.

T2 Thinking Critically

Thinking is not something you choose to do, any more than a fish "chooses" to live in water. To be human is to think. But while the process of thinking may come naturally, awareness of how you think does not. Thinking about thinking is the key to critical thinking.

Understanding critical thinking   T2.a

When you think critically, you take control of your conscious thought processes. Without such control, you risk being controlled by the ideas of others. Indeed, critical thinking is at the heart of a liberal (from the Latin word for *free*) education.

The word *critical* here has a neutral meaning. It does not mean taking a negative view or finding fault, as when someone criticizes another person for doing something wrong. The essence of critical thinking is thinking beyond the obvious, just as critical reading (**T1**) is reading beyond the LITERAL level.

Engaging in critical thinking   T2.b

Critical thinking is a process of contemplation and deliberation. Within this process, it takes time to progress from becoming fully aware of something, to reflecting on it, to reacting to it. You use this sequence often in your life, as when you learn a new job and then evaluate the job itself as well as your ability to do the work.

The general process of critical thinking, as it is applied in academic settings, is described in **QA Box 14**. This process also applies to reading critically (**T1**) and writing critically (**T3**).

STEPS IN THE CRITICAL THINKING PROCESS

QA
Box
14

1 **Analyze:** Consider the whole and then break it into its component parts so that you can examine them separately. By seeing them as distinct units, you can come to understand how they interrelate.

2 **Summarize:** Extract and restate the material's main message or central point at the literal level (see **T1.b**).

3 **Interpret:** Read "between the lines" to make inferences (see **T1.b**) about the unstated assumptions implied by the material. Also evaluate the material for its underlying currents as conveyed by TONE, slant, and clarity of distinctions between fact and opinion (see **T1.b**); by the quality of evidence (see **T2.c**); and by the rigor of its reasoning (see **T2.e**) and logic (see **T2.f**).

4 **Synthesize:** Pull together what you have summarized, analyzed, and interpreted to connect it to what you already know (your prior knowledge) or what you are currently learning. Find links that help you grasp the new material to create a new whole, one that reflects your ability to see and explain relationships among ideas.

5 **Assess critically:** Judge the quality of the material on its own and as it holds up in your synthesis of it with related material.

As with the writing process, the steps of the critical thinking process are not in a rigid order. Each element is described separately in this handbook to help you understand its operation, but in reality the elements are intertwined. Therefore, expect sometimes to combine steps, reverse their order, and even return to earlier parts of the process. Synthesis and assessment, in particular, tend to operate concurrently. Still, they are two different mental activities: *synthesis* is making connections, and *assessment* is making judgments.

! **Alert:** *Summary* (step 2 in **QA Box 14**) and *synthesis* (step 4) are two different processes. Be careful not to think that your summary is a synthesis. For fuller discussion of the differences, see **T3**.

T2.c Assessing evidence critically ▌

The cornerstone of all reasoning is evidence. As a reader, you expect writers to provide solid evidence for any claim made or conclusion reached. As a writer, you want to use evidence well to support your claims or conclusions. Evidence consists of facts, statistical information, examples, and opinions of experts. First-hand evidence is based on **primary sources**—your own or someone else's direct observation or original work. **Secondary sources** report, describe, comment on, or analyze the experiences or work of others. The first-hand evidence of a primary source may be more authoritative than the second-hand evidence of a secondary source, but all evidence requires scrupulous evaluation.

Evaluating Evidence

QA Box 15 gives guidelines for evaluating evidence. Use them for evaluating what you read and for deciding what evidence to include in your own writing.

QA Box 15	**GUIDELINES FOR EVALUATING EVIDENCE** ▌

Is the evidence sufficient? A general rule for both readers and writers is that the more evidence, the better. As a reader, you usually have more confidence in the results of a survey that draws on a hundred respondents rather than on ten. As a writer, you may convince your reader that violence is a serious problem in high schools on the basis of two specific examples, but you will be more convincing if you can give five examples—or, better still, statistics for a school district, a city, or a nation.

Is the evidence representative? As a reader, assess objectivity and fairness; do not assume them because words are in print. Do not trust a claim or conclusion about a group based on only a few members rather than on a truly representative or typical sample. As a writer, make sure

Continued on next page

▶ *QA Box 15, continued from previous page*

the evidence you offer represents your claim fairly; do not base your point on exceptions.

Is the evidence relevant? Determining relevance can demand subtle thinking. Suppose you read evidence that 100 students who had watched television for more than two hours a day throughout high school earned significantly lower scores on a college entrance exam than 100 students who had not. Can you conclude that students who watch less television perform better on college entrance exams? What other differences exist between the two groups—geographical region, family background, socioeconomic group, quality of schools attended? The evidence leading to the conclusion about TV watching and college entrance exams is not relevant unless both groups are identical except for their TV-watching practices.

Is the evidence accurate? Inaccurate evidence is useless. Evidence must come from reliable sources. Equally important, reliable evidence must be carefully presented so that it does not misrepresent or distort information.

Is the evidence reasonable? Evidence rarely justifies claims that include words such as *all*, *certainly*, *always*, or *never*. Conclusions are more reasonable when qualified with words such as *some*, *many*, *a few*, *probably*, *possibly*, *perhaps*, *may*, *usually*, and *often*. Remember that today's "facts" may be revised as time passes, information changes, and knowledge grows.

Assessing cause and effect critically

T2.d

Cause and effect is a mode of thinking that seeks to establish some relationship, or link, between two or more specific pieces of evidence. Regardless of whether you begin with a cause or an effect, you are working with this basic pattern:

Basic Pattern for Cause and Effect

Cause A ⟶ produces ⟶ effect B

You may seek to understand the effects of a known cause (for example, studying two more hours each night):

More studying ⟶ produces ⟶ ?

Or you may attempt to determine the cause or causes of a known effect (for example, recurrent headaches):

? ⟶ produces ⟶ recurrent headaches

If you want to use reasoning based on a relationship of cause and effect, evaluate the connections carefully by keeping in mind the guidelines in **QA Box 16**.

GUIDELINES FOR ASSESSING CAUSE AND EFFECT

Is there a clear relationship between events? When you read or write about causes and effects, carefully think through the reasoning. Related causes and effects happen in sequence, a cause exists or occurs before an effect. First the wind blows; then a door slams; then a pane of glass in the door breaks. But just because the order of events implies a cause-and-effect relationship, that relationship does not necessarily exist. Perhaps someone slammed the door shut. Perhaps someone threw a baseball through the glass pane. A cause-and-effect relationship must be linked by more than chronological sequence. The fact that B happens after A does not prove that A causes B.

Is there a pattern of repetition? To establish that A causes B, there must be proof that every time A is present, B occurs—or that B never occurs unless A is present. The need for a pattern of repetition explains why the Food and Drug Administration performs thousands of tests before declaring a new food or medicine safe for human consumption.

Are there multiple causes and/or effects? Avoid oversimplification. The basic pattern of cause and effect—single cause, single effect (A causes B)—rarely represents the full picture. For example,

A $\longrightarrow$ causes $\longrightarrow$ B
Driving $\longrightarrow$ causes $\longrightarrow$ air pollution

is an oversimplification. It is more accurate to acknowledge that

A and others $\longrightarrow$ cause $\longrightarrow$ B
Driving
Heating with fossil fuels
Clearing forests by burning $\Big\} \longrightarrow$ cause $\longrightarrow$ air pollution
Trees "exhaling" carbon dioxide
Volcanic eruptions

Similarly, a cause or outcome usually produces multiple effects.

T2.e Assessing reasoning processes critically

To think critically, you need to understand reasoning processes so that you can recognize and evaluate them in your reading and use them correctly in your writing. Induction and deduction are reasoning processes. They are natural thought patterns that people use every day to think through ideas and make decisions.

Inductive reasoning moves from the specific to the general. It begins with the evidence of specific facts, observations, or experiences and, from these specific cases, draws a general observation. If, for example, you see your neighbor leave the house at 7:45 every morning, you may eventually say, "My neighbor leaves his house every morning at 7:45." That statement is an inductive conclusion from evidence you have observed. On the basis of it, you can make statements predicting the likelihood of your neighbor's leaving the house at 7:45 today, tomorrow, and into the future. But inductive reasoning is not "true." After all, it takes only one occurrence of your neighbor's leaving at a time other than 7:45 A.M. or not at all to make the inductive conclusion unreliable.

Deductive reasoning moves from the general to the specific, relating two statements in such a way that a valid conclusion can be drawn from them. The deductive process works like this: *When it rains, the streets get wet* [first premise]. *It's raining* [second premise]. *The streets are getting wet* [conclusion]. Deduction is valid as long as premises and conclusions are properly constructed. But deduction is "true" only if the premises are true and the argument is properly constructed. Consider this set of premises and conclusion, for example: *When it rains, fire falls from the sky* [first premise]. *It's raining* [second premise]. *Fire is falling from the sky* [conclusion]. This argument is valid but untrue.

The differences between inductive and deductive reasoning are summarized in **QA Box 17**.

COMPARISON OF INDUCTIVE AND DEDUCTIVE REASONING			QA Box 17
	Inductive Reasoning	**Deductive Reasoning**	
Argument begins	with specific evidence	with a general claim	
Argument concludes	with a general claim	with a specific statement	
Conclusion is	reliable or unreliable	true or false	
Reasoning is used	to discover something new	to apply what is known	

Recognizing and avoiding logical fallacies

T2.f

Logical fallacies are flaws in reasoning that lead to illogical statements. Logical fallacies tend to occur most often when ideas are being argued, but they can be found in all types of writing. Most logical fallacies masquerade as reasonable statements, but they are in fact attempts to manipulate readers by reaching their emotions instead of their intellects, their hearts rather than their heads. Most logical fallacies are given labels that indicate in what way the thinking has gone wrong during the reasoning process.

Hasty generalization occurs when someone generalizes from inadequate evidence. If the statement "My hometown is the best place in the state to live" is supported with only two examples of why the town is pleasant, the generalization is hasty. **Stereotyping** occurs when someone makes prejudiced hasty generalizations about all members of a particular religious, ethnic, racial, or political group: "Everyone from country X is dishonest."

Sexism occurs when someone discriminates against people on the basis of gender. See **E5**, especially **QA Box 40**.

False analogy makes a comparison in which the differences outweigh the similarities, or the similarities are irrelevant to the claim that the analogy is intended to support. "X is too old to be President because an old dog cannot learn new tricks."

Begging the question occurs when an argument states a claim but bases the support on the claim, so the reasoning is circular. Sometimes the support simply restates the claim: "Wrestling is a dangerous sport because it is unsafe." "Unsafe" conveys the same idea as "dangerous"; it does not provide evidence to support the claim that wrestling is dangerous. Another question-begging argument offers as support a second statement but one whose support is the argument in the first statement: "Wrestling is a dangerous sport because wrestlers get injured. Anyone as big and strong as a wrestler would not get injured if the sport were safe." Begging the question also occurs in statements such as "Wrestlers love danger." There is an unstated assumption that wrestling is dangerous as well as an assumption that no proof is called for because the audience shares the opinion that wrestling is dangerous.

Irrelevant argument is called *non sequitur* in Latin, which translates as "it does not follow." This flaw occurs when a conclusion does not follow from the premises: "Jane Jones is a forceful speaker, so she will make a good mayor." It does not follow that someone's ability to be a forceful speaker will make that person a good mayor.

False cause is called *post hoc, ergo propter hoc* in Latin—which means "after this, therefore because of this." It is a reasoning error in assessing cause and effect, for it assumes that because two events are related in time, the first one causes the second one. "A new weather satellite was launched last week, and it has been raining ever since" implies—illogically—that the rain (the second event) is a result of the satellite launch (the first event).

Self-contradiction occurs when two premises are used that cannot simultaneously be true: "Only when nuclear weapons have finally destroyed us will we be convinced of the need to control them." This statement is self-contradictory in that no one would be around to be convinced if everyone had been destroyed.

Red herring, sometimes referred to as *ignoring the question*, sidetracks an issue by bringing up a totally unrelated issue: "Why worry about pandas becoming extinct when we should be concerned about the plight of the homeless?" Someone who introduces an irrelevant issue hopes to distract the audience as a red herring might distract bloodhounds from a scent.

Argument to the person, also known as *ad hominem*, attacks a person's appearance, personal habits, or character instead of dealing with the merits of the individual's arguments, ideas, or opinions. "We could take her position in favor of jailing child abusers seriously if she were not so nasty to the children who live next door to her" is one type of *ad hominem* attack. It seems so reasonable to belittle suggestions about dealing with child abusers from someone who may (or may not) be nasty to the children next door. In truth, however, the suggestions, not the person who makes them, must be dealt with. The person who argues is not the argument.

Guilt by association is a kind of *ad hominem* attack implying that an individual's arguments, ideas, or opinions lack merit because of that person's activities, interests, or associates. The claim that because Jack belongs to the International Hill Climbers Association, which declared bankruptcy last month, he is unfit to be mayor uses guilt by association.

Bandwagon, also known as *going along with the crowd* or *ad populum*, implies that something is right because everyone is doing it, that truth is determined by majority vote: "Smoking is not bad for people because millions of people smoke."

False or irrelevant authority, sometimes called *ad verecundiam*, means citing the opinion of an "expert" who has no claim to expertise about the subject at hand. This fallacy attempts to transfer prestige from one area to another. Many television commercials rely on this tactic—a famous tennis player praising a brand of motor oil or a popular movie star lauding a brand of cheese.

Card-stacking, also known as *special pleading*, ignores evidence on the other side of a question. From all the available facts, the person arguing selects only those that will build the best (or worst) possible case. Many television commercials use this strategy. When three slim, happy consumers rave about a new diet plan, they do not mention (a) the plan does not work for everyone and (b) other plans work better for some people. The makers of the commercial select evidence that helps their cause and ignore any that does not.

The either-or fallacy, also known as *false dilemma*, offers only two alternatives when more exist. Such fallacies often touch on emotional issues and can therefore seem accurate at first, but when people reflect, they quickly come to realize that more alternatives are available: "Either go to college or forget about getting a job." This statement implies that a college education is a prerequisite for all jobs, which is not true.

Taking something out of context separates an idea or fact from the material surrounding it, thus distorting it for special purposes. Suppose a critic writes about a movie, "The plot was predictable and boring but the music was sparkling," and then an advertisement for the movie says, ". . . sparkling" and puts the critic's name by the quotation. The critic's words have been taken out of context and the meaning distorted.

Appeal to ignorance assumes that an argument is valid simply because it has not been shown to be false. Conversely, something is not false simply because it has not been shown to be true. Appeals to ignorance can be very persuasive because they prey on people's superstitions or lack of knowledge. Here is a typical example of such flawed reasoning: "Since no one has proven that depression does not cause cancer, we can assume that it does." In fact, the absence of opposing evidence proves nothing.

Ambiguity and **equivocation** characterize expressions that are unclear because they have more than one meaning. An *ambiguous* expression is one that may be taken either way by the reader. The statement "They were entertaining guests" is an example. Were the guests amusing to be with or were people giving hospitality to guests? An *equivocal* expression, by contrast, is one used in two or more ways within a single argument. If someone argued that the President played a role in arms control negotiations and then, two sentences later, said that the President was playing a role when he called himself "the education President," the person would be equivocating.

T3 Distinguishing Between Summary and Synthesis

A crucial distinction in critical thinking, critical reading, and critical writing resides in the differences between summary and synthesis.

T3.a Understanding summary ▌

Summary comes before synthesis (see **QA Box 14** in **T2.b**). To **summarize** is to extract the main message or central point of a passage. A summary does not include supporting evidence or details. It is the gist, the hub, the seed of what the author is saying; it is not your reaction to it.

Most people summarize informally in conversation (and more formally in a speech). When you write a summary, use the guidelines in **QA Box 53** in section **R3.e**. They apply generally to summarizing, as in content annotations (see **T1.c**) and in papers using sources (see especially **Research Writing**).

Understanding synthesis

Synthesis comes after ANALYSIS, SUMMARY, and interpretation (see **QA Box 14** in **T2.b**). To **synthesize** is to weave together ideas from more than one source; to connect ideas from one or more sources to what you already know from what you have read, listened to, and experienced; to create a new whole that is your own as a result of your thinking about diverse yet related ideas. Many techniques can help that thinking along. When you synthesize unconsciously, your mind connects ideas by thought processes mirrored in the rhetorical strategies discussed in **W4.f**.

Synthesizing

To synthesize deliberately, consciously apply RHETORICAL STRATEGIES to the material. For example:

- Compare ideas in sources.
- Contrast ideas in sources.
- Create definitions that combine and extend definitions in individual sources.
- Apply examples or descriptions from one source to illustrate ideas in another.
- Find causes and/or effects or other processes described in one source that explain another.

Unsynthesized ideas and information are like separate spools of thread, neatly lined up, possibly coordinated, but not integrated. Synthesized ideas and information become threads woven into a tapestry that creates a new whole. Synthesizing is the core of critical thinking. Synthesis is the evidence of your ability to tie ideas together in the tapestry of what you learn and know and experience.

Alert: "Synthesis by summary"—a mere listing of who said what about a topic—is not true synthesis. It does not create new connections among ideas. **!**

When you have only one source to think about, try the following techniques for stimulating your mind to recall prior knowledge and work toward creating a synthesis.

SYNTHESIZING WITH ONE SOURCE

- Use the technique of clustering (see **W1.e**) to lay out and discover relationships among elements in the material and between the material and other ideas that come to mind.
- Use your powers of play. Mentally toss ideas around, even if you make connections that seem outrageous. Try opposites

(for example, read about athletes and think about the most unathletic person you know). Try turning an idea upside down (for example, read about the value of being a good sport and list the benefits of being a bad sport). Try visualizing what you are reading about, and then tinker with the mental picture (for example, picture two people playing tennis and substitute dogs playing Frisbee or seals playing Ping Pong). The possibilities are endless—make word associations, think up song lyrics, draft a TV commercial. The goal is always to jump-start your thinking so that you see ideas in new ways.

■ Discuss your reading with someone else. Summarize its content and elicit the other person's opinion or ideas. Deliberately debate that opinion or challenge those ideas. Discussions and debates can get your mind moving.

■ Write a critical response to the material. Summarize its content and then write out your response to it. Include not just whether you agree or disagree but the reasons why you respond as you do. Think about your prior knowledge and experience, and write about how you connect what you have read to what you know, and how you have made this reading your own.

Grammar Basics

if

as if

as though

and

unless

clauses

noun reference

Parts of speech

using bad and badly

Who, Which, and That

using

good

and

well

AGREEMENT

verb tenses

Phrases

G GRAMMAR BASICS

G1 Parts of Speech

Knowing the parts of speech gives you a basic vocabulary for identifying words and understanding how language works. No part of speech exists in a vacuum. To identify a word's part of speech correctly, you need to see how the word functions in the sentence you are analyzing. Often, the same word functions differently in different sentences.

- We ate **fish**.   [*Fish* is a NOUN.* It names a thing.]
- We **fish** on weekends.   [*Fish* is a VERB. It names an action.]

Recognizing nouns   G1.a

A **noun** names a person, place, thing, or idea: *student, college, textbook, education*. For types of nouns, see **QA Box 18**, below.

Alert: Words often appear with nouns to tell how much or how many, whose, which one, and similar information about the noun. These words include ARTICLES (*a, an, the*) and other DETERMINERS. For more about these words, see **G1.e** and **F2**.   **!**

ESL Note: Sometimes a SUFFIX (a word ending) can help you identify the part of speech. Words with these suffixes are usually nouns: *-ance, -ence, -ment, -ness,* and *-ty*.   **!**

NOUNS			QA Box 18
Proper	names specific people, places, or things (first letter is always capitalized)	*John Lennon, Paris, Buick*	
Common	names general groups, places, people, or things	*singer, city, automobile*	
Concrete	names things experienced through the senses: sight, hearing, taste, smell, and touch	*landscape, pizza, thunder*	
Abstract	names things not knowable through the senses	*freedom, shyness*	
Collective	names groups	*family, team*	
Noncount or mass	names "uncountable" things	*water, time*	
Count	names countable items	*lake (lakes), minute (minutes)*	

*Words printed in small capital letters (such as NOUN) are defined in the Terms Glossary on pages 295–313.

G1.b Recognizing pronouns

A **pronoun** takes the place of a NOUN. The word or words that a pronoun replaces is called its **antecedent**.

- **David** is an accountant. [noun]
- **He** is an accountant. [pronoun]
- The budget committee needs to consult **him**. [The pronoun *him* refers to its antecedent, *David*.]

For types of pronouns, see **QA Box 19**. For more about using pronouns, see **G5–G7**.

QA Box 19	**PRONOUNS**		
	Personal *I, you, they, her, its, ours,* and others	refers to people or things	I saw **her** take a book to **them**.
	Relative *who, which, that*	introduces certain NOUN CLAUSES and ADJECTIVE CLAUSES	The book **that** I lost was valuable.
	Interrogative *who, whose, what, which,* and others	introduces a question	**Who** called?
	Demonstrative *this, these, that, those*	points out the antecedent	Whose books are **these**?
	Reflexive; Intensive *myself, themselves,* and other *-self* or *-selves* words	reflects back to the antecedent; intensifies the antecedent	They claim to support **themselves.** I **myself** doubt it.
	Reciprocal *each other, one another*	refers to individual parts of a plural antecedent	We respect **each other.**
	Indefinite *all, anyone, each,* and others	refers to nonspecific persons or things	**Everyone** is welcome here.

G1.c Recognizing verbs

Main verbs express action, occurrence, or state of being.

- I **dance**. [action]
- The audience **became** silent. [occurrence]

- Your dancing **was** excellent.   [state of being]

For more about verbs, see **G3**; for MODAL AUXILIARY VERBS, see **F6**.

Alert: If you are not sure whether a word is a verb, try putting the word into a different TENSE. If the sentence still makes sense, the word is a verb. (For an explanation of verb tense, see **G3.d**.)

No   He is a **changed** person. He is a **will change** person.   [The sentence does not make sense when the verb *will change* is substituted, so *changed* is not functioning as a verb.]

Yes   The store **changed** owners. The store **will change** owners. [Because the sentence still makes sense when the verb *will change* is substituted, *changed* is functioning as a verb.]

Recognizing verbals   G1.d

Verbals are verb parts functioning as NOUNS, ADJECTIVES, or ADVERBS; see **QA Box 20**.

VERBALS		QA Box 20
Infinitive *to* + SIMPLE FORM of verb	1. Noun: names an action, state, or condition 2. Adjective or adverb: describes or modifies	**To eat** soon is our goal. Still, we have nothing **to eat**.
Past participle -*ed* form of REGULAR VERB or equivalent in IRREGULAR VERB	Adjective: describes or modifies	**Boiled, filtered** water is usually safe to drink.
Present participle -*ing* form of verb	1. adjective: describes or modifies 2. noun: names an action, state, or condition	**Running** water may not be safe. **Drinking** contaminated water is dangerous.

ESL Note: For information about GERUNDS and INFINITIVES used as objects, see **F5**.

Recognizing adjectives   G1.e

Adjectives modify—that is, they describe or limit—NOUNS, PRONOUNS, and word groups that function as nouns.

- I saw a **green** and **leafy** tree.   [*Green* and *leafy* modify the noun *tree*.]

Descriptive adjectives, such as *green* and *leafy*, can show levels of intensity: *green, greener, greenest; leafy, more leafy, most leafy;* see **G8.d**. **Proper adjectives** are formed from proper nouns: *American, Victorian*.

! **ESL Note:** Words with these SUFFIXES (word endings) are usually adjectives: *-ful, -ish, -less,* and *-like*. For more about suffixes, see **E4.c**.

Determiners, sometimes called *limiting adjectives*, "limit" nouns by conveying information such as whether a noun is general (*a tree*) or specific (*the tree*). They also tell which one (*this tree*), how many (*twelve trees*), whose (*our tree*), and similar information about nouns. For types of determiners, see **QA Box 21**. For more on determiners, see **F1** and **F2**.

QA Box 21	**DETERMINERS**	
	Articles *a, an, the*	**A** reporter working on **an** assignment is using **the** telephone.
	Demonstrative *this, these, that, those*	**Those** students rent **that** house.
	Indefinite *any, each, few, other, some,* and others	**Few** films today have complex plots.
	Interrogative *what, which, whose*	**What** answer did you give?
	Numerical *one, first, two, second,* and others	The **fifth** question was tricky.
	Possessive *my, your, their,* and others	**My** violin is older than **your** cello.
	Relative *what, which, whose, whatever,* and others	We do not know **which** road to take.

For more about adjectives, see **G8**.

G1.f Recognizing adverbs

An **adverb** modifies—that is, describes or limits—VERBS, ADJECTIVES, other adverbs, and entire sentences.

- Chefs plan meals **carefully**.   [*Carefully* modifies the verb *plan*.]
- Vegetables provide **very** important vitamins.   [*Very* modifies the adjective *important*.]

- Those potato chips are **too** heavily salted.   [*Too* modifies the adverb *heavily*.]
- **Fortunately**, people realize that salt can do harm.   [*Fortunately* modifies the entire sentence.]

Descriptive adverbs can show levels of intensity, usually by adding *more* (or *less*) and *most* (or *least*): *more happily, least clearly*. Many descriptive adverbs are formed by adding *-ly* to adjectives: *sadly, loudly, normally*. Some adjectives, however, end in *-ly*: *brotherly, lovely*. Also many adverbs do not end in *-ly*: *very, always, not, yesterday*, and *well* are a few that do not. For more about descriptive adverbs, see **G8**.

Conjunctive adverbs modify by creating logical connections in meaning, as shown in **QA Box 22**.

When words such as *where, why*, and *when* are used to introduce ADJECTIVE CLAUSES (see **G2.e**), they are called **relative adverbs**.

CONJUNCTIVE ADVERBS AND THE RELATIONSHIPS THEY EXPRESS		QA Box 22
Relationship	**Words**	
Addition	*also, furthermore, moreover, besides,*	
Contrast	*however, still, nevertheless, conversely, nonetheless, instead, otherwise,*	
Comparison	*similarly, likewise,*	
Result or summary	*therefore, thus, consequently, accordingly, hence, then,*	
Time	*next, then, meanwhile, finally, subsequently,*	
Emphasis	*indeed, certainly,*	

Recognizing prepositions   G1.g

Prepositions include common words such as *in, under, by, after, to, on, over*, and *since*. **Prepositions** function with other words in PREPOSITIONAL PHRASES and these phrases often set out relationships in time or space: *in April, under the orange umbrella*. For more about prepositions, including a list, see **F4**.

- **In** the fall, we will hear a concert **by** our favorite tenor.
- **After** the concert, he will fly **to** Paris.

Recognizing conjunctions   G1.h

A **conjunction** connects words, PHRASES, or CLAUSES. **Coordinating conjunctions** join two or more grammatically equivalent structures.

<table>
<tr><td>QA Box 23</td><td colspan="2">COORDINATING CONJUNCTIONS AND THE RELATIONSHIPS THEY EDXPRESS</td></tr>
</table>

Relationship	Words
Addition	*and*
Contrast	*but, yet*
Result or effect	*so*
Reason or cause	*for*
Choice	*or*
Negative choice	*nor*

- We hike **and** camp every summer. [*And* joins two words.]
- I love the outdoors, **but** my family does not. [*But* joins two independent clauses.]

Correlative conjunctions function in pairs to join equivalent grammatical structures. They include *both . . . and, either . . . or, neither . . . nor, not only . . . but (also), whether . . . or,* and *not . . . so much as.*

- **Not only** students **but also** business people should study a second language.

Subordinating conjunctions introduce DEPENDENT CLAUSES, structures that are grammatically less important than those in an independent clause within the same sentence. **QA Box 24**, below, lists subordinating conjunctions.

<table>
<tr><td>QA Box 24</td><td colspan="2">SUBORDINATING CONJUNCTIONS AND THE RELATIONSHIPS THEY EXPRESS</td></tr>
</table>

Relationship	Words
Time	*after, before, once, since, until, when, whenever, while*
Reason or cause	*as, because, since*
Result or effect	*in order that, so, so that, that*
Condition	*if, even if, provided that, unless*
Contrast	*although, even though, though, whereas*
Location	*where, wherever*
Choice	*rather than, than, whether*

- Many people were happy **after** they heard the news.
- **Because** it snowed, school was canceled.

Recognizing interjections   G1.i

An **interjection** is a word or expression that conveys surprise or another strong emotion. Alone, an interjection is usually punctuated with an exclamation point: ***Hooray!*** *I got the promotion.* As part of a sentence, an interjection is set off with a comma (or commas): ***Oh,*** *you knew yesterday.* In academic writing, use interjections sparingly, if at all.

G2 Sentence Structures

When you know how sentences are formed, you have one tool for understanding the art of writing.

Recognizing subjects and predicates   G2.a

A sentence consists of two basic parts: a subject and a predicate; see **QA Box 25**, below.

The **simple subject** is the word or group of words that acts, is described, or is acted upon: *The **telephone** rang.* The **complete subject** is the subject and all its MODIFIERS.

The **predicate** is the part of the sentence that contains the verb. The predicate tells what the subject is doing or experiencing or what is being done to the subject: *The telephone **rang**.* The **complete predicate** is the verb and all its modifiers.

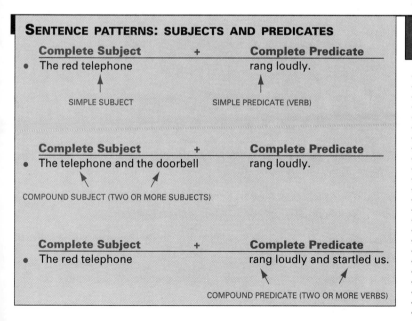

SENTENCE PATTERNS: SUBJECTS AND PREDICATES

QA
Box
25

Complete Subject	+	Complete Predicate
• The red telephone		rang loudly.

SIMPLE SUBJECT — SIMPLE PREDICATE (VERB)

Complete Subject	+	Complete Predicate
• The telephone and the doorbell		rang loudly.

COMPOUND SUBJECT (TWO OR MORE SUBJECTS)

Complete Subject	+	Complete Predicate
• The red telephone		rang loudly and startled us.

COMPOUND PREDICATE (TWO OR MORE VERBS)

! **ESL Note:** Avoid repeating a subject with a personal pronoun in the same clause.

No   My grandfather he lived to be eighty-seven.

Yes   My grandfather lived to be eighty-seven.

G2.b Recognizing direct and indirect objects ▌

A **direct object** receives the action—it completes the meaning—of certain VERBS called TRANSITIVE VERBS. To find a direct object, make up a *whom?* or *what?* question about the verb: *Keisha bought* [what?] ***a sweater.***

An **indirect object** answers a *to whom? for whom? to what?* or *for what?* question about the verb: *Keisha bought* [for whom?] ***me*** *a sweater.* **QA Box 26** shows the relationships of direct and indirect objects in sentences.

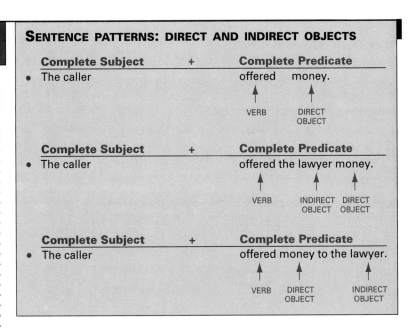

QA Box 26

SENTENCE PATTERNS: DIRECT AND INDIRECT OBJECTS

Complete Subject	+	Complete Predicate
• The caller		offered money.

                ↑   ↑
    VERB   DIRECT OBJECT

Complete Subject	+	Complete Predicate
• The caller		offered the lawyer money.

   ↑   ↑   ↑
VERB INDIRECT OBJECT DIRECT OBJECT

Complete Subject	+	Complete Predicate
• The caller		offered money to the lawyer.

   ↑   ↑   ↑
VERB DIRECT OBJECT INDIRECT OBJECT

! **ESL Notes:** (1) In sentences with indirect objects that follow the word *to* or *for*, always put the direct object before the indirect object.

No   Will you please give to John this letter?

Yes   Will you please give this letter to John?

(2) When a PRONOUN is used as an indirect object, some verbs require *to* or *for* before the pronoun, and others do not.

No   Please explain me the rule.   [*Explain* requires *to* before an indirect object.]

Yes   Please explain the rule to me.

Yes   Please give me the letter.   [*Give* does not require *to* before an indirect object.]

Even though a verb does not require *to* before an indirect object, you may use *to* if you prefer. Just be sure, if you do, to put the direct object before the indirect object.

Yes   Please give the letter to me.

Recognizing complements, modifiers, and appositives   G2.c

Recognizing Complements

A **complement** renames or describes a SUBJECT or an OBJECT. It occurs in the PREDICATE of a sentence.

A **subject complement** is a NOUN, PRONOUN, or ADJECTIVE that follows a LINKING VERB (for an explanation of linking verbs, see **QA Box 31** in section **G3**).

An **object complement** is a noun or an adjective that follows a DIRECT OBJECT (see **G2.b**) and either describes or renames it. **QA Box 27** shows the relationships of subject and object complements in sentences.

SENTENCE PATTERNS: COMPLEMENTS   QA Box 27

Complete Subject	+	**Complete Predicate**
• The caller		was a student.

    ↑ ↑
LINKING   SUBJECT
VERB   COMPLEMENT

Complete Subject	+	**Complete Predicate**
• The student		called himself a victim.

    ↑ ↑ ↑
VERB   DIRECT   OBJECT
OBJECT   COMPLEMENT

Recognizing Modifiers

A **modifier** is a word or group of words that functions as an adjective or adverb. Modifiers can appear anywhere in a sentence.

- The **large red** telephone rang.   [Adjectives *large* and *red* modify the noun *telephone*.]
- The lawyer answered **quickly**.   [The adverb *quickly* modifies the verb *answered*.]
- The person **on the telephone** was **extremely** upset.   [The PREPOSITIONAL PHRASE *on the telephone* modifies the noun *person*; the adverb *extremely* modifies the adjective *upset*.]

- **Therefore**, the lawyer spoke gently. [The adverb *therefore* modifies the INDEPENDENT CLAUSE *the lawyer spoke gently*.]
- **Because the lawyer's voice was calm**, the caller felt reassured. [*Because the lawyer's voice was calm* is called an **adverb clause**; it modifies the independent clause *the caller felt reassured*.]

Recognizing Appositives

An **appositive** is a word or group of words that renames the noun or pronoun preceding it.

! Alert: When an appositive is not essential for identifying the noun or pronoun it renames (that is, when an appositive is NONRESTRICTIVE), use a comma or commas to set the appositive off from whatever it renames and from any words following it; see **P2.e**).

- The student's story, **a tale of broken promises**, was complicated. [*A tale of broken promises* is an appositive that renames the noun *story*.]
- The lawyer consulted an expert, **her law professor**. [*Her law professor* is an appositive that renames the noun *expert*.]

G2.d Recognizing phrases ▌

A **phrase** is a group of related words that may contain a SUBJECT or a PREDICATE, but not both. A phrase cannot stand alone as an independent unit. Phrases function as parts of speech.

A **noun phrase** functions as a NOUN in a sentence: *The modern population census dates back to the seventeenth century.*

A **verb phrase** functions as a VERB in a sentence: *The Romans had been conducting censuses every five years.*

A **prepositional phrase** starts with a PREPOSITION, contains a noun or PRONOUN, and functions as a MODIFIER: *After the collapse of Rome, censuses were discontinued until modern times.* (*After the collapse, of Rome,* and *until modern times* are all prepositional phrases.)

An **absolute phrase** contains a noun or pronoun and a PARTICIPLE. It modifies the entire sentence: *Censuses being the fashion, Quebec and Nova Scotia took sixteen counts between 1665 and 1754.*

A **verbal phrase** is a word group that contains a verbal—an INFINITIVE (infinitive phrase), a PRESENT PARTICIPLE (participial phrase or gerund phrase), or a PAST PARTICIPLE (participial phrase); see **G1.d**. Verbal phrases function as nouns or modifiers.

- In 1624, Virginia began **to count** its citizens in a census. [infinitive phrase = direct object]
- **Going from door to door**, census takers interview millions of people. [participial phrase = adjective modifying *census takers*]

- **Amazed by some people's answers**, the census takers always listen carefully. [participial phrase = adjective modifying *census takers*]

Telling the difference between a gerund phrase and a participial phrase using a present participle can be tricky because both use the *-ing* verb form. The key is to determine how the verbal phrase is functioning: a gerund phrase functions only as a noun, and a participial phrase functions only as a modifier.

- **Including each person** in the census was important. [gerund phrase = noun used as the subject]
- **Including each person in the census**, Abby spent many hours on the crowded city block. [participial phrase = modifier used as adjective describing *Abby*]

Recognizing clauses   G2.e

A **clause** is a group of words that contains a SUBJECT and a PREDICATE. Clauses are divided into two categories: *independent clauses* (also known as *main clauses*) and *dependent clauses* (also known as *subordinate clauses*).

Recognizing Independent Clauses

An **independent clause** contains a subject and a predicate. It can stand alone as a sentence because it is an independent grammatical unit. **QA Box 28**, below, shows the basic pattern.

SENTENCE PATTERNS: INDEPENDENT CLAUSES	QA Box 28

INDEPENDENT CLAUSE	
Complete Subject +	**Complete Predicate**
• The telephone	rang.

Recognizing Dependent Clauses

A **dependent clause**, like all clauses, contains a subject and a predicate, but it cannot stand alone as a sentence. A dependent clause must be joined to an independent clause.

Some dependent clauses start with SUBORDINATING CONJUNCTIONS, words such as *although, because, when, until*; see **QA Box 24** on page 52. These clauses are called **adverb clauses** (or sometimes **subordinate clauses**). They function as ADVERBS, usually answering some question about the independent clause: *how? why? when? under what circumstances?* Adverb clauses modify VERBS, ADJECTIVES, other adverbs, and entire independent clauses.

! **Alert:** When an adverb clause comes before its independent clause, the clauses are usually separated by a comma; see **P2.b.**

- **If the bond issue passes**, the city will install sewers.   [The adverb clause modifies the verb *install,* explaining under what circumstances.]

- They are drawing up plans **as quickly as they can**.   [The adverb clause modifies the verb *drawing up,* explaining how.]

- The homeowners feel happier **because they know the flooding will soon be better controlled**.   [The adverb clause modifies the entire independent clause, explaining why.]

Adjective clauses (also called **relative clauses**) are dependent clauses that start with RELATIVE PRONOUNS (*who, whom, which, whose,* and *that*) or occasionally with RELATIVE ADVERBS such as *when* or *where.* An adjective clause modifies the NOUN or PRONOUN that it follows.

- The car **that Jack bought** is practical.   [The adjective clause describes the noun *car; that* refers to *car.*]

- The day **when I can buy my own car** is getting closer.   [The adjective clause modifies the noun *day; when* refers to *day.*]

QA Box 29 shows common sentence patterns for adverb and adjective (dependent) clauses.

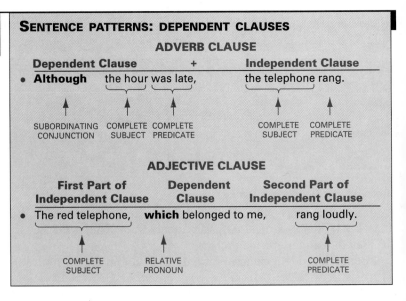

QA Box 29

SENTENCE PATTERNS: DEPENDENT CLAUSES

ADVERB CLAUSE

| Dependent Clause | + | Independent Clause |

- **Although** the hour was late,   the telephone rang.

| SUBORDINATING CONJUNCTION | COMPLETE SUBJECT | COMPLETE PREDICATE | COMPLETE SUBJECT | COMPLETE PREDICATE |

ADJECTIVE CLAUSE

| First Part of Independent Clause | Dependent Clause | Second Part of Independent Clause |

- The red telephone,   **which** belonged to me,   rang loudly.

| COMPLETE SUBJECT | RELATIVE PRONOUN | COMPLETE PREDICATE |

Noun clauses, like adjective clauses, often begin with *that, who,* or *which,* as well as *whoever, whichever, when, where, whether, why,* or *how.* Noun clauses replace nouns.

- **Promises** are not always dependable.   [noun]

- **What politicians promise** is not always dependable.   [noun clause]
- Often, voters do not know **the truth**.   [noun]
- Often, voters do not know **that the truth is being manipulated**.   [noun clause]

Because they start with similar words, noun clauses and adjective clauses are sometimes confused with each other. A noun clause *is* a SUBJECT, OBJECT, or COMPLEMENT; an adjective clause *modifies* a subject, object, or complement. The word starting an adjective clause has an antecedent in the sentence; the word starting a noun clause does not.

- Politicians understand **whom they must please**.   [Noun clause is an object; *whom* does not need an antecedent here.]
- Politicians **who make promises** sometimes fail to keep them. [Adjective clause modifies *politicians*, which is the antecedent of *who*.]

Alert: Use a singular verb to agree with a noun clause functioning as a subject: *What most politicians try to do is* [not *are*] *serve the public. What most politicians need is* [not *are*] *new careers.*   **!**

ESL Note: Noun clauses in indirect questions are phrased as statements, not questions. TENSE, pronoun, and other changes may be necessary when a direct question is rephrased as an indirect question; see **C3.d**. Suppose you are reporting that Kara said "Why do you need the purple paint?"   **!**

No Kara asked why **did** [*or* **do**] **we need** the purple paint?

Yes Kara asked why **we needed** the purple paint.

Recognizing sentence types G2.f

A sentences can be simple, compound, complex, or compound-complex.

A **simple sentence** is composed of a single INDEPENDENT CLAUSE with no DEPENDENT CLAUSES.

- Charlie Chaplin was born in London on April 16, 1889.
- A mime, he became famous for his character the Little Tramp.

A **compound sentence** is composed of two or more independent clauses.

- Chaplin's father died early, and his mother spent time in mental hospitals.
- Many people enjoy Chaplin films; others do not.

A **complex sentence** is composed of one independent clause and one or more dependent clauses.

- When Chaplin was performing with a troupe that was touring the United States, he was hired by Mack Sennett, who owned the Keystone Comedies.   [dependent clause starting *When*; dependent clause starting *that*; independent clause starting *he*; dependent clause starting *who*]

A **compound-complex** sentence joins a compound sentence and a complex sentence. It contains two or more independent clauses and one or more dependent clauses.

- Once studios could no longer afford him, Chaplin cofounded United Artists, and then he was able to produce and distribute his own films.   [dependent clause starting *Once*; independent clause starting *Chaplin*; independent clause starting *then he was able*]

G3 Verbs

A **verb** conveys information about an action (*Many people **overeat***), an occurrence (*Thanksgiving **falls** on a Thursday*), or a state of being (*Thanksgiving **is** a national holiday*). Verbs also convey the information described in **QA Box 30**, below.

QA Box 30	INFORMATION VERBS CONVEY	
Person	Who or what acts or experiences an action—first person (the speaker: *I dance*), second person (the one spoken to: ***you** dance*), or third person (the one spoken about: ***the dog** dances*).	
Number	How many subjects act or experience an action—singular (one) or plural (more than one).	
Tense	When an action occurs—past (*we **danced***), present (*we dance*), or future (*we **will dance***); see **G3.d.**	
Mood	What attitude is expressed toward the action—imperative (commands and polite requests: *Dance*), conditional (speculation, wishes, unreality: *if we were dancing . . .*), or indicative (*we dance*); see **G3.e.**	
Voice	Whether the subject acts or is acted upon—active voice or passive voice; see **G3.f.**	

Verbs vary in type, as explained in **QA Box 31**, below.

TYPES OF VERBS

QA Box 31

Main verb   The word in a PREDICATE that says something about the SUBJECT: *She **danced** for the group.*

Auxiliary verb   A verb that combines with a main verb to convey information about tense, mood, or voice (see **QA Box 30**): *She has danced for them before.* *Be*, *do*, and *have* can be auxiliary verbs or main verbs. The verbs *can*, *could*, *may*, *might*, *should*, *would*, *must*, and others are MODAL AUXILIARY VERBS that add shades of meaning such as ability or possibility to verbs: *She **might dance** for them again.* See **G3.b** for more about *be*, *do*, and *have* and **F6** for more about modals.

Linking verb   A verb that links a subject to a **complement**, a word or words that rename or describe the subject: *She **was** happy dancing.* Linking verbs indicate a state or condition. *Be* is the most common linking verb; sometimes sense verbs (for example, *smell*, *taste*) or verbs of perception (for example, *seem*, *feel*) function as linking verbs. For a sentence pattern with linking verbs, see **QA Box 27**, page 55.

Transitive verb   A verb followed by a DIRECT OBJECT—a NOUN or PRONOUN that completes the verb's message: *They **sent** her a thank-you note for her performance.* For sentence patterns with objects, see **QA Box 26**, page 54.

Intransitive verb   A verb that does not require a direct object: *Yesterday she **danced**.*

Recognizing forms of main verbs   G3.a

- The simple form conveys an action, occurrence, or state of being taking place in the present (*I laugh*) or, with an AUXILIARY VERB, in the future (*I will laugh*).
- The past-tense form is the basis for conveying an action, occurrence, or state completed in the past (*I laughed*). Regular verbs add *-ed* or *-d* to the simple form. Irregular verbs vary; see **QA Box 32** on page 63.

- The past participle form in regular verbs uses the same form as the past tense. Irregular verbs vary; see **QA Box 32** on page 63. To function as a verb, a past participle combines with one or more auxiliary verbs: *I have laughed.* Used alone, past participles function as ADJECTIVES: *crumbled cookies.*

- The present participle is formed by adding *-ing* to the simple form (*laughing*). To function as a verb, a present participle combines with one or more auxiliary verbs (*I was laughing*). Used alone, present participles function as NOUNS (*laughing is healthy*) or as adjectives (*my laughing friends*).

- The infinitive uses the simple form, usually but not always following *to* (*I started to laugh*). The infinitive functions as a noun or an adjective, not a verb.

Using the -s Form

The *-s* form of a verb occurs in the third-person singular of the present tense. The *-s* ending attaches to the verb's simple form (*laugh, laughs*). For the *-s* form in SUBJECT–VERB AGREEMENT, see the start of **G4**.

! **Alert:** Only the verbs *be* and *have* have irregular forms for third-person singular of the present tense: *is* and *has*. They are the standard third-person singular forms to use in edited American English.

No	Jasper be studying hard every day, so he have a chance to win a scholarship.
Yes	Jasper **is** studying hard every day, so he **has** a chance to win a scholarship.

Using Regular and Irregular Verbs

Most verbs in English are regular, forming the past tense and past participle by adding *-ed* or *-d* to the simple form: *enter, entered, entered; smile, smiled, smiled.*

! **Alert:** Speakers sometimes skip over the *-ed* sound in the past tense, hitting the sound lightly or not at all. If you are unused to hearing or pronouncing this sound, you may forget to add it when you write.

- The birthday cake was suppose^d to be ready.

About two hundred of the most common verbs in English are irregular. You can always look in a dictionary for the principal parts of any verb, but memorizing them from **QA Box 32** is more efficient in the long run.

COMMON IRREGULAR VERBS

Simple Form	Past Tense	Past Participle
awake	awoke *or* awaked	awaked *or* awoken
be	was, were	been
become	became	become
begin	began	begun
blow	blew	blown
break	broke	broken
bring	brought	brought
build	built	built
buy	bought	bought
catch	caught	caught
choose	chose	chosen
come	came	come
cost	cost	cost
deal	dealt	dealt
dive	dived *or* dove	dived
do	did	done
drink	drank	drunk
drive	drove	driven
eat	ate	eaten
fall	fell	fallen
fight	fought	fought
find	found	found
fly	flew	flown
freeze	froze	frozen
get	got	got *or* gotten
give	gave	given
go	went	gone
grow	grew	grown
have	had	had
hear	heard	heard
hide	hid	hidden
hurt	hurt	hurt
keep	kept	kept
know	knew	known
lay	laid	laid
lead	led	led
lend	lent	lent
lie	lay	lain
lose	lost	lost

Continued on next page

➤ QA Box 32, continued from previous page

Simple Form	Past Tense	Past Participle
make	made	made
read	read	read
ring	rang	rung
rise	rose	risen
run	ran	run
say	said	said
see	saw	seen
send	sent	sent
shake	shook	shaken
shoot	shot	shot
sing	sang	sung
sink	sank	sunk
sit	sat	sat
sleep	slept	slept
speak	spoke	spoken
stand	stood	stood
steal	stole	stolen
strike	struck	struck
swear	swore	sworn
swim	swam	swum
take	took	taken
teach	taught	taught
throw	threw	thrown
wear	wore	worn
write	wrote	written

G3.b Using auxiliary verbs

Auxiliary verbs, also called **helping verbs**, combine with MAIN VERBS to make verb phrases.

```
        AUXILIARY          MAIN
          VERB             VERB
           ↓                ↓
    ● I    am           shopping      for new shoes.
           ⏝_____⏝
              VERB PHRASE
```

- Clothing prices **have** [auxiliary verb] **soared** [main verb] recently.
  [*have soared* = verb phrase]

- Leather shoes **can** [auxiliary verb] **be** [main verb] expensive.
  [*can be* = verb phrase]

Three verbs—*be, do,* and *have*—deserve special attention. They occur very frequently in English, both as auxiliary verbs and as main verbs, and they vary more than most irregular verbs.

FORMS OF *BE, DO,* AND *HAVE*

	be	do	have
Simple form	be	do	have
Past tense	was, were	did	had
Past participle	been	done	had
***-s* form**	is	does	has
Present participle	being	doing	having

Alert: Academic writing requires standard uses of the forms of *be,* whether it is an auxiliary or a linking (main) verb. **!**

- The gym **is** [*not* be] a busy place.
- The gym **is** [*not* be] filling with spectators.

ESL Note: When an auxiliary verb is used with a main verb, the **!** auxiliary may change to an *-s* form to agree with a third-person singular subject, but the main verb does not change: *Does the gym close* [not *closes*] *at midnight?*

The verbs *can, could, may, might, must, shall, should, will, would,* and others are **modal auxiliary verbs**. Modals communicate meanings of ability, permission, obligation, advisability, necessity, or possibility. For more about modals, see **F6**.

Using *lie* and *lay* G3.c

Use the irregular verbs *lie* ("to recline") and *lay* ("to place something down") with care. *Lie* is intransitive (it cannot be followed by a DIRECT OBJECT). *Lay* is transitive (it must be followed by a direct object). Confusion arises because *lay* is both the SIMPLE FORM of *lay* and the PAST-TENSE FORM of *lie* and many people use the words as though they share other parts as well. Become completely familiar with the PRINCIPAL PARTS of *lie* and *lay* so that you can use them with ease.

FORMS OF *LIE* AND *LAY*

	lie	lay
Simple form	lie	lay
Past tense	lay	laid
Past participle	lain	laid
***-s* form**	lies	lays
Present participle	lying	laying

- The hikers are ~~laying~~ _lying_ down to rest.
- The hikers ~~laid~~ _lay_ down to rest.
- The hikers took off their gear and ~~lay~~ _laid_ it on the rocks.

G3.d Understanding verb tense

Verbs use tense to express time. MAIN VERBS change form and combine with AUXILIARY VERBS to do this. PROGRESSIVE FORMS show ongoing actions or conditions.

SUMMARY OF TENSES

SIMPLE TENSES

		PROGRESSIVE FORMS
Present	I talk	I am talking
Past	I talked	I was talking
Future	I will talk	I will be talking

PERFECT TENSES

		PROGRESSIVE FORMS
Present perfect	I have talked	I have been talking
Past perfect	I had talked	I had been talking
Future perfect	I will have talked	I will have been talking

Using the Simple Present Tense

The simple present tense uses a verb's simple form to describe what is happening now, what is true at the moment, and what is generally or consistently true, and to express that an event will take place at a fixed time in the future.

- The tourists **are** on vacation. [Happening now]
- They **enjoy** the sunshine. [True at the moment]
- Ocean voyages **make** them seasick. [Consistently true]
- A cruise **is** an expensive vacation. [Generally true]
- Their ship **departs** at midnight. [Fixed-time future event]

! **Alert:** Use the present tense to discuss action in a work of literature.

- In _Romeo and Juliet_, Juliet's father wants her to marry Paris, but Juliet loves Romeo.
- Shakespeare's play depicts the tragedy of ill-fated love.

Using Accurate Tense Sequences

When you want your sentences to deliver messages about actions, occurrences, or conditions that take place over time, use accurate tense sequences—that is, show the time relationships correctly—to deliver your message clearly; see **QA Box 33**, below.

SEQUENCE OF TENSES

QA
Box
33

- **When the independent-clause verb is in the simple present tense, for the dependent-clause verb:**

  Use the present tense to show same-time action.
  - I **avoid** shellfish because I **am** allergic to it.

  Use the past tense to show earlier action.
  - I **am** sure that I **deposited** the check.

  Use the present perfect tense to show a period of time extending from some point in the past to the present.
  - They **claim** that they **have visited** the planet Venus.

  Use the future tense for action to come.
  - The Surgeon General **says** that flu **will strike** hard this winter.

- **When the independent-clause verb is in the past tense, for the dependent-clause verb:**

  Use the past tense to show another completed past action.
  - I **closed** the door because you **told** me to.

  Use the past perfect tense to show earlier action.
  - The sprinter **knew** that she **had broken** the record.

  Use the present tense to state a general truth.
  - Christopher Columbus **discovered** that the world **is** round.

- **When the independent-clause verb is in the present perfect or past perfect tense, for the dependent-clause verb:**

  Use the past tense.
  - The agar plate **has become** moldy since I **poured** it.
  - Sugar prices **had** already **declined** when artificial sweeteners first **appeared**.

- **When the independent-clause verb is in the future tense, for the dependent-clause verb:**

  Use the present tense to show action happening at the same time.
  - You **will be** rich if you **win** [*not* will win] the prize.

Continued on next page

> *QA Box 33, continued from previous page*

Use the past tense to show earlier action.

- You **will** surely **win** the prize if you **remembered** to mail the entry form.

Use the present perfect tense to show future action earlier than the action of the independent-clause verb.

- The river **will flood** again next year unless we **have built** [*not* will build] a better dam by then.

■ **When the independent-clause verb is in the future perfect tense, for the dependent-clause verb:**

Use either the present tense or the present perfect tense.

- Dr. Change **will have delivered** 5,000 babies by the time she **retires**.

- Dr. Change **will have delivered** 5,000 babies by the time she **has retired**.

G3.e Understanding the indicative, imperative, and subjunctive moods

The **indicative mood** expresses statements about real things (*The door opened*) or highly likely ones (*She seemed lost*) or questions about fact (*Do you need help?*).

The **imperative mood** expresses commands and direct requests: *Please shut the door.* *Watch out!* The SUBJECT, omitted in an imperative sentence, is assumed to be *you*.

The **subjunctive mood** expresses conditions including wishes, recommendations, demands, indirect requests, and speculations: *If I were you, I would ask for directions.*

Using the Subjunctive with *if, as if, as though,* and *unless* Clauses

Not all CLAUSES introduced by *if, as if, as though,* and *unless* require the subjunctive. Use the subjunctive only when such clauses describe a speculation or condition contrary to fact.

Indicative	If she **leaves** late, I will drive her to the track meet. [Fact, not speculation]
Subjunctive	If she **were going to leave** late, I would drive her to the track meet. [Speculation]

- If it ~~was~~ raining, fewer people would be at the race.
  were
  [Condition contrary to fact—it is not raining.]

- Unless the temperature ~~was~~ *were* to rise above 70°, no runner would
  ^
  become dehydrated.

Alert: When you use *would, could,* or *should* to express speculation
or conditions contrary to fact, be careful to use these words in the
independent clause only, not in both the *if* (or *unless*) clause and the
independent clause. **!**

- If he ~~would have~~ *had* trained, he would have won the race.
  ^

Using the Subjunctive in *that* Clauses

When *that* clauses express wishes, indirect requests, recommendations, and demands, use the subjunctive.

- I wish that this race ~~was~~ *were* over.
  ^
- It is important that the doctor ~~is~~ *be* present because someone is
  ^
  insisting that she examines the runners.

Using active and passive voices **G3.f**

Voice refers to verbs' ability to show whether the sentence SUBJECT
acts or receives the action named by the verb. In the **active voice**, the
subject performs the action. In the **passive voice**, the subject is acted
upon.

Active	**Svetlana considers** clams a delicacy. [The subject, *Svetlana*, performs the action: she *considers*.]
Passive	**Clams are considered** a delicacy by Svetlana. [The subject, *clams*, is acted upon—they *are considered*—by Svetlana.]

Because the active voice emphasizes the doer of an action, active
constructions are usually more direct and dramatic than passive ones.
They are often more concise as well; see **E1.c.**

When no one knows who or what did something or when that
information is unimportant, the passive voice may be appropriate.

- The lock **was broken** sometime last night.

When the doer of an action is less important than the action, the
passive voice may deliver the appropriate emphasis.

- Oxygen was discovered in 1774 by Joseph Priestley.

However, if you use the passive voice unintentionally or to make writing seem "lofty" or to hide the doer of some action, revise to the active
voice.

Pointless passive	An experiment was conducted by me to demonstrate the existence of carbon.
Revised to active	I conducted an experiment to demonstrate the existence of carbon.

G4 Subject–Verb Agreement

SUBJECTS and VERBS must agree, or match, in NUMBER (singular or plural). Singular subjects require singular verbs, and plural subjects require plural verbs. Subjects and verbs must also match in PERSON. That is, both subject and verb must be in the first person (*I* or *we*), second person (*you*), or third person (*he, she, it,* or *they*).

Problems can arise with the letter *s* at the end of words. Most NOUNS add -*s* (or -*es*) to change from singular to plural. All verbs, on the other hand, use an -*s* form for third-person singular in the present tense. In **QA Box 34**, below, the memory device at the top shows how the *s* works in most cases of agreement. The -*s* or -*es* can take only one path at a time, going either to a noun subject at the top or to a verb at the bottom.

QA Box 34

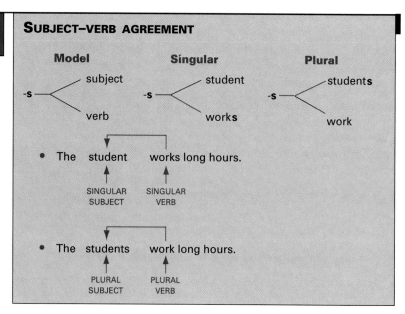

SUBJECT–VERB AGREEMENT

Ignoring words between a subject and verb

G4.a

Words that intervene between a SUBJECT and VERB do not influence verb agreement.

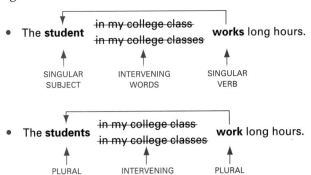

No The **winners** in the state competition **goes** to the national finals.
[*Winners* is the subject, so the verb must agree with it; *in the state competition* is an intervening PREPOSITIONAL PHRASE that does not alter basic subject–verb agreement.]

Yes The **winners** in the state competition **go** to the national finals.

To locate the subject of a sentence, eliminate PHRASES that start with PREPOSITIONS or with the words *including, together with, along with, accompanied by, in addition to, except*, and *as well as*.

No The **moon**, as well as Venus, **are** visible in the night sky. [*Moon* is the subject, so the verb must agree with it; ignore *as well as Venus*.]

Yes The **moon**, as well as Venus, **is** visible in the night sky.

Using *one of the*

A construction that starts with the words *one of the* takes a singular verb, to agree with the word *one*. Agreement does not apply to the plural noun in the *of* phrase. For *one of the . . . who*, see **G4.d**.

- **One** of the problems **is** [*not* are] broken equipment.

Using the correct verb for subjects connected by *and*

G4.b

Two or more SUBJECTS joined by *and* become plural as a group and therefore require a plural verb.

- **The student and the instructor work** long hours.

COMPOUND SUBJECT
(USES *and*)

PLURAL
VERB

- **The Cascade Diner and the Wayside Diner have** [*not* has] fried catfish today.

An exception occurs when subjects joined by *and* combine to form a single thing or person; in this case use a singular verb.

- **Spaghetti and meatballs has** [*not* have] a place on many menus.

Using *each* and *every*

Each and *every* are singular PRONOUNS and require singular verbs. Even when *each* or *every* precedes subjects joined by *and,* use a singular verb.

- **Each** human hand and foot **leaves** a distinctive print.

G4.c Making a verb agree with the nearest subject

When SUBJECTS are joined with *or, nor, either . . . or, neither . . . nor,* or *not only . . . but (also),* the verb agrees with the subject nearest to it. Ignore everything before the final subject.

- ~~Either the instructor or~~
  ~~Either the instructors or~~ **the student knows** the answer.

  SINGULAR   SINGULAR
  SUBJECT   VERB

- ~~Either the instructor or~~
  ~~Either the instructors or~~ **the students know** the answer.

  PLURAL   PLURAL
  SUBJECT   VERB

G4.d Making verbs agree with pronoun subjects

Using Singular Verbs with Most Indefinite Pronouns

INDEFINITE PRONOUNS are usually singular, so they usually take singular verbs.

COMMON INDEFINITE PRONOUNS

another	each	neither	somebody
anybody	either	nobody	someone
anyone	every	no one	something
anything	everyone	nothing	
	everything		

- Whenever **anyone says** anything, **nothing is** done.
- **Everything** about these roads **is** [*not* are] dangerous.
- **Each** of the roads **has** [*not* have] to be resurfaced.

A few indefinite pronouns—*none, some, more, most, any,* and *all*—can be either singular or plural, depending on the meaning of the sentence.

- **Some** of our streams **are** polluted, **some** pollution **is** reversible, but **all** pollution **is** a threat to the balance of nature. [The first *some* refers to the plural *streams,* so the plural verb agrees with it; the second *some* and *all* refer to the singular word *pollution,* so the singular verbs agree with it.]

Making Verbs Agree with the Antecedents of *who, which,* and *that*

When *who, which,* or *that* starts an ADJECTIVE CLAUSE, the verb agrees with the noun or pronoun to which *who, which,* or *that* refers (its ANTECEDENT).

- The scientist will share the income from her new patent with the graduate students **who work** with her. [*Who* refers to the plural *students,* and *work* is a plural verb.]
- George Jones is the student **who works** in the science lab. [*Who* refers to the singular *student,* and *works* is a singular verb.]

Using *one of the . . . who*

In *one of the . . . who* (*which, that*) phrases, the antecedent of *who* is the plural noun in the *one of the . . .* phrase, making a plural verb correct.

- Tracy is one of the **students who talk** [*not* talks] in class. [*Who* refers to plural *students* and requires the plural verb *talk.*]

If the phrase is *the only one of the . . . who,* the antecedent of *who* is the singular word *one,* making a singular verb correct.

- Tracy is **the only one** of the students **who talks** [*not* talk] in class. [*Who* refers to the singular *one* and requires the singular verb *talks.*]

Making verbs agree with subjects in inverted sentences, in expletive constructions, and in sentences containing subject complements

G4.e

Finding the Subject in Inverted Word Order

In English, the subject of a sentence normally precedes its verb: *The mayor walked in.* Inverted word order changes the usual order: *In walked the mayor.* Most questions use inverted word order: *Is the mayor here?* In inverted word order, be sure to look *after* the verb, not before it, to check that the subject and verb agree.

- Across the street **stand** [*not* stands] the **picketers**.

Finding the Subject with an Expletive Construction

Expletive constructions, such as *There is, It is, There were,* put a sentence's verb before the subject. Check ahead to identify the subject, and make sure that the verb agrees with it.

- There **are** nine **planets** in our solar system. [For agreement purposes, think of this sentence as *Nine planets are in our solar system.*]

Agreeing with the Subject, Not the Subject Complement

LINKING VERBS connect the subject to a **complement**—a word that renames or describes the subject. Always make the verb agree with the subject, not the subject complement.

No	The worst part of owning a car are the bills. [The subject is the singular noun *part*, which requires the singular verb *is*; *bills* is a subject complement and should be ignored.]
Yes	The worst **part** of owning a car **is** the bills.
Yes	**Bills are** the worst part of owning a car. [The plural noun *bills* is now the subject and requires the plural verb *are*.]

G4.f Making verbs agree with collective nouns, with nouns that specify amounts, with singular subjects in plural form, and with titles and terms

Making Verbs Agree with Collective Nouns

A **collective noun** names a group of people or things, such as *family, group, audience, class, number.* When you want to convey that the group is acting as one unit, use a singular verb. When you want to convey that the members of the group are acting individually, use a plural verb.

- The senior **class has** 793 people in it. [*Class* is meant as one unit, so the singular verb *has* agrees with it.]
- The senior **class were fitted** for their graduation robes today. [The people in the class are meant as individual members within the group, so the plural verb *were fitted* agrees with it.]

Making Verbs Agree with Subjects That Specify Amounts

Use a singular verb with a subject that specifies an amount of money, time, weight, or distance considered as one unit.

- **Ninety cents is** the current bus fare.
- **Two miles passes** quickly for a serious jogger.

But when a subject refers to units of measurement considered individually rather than as one amount, use a plural verb.

- **Eighteen inches are** marked off on that ruler.
- **Fifty percent** of these peaches **are** bruised.

Making Verbs Agree with Singular Subjects in Plural Form

Some words that end in *-s* or *-ics* are singular in meaning and therefore need singular verbs, despite their plural appearance. These words include *news*, *ethics*, and *measles*, as well as *economics*, *mathematics*, *physics*, and *statistics* when they refer to a course of study.

- **Statistics is** a requirement for science majors. [*Statistics* refers to a course of study, so the singular verb agrees with it.]
- **Statistics show** that a recession is coming. [*Statistics* refers to items of data, so the plural verb agrees with it.]

Series and *means* have the same form in singular and plural. Context determines whether the verb is singular or plural.

- Six new television **series are** beginning this week.
- A **series** of disasters **is** delaying our production.

Using Singular Verbs with Titles and Terms

A work referred to by its title or a word referred to as a term is a single thing. Use a singular verb even when the title or term contains plural words.

- *Cats* **was** a popular musical.
- **"Our" implies** that I am included.
- **"Protective reaction strikes" is** a euphemism for bombing.

Alert: The word *states* is always plural, but names such as *the United States* or the *Organization of American States* refer to singular things—a country and an organization—so they require singular verbs: *The United States has* [not *have*] *a large television industry.* **!**

G5 Pronoun–Antecedent Agreement

Pronoun–antecedent agreement means that a pronoun must match the grammatical form of the word or words it refers to (its antecedent). For example, if the antecedent is third-person singular, the pronoun must be third-person singular too. **QA Box 35** on page 76 summarizes pronoun–antecedent agreement.

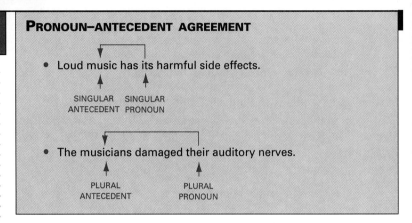

QA Box 35

PRONOUN–ANTECEDENT AGREEMENT

- Loud music has its harmful side effects.

  SINGULAR SINGULAR
  ANTECEDENT PRONOUN

- The musicians damaged their auditory nerves.

  PLURAL   PLURAL
  ANTECEDENT   PRONOUN

Pronouns and antecedents must match in NUMBER. Singular pronouns refer to singular antecedents, and plural pronouns to plural antecedents. They must also match in CASE; see **G7**.

G5.a Using plural pronouns for antecedents joined by *and*

Two or more antecedents joined by *and* require a plural pronoun, even if each antecedent is singular.

- **The United States and Canada** maintain **their** border as the world's longest open frontier.
- **The Cascade Diner and the Wayside Diner** closed for New Year's Eve to give **their** employees the night off.

An exception occurs when *each* or *every* precedes singular nouns joined by *and*. Here a singular pronoun is correct.

- **Every car and truck** that comes through the border station has **its** contents inspected.

Another exception occurs when singular nouns joined by *and* refer to a single person or thing. Here a singular pronoun is correct.

- Our **guide and translator** told us to watch out for traffic as **she** helped us off the tour bus.   [The guide is the same person as the translator; if the guide and translator were two people, *our* would also appear before *translator* and *she* would be *they*.]

G5.b Agreeing with the nearest antecedent

Antecedents joined by *or, nor,* or CORRELATIVE CONJUNCTIONS such as *either . . . or, not only . . . but (also)*, can mix the masculine and feminine as well as singular and plural. For the purposes of agreement, however, ignore everything before the final antecedent.

- ~~Either the loudspeakers or the~~ **microphone** needs **its** wiring repaired.

  SINGULAR ANTECEDENT   SINGULAR PRONOUN

- ~~Either the microphone or the~~ **loudspeakers** need **their** wiring repaired

  PLURAL ANTECEDENT   PLURAL PRONOUN

Agreeing with indefinite-pronoun antecedents   G5.c

Indefinite pronouns (for a list, see **G4.d**) are pronouns that do not refer to any particular person, thing, or idea. They take on clear meanings and identities only in context with other words. Indefinite pronouns are usually singular: *Anyone who knows the answer should raise **his or her** hand.* For advice about avoiding sexist use of indefinite pronouns, see **E5**.

Alert: Note that *he or she* always functions as a singular pronoun.   **!**

Some indefinite pronouns can be either singular or plural (*none, some, more, most, any, all*) depending on the meaning of the sentence. When an indefinite pronoun is plural, pronouns referring to it should be plural.

- **None** fear that **they** will fail.   [All the people in the group expect to succeed; using a plural pronoun reflects this meaning.]
- **None** fears that **he or she** will fail.   [No individual expects to fail; using singular pronouns reflects this meaning.]

The indefinite pronouns *each* and *every* are singular, no matter what words follow.

- Each of the students handed in ~~their~~ *his or her* final term paper.
- Every student in my classes is studying ~~their~~ *his or her* hardest.

Be especially careful about agreement when you use the words *this* (singular) and *these* (plural): ***This** kind of hard work has **its** advantages. **These** kinds of difficult jobs have **their** advantages.*

Agreeing with collective-noun antecedents   G5.d

A **collective noun** names a group of people or things, such as *family, group, audience, class, number*. When the group acts as one unit, use a singular PRONOUN to refer to it. When the members of the group act individually, use a plural pronoun.

- The **audience** cheered as **it** rose to applaud.   [The singular pronoun *it* conveys that the audience is acting as one unit.]
- The **audience** put on **their** coats and walked to the exits.   [The plural pronoun *their* conveys that the audience is acting as many individuals.]

G6 Pronoun Reference

The word (or words) a pronoun replaces is called its **antecedent**. In order for your writing to communicate its message clearly, each pronoun must relate precisely to an antecedent.

G6.a Avoiding unclear pronoun reference

In sentences that contain more than one logical antecedent, pronouns can become ambiguous.

Unclear pronoun reference

In 1911, Roald Amundsen reached the South Pole just thirty-five days before Robert F. Scott arrived. He [Who, Amundsen or Scott?] had told people that he was going to sail north to the Arctic, but then he turned south for the Antarctic. On the journey home, he [Who, Amundsen or Scott?] and his party froze to death just a few miles from safety.

Revised

In 1911, Roald Amundsen discovered the South Pole just thirty-five days before Robert F. Scott arrived. Amundsen had told people that he was going to sail north to the Arctic, but then he turned south for the Antarctic. On the journey home, Scott and his party froze to death just a few miles from safety.

If too much material comes between a pronoun and its antecedent, readers can also lose track of the meaning.

- Alfred Wegener, a German meteorologist and professor of geophysics at the University of Graz, was the first to suggest that all the continents on earth were originally part of one large land mass. According to this theory, the supercontinent broke up long ago and the fragments drifted apart. ~~He~~ Wegener named this supercontinent Pangaea.

[*He* can refer only to Wegener, but material about Wegener's theory intervenes, so using *Wegener* again instead of *he* jogs the reader's memory and makes reading easier.]

Avoiding adjectives as antecedents   G6.b

An ADJECTIVE cannot serve as a NOUN, so using an adjective as a pronoun's ANTECEDENT is imprecise.

No   Dan likes to study geological records. That is his major.   [*That* must refer to a noun or pronoun; *geological* is an adjective.]

Yes   Dan likes to study geological records. **Geology** is his major.

Using *it, that, this,* and *which* precisely   G6.c

When you use *it, that, this,* and *which,* be sure that your readers can easily understand what each word refers to.

No   Comets usually fly by the earth at 100,000 m.p.h., whereas asteroids sometimes collide with the earth. **This** interests scientists.   [*This* could refer to the speed of comets, comets flying by the earth, or asteroids colliding with the earth.]

Yes   Comets usually fly by the earth at 100,000 m.p.h., whereas asteroids sometimes collide with the earth. **This difference** interests scientists.

In speech, statements sometimes begin with "It said on the news . . ." or "In Washington they say . . . ." Avoid such inexact and wordy expressions in academic writing.

No   In California they say that no one feels a minor earthquake.

Yes   Californians say that no one feels a minor earthquake.

Using *you* for direct address only   G6.d

In academic writing, *you* is not a suitable substitute for specific words that refer to people, situations, or occurrences. Exact language is always preferable. Reserve *you* for writing that addresses the reader directly.

No   Prison uprisings often happen when you allow overcrowding. [The reader, *you,* did not allow the overcrowding.]

Yes   Prison uprisings often happen when prisons are overcrowded.

Using *who, which,* and *that*   G6.e

Who refers to people and to animals mentioned by name.

- **Theodore Roosevelt, who** served as the twenty-sixth U.S. President, inspired the creation of the stuffed animal called the "teddy bear."

- **Lassie, who** was known for her intelligence and courage, was actually played by a series of male collies.

Which and *that* refer to animals, things, and sometimes anonymous or collective groups of people. To choose between *that* and *which*, decide whether the pronoun introduces a RESTRICTIVE CLAUSE (use *that* or *which*, but be consistent) or a NONRESTRICTIVE CLAUSE (use *which*).

! **Alert:** Set off nonrestrictive clauses with commas; see **P2.e**.

G7 Pronoun Case

Case refers to the different forms that NOUNS and PRONOUNS take, according to their function in the sentence. English has three cases: **subjective** (noun or pronoun SUBJECTS), **objective** (noun or pronoun OBJECTS), and **possessive** (nouns or pronouns showing possession).

Most questions about pronoun case concern PERSONAL PRONOUNS or *who/whom* and *whoever/whomever*.

CASE FORMS OF PERSONAL PRONOUNS

	Subjective	Objective	Possessive
Singular	I, you, he, she, it	me, you, him, her, it	mine, yours, his, hers, its
Plural	we, you, they	us, you, them	ours, yours, theirs

The case forms for *who* are the same for singular and plural: *who* (subjective); *whom* (objective); *whose* (possessive).

G7.a Using accurate pronoun case in compound subjects and objects

A compound subject or a compound object contains more than one noun and/or pronoun. Compounding does not affect pronoun case.

Compound subject	**He and I** saw the solar eclipse.
Compound object	That eclipse astonished **him and me**.

If you are unsure which case to use, try the "drop test": Temporarily drop everything in a compound element except the pronoun in question to see which sounds correct.

> ● ~~Janet and me~~
> ~~Janet and I~~ ⟩ learned about the moon.

After *Janet and* is dropped, it is clear that *I learned about the moon* is correct; therefore, *Janet and I* is the right choice.

The same drop test also works when

- a compound subject contains only pronouns:
  - **She and I** [*not* Her and me, She and me, *or* Her and I] learned about the moon.

- a compound object contains pronouns:
  - The instructor told **Janet and me** [*not* Janet and I] that the moon's volume is one fiftieth of the earth's volume.
  - The instructor told **her and me** [*not* she and I, her and I, *or* she and me] that the moon's volume is one-fiftieth of the earth's volume.

Alert: In PREPOSITIONAL PHRASES, pronoun objects should always be in the objective case. **!**

No   Mrs. Parks gave an assignment to **Sam and I**.   [*I* is in the subjective case and cannot be used as the object of the PREPOSITION, *to*.]

Yes   Mrs. Parks gave an assignment to **Sam and me**.

Be especially careful when a pronoun object follows the preposition *between*.

No   Mrs. Parks divided the work between **he and I**.   [*He* and *I* are in the subjective case and cannot be used as objects of the preposition, *between*.]

Yes   Mrs. Parks divided the work between **him and me**.

Matching the case of pronouns and nouns in appositives G7.b

When pronouns are renamed by NOUN APPOSITIVES and when pronouns are appositives themselves, the pronouns and nouns must be in the same case. To check, try the drop test: Temporarily drop the noun to see which pronoun reads correctly.

- **We** ~~tennis players~~
  Us ~~tennis players~~ practice hard.

After *tennis players* is dropped, *we practice hard* is correct; therefore, *We tennis players practice hard* is the right choice.

The same drop test also works when

- The pronouns function as the appositive, coming after the noun:
  - The winners, **she and I** [*not* her and me], advanced to the finals. [Because the pronouns rename *winners*, which is the subject, the pronouns must be in the subjective case.]

■ The nouns and pronouns are in the objective case:

- The coach tells us [*not* we] tennis players to practice hard.

- The crowd cheered the winners, her and me [*not* she and I].

G7.c Using the subjective case after linking verbs

A pronoun coming after any LINKING VERB either renames the SUBJECT or shows possession by the subject. An objective-case pronoun is incorrect in such constructions.

- **The contest winner was I.** [*I* renames *contest winner*, the subject, so the subjective case is correct.]

- **The prize was mine.** [*Mine* shows possession, so the possessive case is correct.]

G7.d Using *who, whoever, whom,* and *whomever*

The pronouns *who* and *whoever* are in the SUBJECTIVE CASE. The pronouns *whom* and *whomever* are in the OBJECTIVE CASE. Informal spoken English tends to blur distinctions between *who* and *whom*, so you should not rely entirely on what sounds right. To check, use a variation of the drop test introduced on page 80: Temporarily drop everything in the sentence up to the pronoun in question, and then make substitutions. For *who* and *whoever*, test with *he, she,* or *they*. For *whom* and *whomever*, test with *him, her,* or *them*.

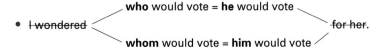

He would vote is correct, and *he* was used as a substitute for *who*: Therefore, *I wondered who would vote for her* is the right choice.

The drop test also works for *whoever*:

- Volunteers enroll **whoever** is eligible to vote. [The words *is eligible to vote* work with *he* (not *him*), so *whoever* is right.]

The drop test also shows when the objective case is called for.

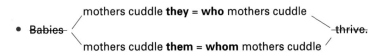

Mothers cuddle them is correct, and *them* was used as a substitute for *whom*: Therefore, *Babies whom mothers cuddle thrive* is the right choice.

The drop test works similarly for *whomever*:

- The senior citizens can nominate whomever they wish.
  [*The senior citizens can nominate him* (not *he*) shows that the objective case, *whomever*, is right.]

At the beginning of questions, use *who* if the question is about the subject and *whom* if the question is about the object. To determine case, recast the question into a statement, temporarily substituting *he* or *him* (or *she* or *her*).

- **Who** watched the space shuttle liftoff? [*He* (not *Him*) *watched the space shuttle liftoff* uses the subjective case, so *Who* is correct.]
- Ted admires **whom**? [*Ted admires him* (not *he*) uses the objective case, so *whom* is correct.]
- **Whom** does Ted admire? [*Ted admires him* (not *he*) uses the objective case, so *whom* is correct.]
- To **whom** does Ted speak about becoming an astronaut? [*Ted speaks to them* (not *they*) uses the objective case, so *whom* is correct.]

Using accurate case after *than* and *as*   G7.e

A sentence of comparison can be clear even when some of the words following *than* or *as* are implied rather than directly stated: *My Saint Bernard pup is larger than most full-grown dogs.* The word *are* is implied after *dogs*.

When a PRONOUN follows *than* or *as*, the pronoun case carries essential information about what is meant. For example, these two sentences convey very different messages simply because of the choice between the words *me* and *I* after *than*.

1. My sister loved that dog more than me.
2. My sister loved that dog more than I.

Because the pronoun *me* functions as an OBJECT, sentence 1 means "My sister loved that dog more than she loved me." Because the pronoun *I* functions as a SUBJECT, sentence 2 means "My sister loved that dog more than I loved it."

To make sure that your sentences of comparison deliver the message you intend, mentally fill in the implied words.

Using pronouns with infinitives and gerunds   G7.f

An **infinitive** is the simple form of a verb, usually but not always following *to*: *to laugh.* OBJECTIVE-CASE pronouns are used both as SUBJECTS and as OBJECTS of infinitives.

- Our tennis coach expects me to serve well. [The word *me* is the subject of the infinitive *to serve*; it is in the objective case.]

- Our tennis coach expects him to beat **me**. [The word *him* is the subject of the infinitive *to beat*, and *me* is the object of the infinitive; both are in the objective case.]

The possessive case communicates important information with *-ing* words. For example, these two sentences convey two different messages because of the possessive.

1. The detective noticed the **man** staggering.
2. The detective noticed the **man's** staggering.

Sentence 1 means that the detective noticed the *man*; sentence 2 means that the detective noticed the *staggering*.

The same distinction applies to pronouns:

1. The detective noticed **him** staggering.
2. The detective noticed **his** staggering.

G7.g Using *-self* pronouns █

Reflexive pronouns reflect back on the SUBJECT or OBJECT: *The detective disguised **himself**; he relied on **himself** to solve the mystery.*

Intensive pronouns provide emphasis by making another word more intense in meaning: *The detective felt that his career **itself** was at risk.*

Do not use reflexive pronouns as substitutes for subjects or objects.

No   The detective and myself had a long talk. He wanted my partner and myself to help him.

Yes   The detective and I had a long talk. He wanted my partner and **me** to help him.

G8 Adjectives and Adverbs

Both adjectives and adverbs are modifiers; that is, they describe other words. The key to distinguishing between adjectives and adverbs is understanding that they modify different words or groups of words.

SUMMARY OF DIFFERENCES BETWEEN ADJECTIVES AND ADVERBS

What Adjectives Modify

Nouns	The *busy* **lawyer** rested.
Pronouns	**She** felt *tired*.

What Adverbs Modify

Verbs	The lawyer **spoke** *quickly*.
Adverbs	The lawyer spoke *very* quickly.
Adjectives	The lawyer was *extremely* busy.
Independent clauses	*Undoubtedly*, the lawyer needed a rest.

Many adverbs end in *-ly* (*run swiftly*), but some do not (*run often*). Also, some adjectives end in *-ly* (*friendly dog*), so an *-ly* ending does not reliably identify an adverb.

Using adverbs—not adjectives—to modify verbs, adjectives, and other adverbs   G8.a

No   The chauffeur drove careless.   [An adjective, *careless*, cannot modify a verb, *drove*.]

Yes   The chauffeur drove **carelessly**.

No   The candidate felt unusual energetic today.   [An adjective, *unusual*, cannot modify another adjective, *energetic*.]

Yes   The candidate felt **unusually** energetic today.

No   The candidate spoke exceptional forcefully today.   [An adjective, *exceptional*, cannot modify an adverb, *forcefully*.]

Yes   The candidate spoke **exceptionally** forcefully today.

Avoiding double negatives   G8.b

A **double negative** is a statement that contains two negative MODIFIERS (for example, *no*, *never*, *not*, *none*, *nothing*, *hardly*, and *scarcely*).

No   The union members did not have no money in the reserve fund.

Yes   The union members did **not** have **any** money in the reserve fund.

Yes   The union members had **no** money in the reserve fund.

No   The union members will never vote for no strike.

Yes   The union members will **never** vote for **a** strike.

Using adjectives—not adverbs—as complements after linking verbs   G8.c

LINKING VERBS use adjectives as COMPLEMENTS. ACTION VERBS use adverbs.

- Anne looks happy.   [*Looks* functions as a linking verb; *happy* is an adjective.]

- Anne looks happily at the sunset.   [*Looks* functions as an action verb; *happily* is an adverb.]

Using *bad* and *badly*

The words *bad* (adjective) and *badly* (adverb) are particularly prone to misuse with linking verbs such as *feel, grow, smell, sound,* and *taste.* Only the adjective *bad* is correct when a verb functions as a linking verb.

No   The student felt badly.

Yes   The student felt bad.

Using *good* and *well*

Good is always an adjective. *Well* is an adjective only when it is referring to health; otherwise, *well* is an adverb.

- You look well.   [This means "You look in fine health"; *well* functions as an adjective.]
- You write well.   [This means "You write skillfully"; *well* functions as an adverb.]

G8.d Using correct comparative and superlative forms

Descriptive adjectives and adverbs often carry a message of comparison, so their forms indicate relative degrees of intensity.

Using Correct Regular Forms

Regular adjectives and adverbs show degrees of intensity by adding *-er* and *-est* endings or by adding the words *more* and *most* or *less* and *least.*

Positive [1]	Comparative [2]	Superlative [3+]
green	greener	greenest
happy	happier	happiest
selfish	less selfish	least selfish
beautiful	more beautiful	most beautiful

[1]   That tree is **green**.
[2]   That tree is **greener** than this tree.
[3+]   That tree is the **greenest** tree on the block.

The choice between using *-er* versus *more* and *-est* versus *most* depends largely on the number of syllables in the adjective or adverb. The *-er* and *-est* endings are most common with one-syllable words: *large, larger, largest* (adjective); *far, farther, farthest* (adverb). Adverbs of two or more syllables use *more* and *most*: *easily, more easily, most easily.* Two-syllable adjectives vary; try checking in the dictionary—most college dictionaries show the comparative and superlative forms in the entry for an adjective's positive form. Adjectives of three or more syllables use *more* and *most*.

Alert: Do not use a double comparative (not *more louder*) or superlative (not *most snappiest*). The words *more* or *most* cannot be used if the *-er* or *-est* ending has been used. !

Using Correct Irregular Forms

A few common adjectives and adverbs have irregular comparative and superlative forms.

Positive [1]	Comparative [2]	Superlative [3+]
good [adjective]	better	best
well [adverb]	better	best
well [adjective]		
bad [adjective]	worse	worst
badly [adverb]	worse	worst
many	more	most
much	more	most
some	more	most
little	less	least

- The Perkinses saw a **good** movie.
- The Perkinses saw a **better** movie than the Smiths did.
- The Perkinses saw the **best** movie that they had ever seen.

- The Millers had **little** trouble finding jobs.
- The Millers had **less** trouble finding jobs than the Smiths did.
- The Millers had the **least** trouble finding jobs of everyone.

Alert: Do not use *less* and *fewer* interchangeably. Use *less* with uncountable items and *fewer* with numbers or other countable things: *They consumed **fewer calories;** the sugar substitute had **less aftertaste.*** !

Avoiding too many nouns as modifiers   G8.e

Sometimes nouns—words that name a person, place, thing, or idea function as MODIFIERS of other nouns: *truck driver, train track, security system.* These very familiar terms create no problems. However, when nouns pile up in a sequence of modifiers, the reader has difficulty figuring out which nouns are being modified, and which nouns are doing the modifying. As you revise such sentences, you can use any of several routes to clarify your material.

SENTENCE REWRITTEN

No	I asked my advisor to write **two college recommendation** letters for me.
Yes	I asked my advisor to write **letters of recommendation** to **two colleges** for me.

ONE NOUN CHANGED TO POSSESSIVE CASE AND ANOTHER TO ADJECTIVE FORM

No   Some students might take the **United States Navy examination** for **navy engineering training.**

Yes   Some students might take the United States **Navy's examination** for **naval engineer training.**

NOUN CHANGED TO PREPOSITIONAL PHRASE

No   Our **student advisor training program** has won awards for excellence.

Yes   Our training program **for student advisors** has won awards for excellence.   [Notice that this change requires the plural *advisors.*]

Correct
Sentences

subject, voice, and mood

dangling modifiers

direct discourse

ambiguous

mma splices

fused sentences

shifts

sentence fragments

faulty predication

indirect discourse

C CORRECT SENTENCES

C1 Sentence Fragments

A **sentence fragment** is a group of words that is capitalized and punctuated like a complete sentence but is not one. In college writing, a sentence fragment usually is considered an error because it can interfere with clarity; therefore, be sure to write complete sentences.

Checking for sentence completeness C1.a

Use **QA Box 36** to check that your sentences are complete.

TEST FOR SENTENCE COMPLETENESS

QA
Box
36

- Does the word group include a SUBORDINATING word and lack an INDEPENDENT CLAUSE? If yes, there is a fragment. To revise, see **C1.b.**

  Fragment Because the ship had to cut a path through the ice.

- Is there a VERB? If not, there is a fragment. To revise, see **C1.c.**

  Fragment Thousands of whales in the Arctic Ocean because of an early winter.

- Is there a SUBJECT? If not, there is a fragment. To revise, see **C1.c.**

  Fragment Raced to reach the whales.

Revising dependent clauses punctuated as sentences C1.b

A **dependent clause** has a SUBJECT and a VERB, but it starts with a subordinating word. A dependent clause cannot stand on its own as a sentence. Subordinating words include SUBORDINATING CONJUNCTIONS, such as *after, although, because, before, until, when, whether, while,* and *unless,* and RELATIVE PRONOUNS, such as *who, which,* and *that;* for a complete list of subordinating words, see **QA Box 24** in **G1.h.**

To revise a dependent clause punctuated as a sentence, you may choose to (1) attach the dependent clause to an INDEPENDENT CLAUSE that comes directly before or after the fragment, (2) compose an independent clause to complete the thought, or (3) drop the subordinating word. Sometimes you will need to add words so that the complete sentence makes sense.

Fragment   **Because the ship had to cut a path through the ice.** The rescue effort would take a few hours.   [*Because the ship had to cut a path through the ice* is a dependent clause, not a sentence.]

Revised	Because the ship had to cut a path through the ice, the rescue effort would take a few hours. [joined to an independent clause]
Revised	The ship had to cut a path through the ice. The rescue effort would take a few hours. [subordinating word dropped]
Fragment	The noise of the rescue effort worried the ship's crew. **Who knew the whales might panic.** [*Who knew the whales might panic* is a dependent clause, not a sentence.]
Revised	The noise of the rescue effort worried the ship's crew, who knew the whales might panic. [joined to an independent clause]
Revised	The noise of the rescue effort worried the ship's crew. They knew the whales might panic. [subordinating word changed to a word that can be a subject in an independent clause]

! **Alert:** When a dependent clause starting with a subordinating conjunction comes before its independent clause, a comma usually separates the two clauses.

C1.c Revising phrases punctuated as sentences ▌

A **phrase** is a group of words that lacks a SUBJECT, a VERB, or both. A phrase cannot stand on its own as a sentence. To revise a phrase punctuated as a sentence, you may choose to (1) rewrite it to become an independent clause or (2) join it to an independent clause that comes directly before or after.

A phrase containing only a verbal (an INFINITIVE, a PAST PARTICIPLE, or a PRESENT PARTICIPLE) but containing no verb is a fragment, not a sentence.

Fragment	The mayor called a news conference last week. **To announce new programs for crime prevention.** [*To announce* starts an infinitive phrase, not a sentence.]
Revised	The mayor called a news conference last week to announce new programs for crime prevention. [joined into one sentence]
Revised	The mayor called a news conference last week. She announced new programs for crime prevention. [rewritten]
Fragment	**Hoping for public support.** She gave examples of problems everywhere in the city. [*Hoping for public support* is a participle phrase, not a sentence.]

Revised	Hoping for public support, she gave examples of problems everywhere in the city. [joined into one sentence]
Revised	She was hoping for public support. She gave examples of problems everywhere in the city. [rewritten]

A prepositional phrase starts with a PREPOSITION. It is not a sentence.

Fragment	Cigarette smoke made the conference room seem airless. **During the long news conference.**
Revised	Cigarette smoke made the conference room seem airless during the long news conference. [joined into one sentence]
Revised	Cigarette smoke made the conference room seem airless. It was hard to breathe during the long news conference. [rewritten]

An **appositive** is one or more words that rename a NOUN. It is not a sentence.

Fragment	Most people respected the mayor. **A politician with fresh ideas and practical solutions.** [*A politician* starts an appositive, not a sentence.]
Revised	Most people respected the mayor, a politician with fresh ideas and practical solutions. [joined into one sentence]
Revised	Most people respected the mayor. She seemed to be a politician with fresh ideas and practical solutions. [rewritten]

A **compound predicate** contains two or more verbs. To be part of a complete sentence, a PREDICATE must have a subject. When the second half of a compound predicate is punctuated as a separate sentence, it is not a sentence.

Fragment	The reporters questioned the mayor about the details of her programs. **And then asked if she planned to run for governor.** [*And then asked* is the start of a compound predicate, not a sentence.]
Revised	The reporters questioned the mayor about the details of her programs and then asked if she planned to run for governor. [joined into one sentence]
Revised	The reporters questioned the mayor about the details of her programs. Then they asked her if she planned to run for governor. [rewritten]

C1.d Being aware of intentional fragments ▌

Professional writers sometimes intentionally use fragments for emphasis and effect. The ability to judge the difference between an acceptable and an unacceptable sentence fragment comes from much exposure to reading the works of skilled writers. Many instructors, therefore, often do not accept sentence fragments in student writing until a student can demonstrate the consistent ability to write well-constructed complete sentences.

C2 Comma Splices and Fused Sentences

Comma splices and fused sentences are two versions of the same problem: incorrect separation of INDEPENDENT CLAUSES. A **comma splice** occurs when only a comma separates independent clauses: For a comma to be correct between independent clauses, it must be followed by a COORDINATING CONJUNCTION (*and, but, for, or, nor, so, yet*).

Comma splice error   The hurricane suddenly intensified, it turned toward land.

A **fused** (or **run-on**) **sentence** occurs when independent clauses are run together without being separated by punctuation.

Fused sentence error   The hurricane suddenly intensified it turned toward land.

Occasionally, experienced writers use a comma to join short independent clauses: *Mosquitoes do not bite, they stab.* Because many instructors consider this practice an error in student writing, avoid it.

C2.a Recognizing causes of comma splices ▌
and fused sentences

Avoiding comma splices and fused sentences is easier when you know the three most common causes for these errors; they are summarized in **QA Box 37.**

QA Box 37

MAJOR CAUSES OF COMMA SPLICES AND FUSED SENTENCES

1 **Pronouns.** A comma splice or fused sentence often occurs when the second independent clause starts with a pronoun.

No Thomas Edison was a productive inventor, he held over 1,300 U.S. and foreign patents.

Yes Thomas Edison was a productive inventor. He held over 1,300 U.S. and foreign patents.

2 **Conjunctive adverbs and other transitional expressions.** A comma splice or fused sentence often occurs when the second independent clause starts with a conjunctive adverb (for a list, see **QA Box 22**). Remember that coordinating conjunctions (*and, but, or, nor, for, so, yet*) can work with a comma to join two independent clauses, but conjunctive adverbs and other transitional expressions cannot.

No Thomas Edison was a brilliant scientist, however, his schooling was limited to only three months.

Yes Thomas Edison was a brilliant scientist. However, his schooling was limited to only three months.

3 **Explanations or examples.** A comma splice or fused sentence often occurs when the second independent clause explains or gives an example of the information in the first independent clause.

No Thomas Edison was the genius behind many inventions, among the best known are the phonograph and the incandescent lamp.

Yes Thomas Edison was the genius behind many inventions. Among the best known are the phonograph and the incandescent lamp.

Correcting comma splices and fused sentences   C2.b

Using Punctuation

A period or a semicolon can separate the INDEPENDENT CLAUSES in a comma splice or fused sentence.

Comma splice A shark is all cartilage, it does not have a bone in its body.

Fused sentence A shark is all cartilage it does not have a bone in its body.

Corrected	A shark is all cartilage. It does not have a bone in its body.
Corrected	A shark is all cartilage; it does not have a bone in its body.

Although using punctuation to correct these errors is never wrong, revising to communicate a coordinate or subordinate relationship between the clauses may deliver your meaning more effectively.

Using a Coordinating Conjunction

When ideas in independent clauses are closely related and grammatically equivalent, you can connect them with a comma followed by a coordinating conjunction (*and, but, for, nor, or, so, yet*).

Comma splice	Every living creature gives off a weak electrical charge in the water, special pores on a shark's skin can detect these signals.
Fused sentence	Every living creature gives off a weak electrical charge in the water special pores on a shark's skin can detect these signals.
Corrected	Every living creature gives off a weak electrical charge in the water, **and** special pores on a shark's skin can detect these signals.

Revising an Independent Clause into a Dependent Clause

When one independent clause expresses information that can logically be subordinated (see **E2.c**), you can use a SUBORDINATING CONJUNCTION to make that clause DEPENDENT.

Comma splice	Homer and Langley Collyer had packed their house from top to bottom with junk, police could not open the front door to investigate a missing-persons report on the brothers.
Fused sentence	Homer and Langley Collyer had packed their house from top to bottom with junk police could not open the front door to investigate a missing-persons report on the brothers.
Corrected	**Because** Homer and Langley Collyer had packed their house from top to bottom with junk, police could not open the front door to investigate a missing-persons report on the brothers.

Another way to create a dependent clause is to use a RELATIVE PRONOUN (*that, which, who*).

Comma splice	The Collyers had been crushed under a pile of newspapers, the newspapers had toppled onto the brothers.

Fused sentence	The Collyers had been crushed under a pile of newspapers the newspapers had toppled onto the brothers.
Corrected	The Collyers had been crushed under a pile of newspapers, **which** had toppled onto the brothers.

Alert: (1) Generally, use a comma after an introductory dependent clause (see **P2.b**), but when the independent clause comes first, use a comma between the clauses only if the dependent clause is NONRESTRICTIVE (see **P2.e**). (2) For an ADJECTIVE CLAUSE starting with *who*, *which*, or *that*, use commas if the clause is nonrestrictive (see **P2.e**). !

Taking Special Care with Conjunctive Adverbs and Other Transitional Expressions

CONJUNCTIVE ADVERBS include such words as *however, therefore, also, next, then, thus, furthermore*, and *nevertheless*. TRANSITIONAL EXPRESSIONS include *for example, for instance*, and others. For a list of conjunctive adverbs, see **QA Box 22** on page 51.

Conjunctive adverbs and transitional expressions link ideas between INDEPENDENT CLAUSES. When a conjunctive adverb or other transitional expression falls between independent clauses, use a period or a semicolon immediately before it.

Comma splice	Buying a car versus leasing one is a matter of individual preference, however, it is wise to consider several points before deciding.
Fused sentence	Buying a car versus leasing one is a matter of individual preference however, it is wise to consider several points before deciding.
Corrected	Buying a car versus leasing one is a matter of individual preference; however, it is wise to consider several points before deciding.

C3 Sentence Shifts and Disjointed Sentences

Grammatical shifts and mixed sentences create inconsistent and illogical writing that blurs meaning and confuses readers.

C3.a Staying consistent in person and number

PERSON is conveyed by NOUNS, PRONOUNS, and VERBS. **First person** (using such pronouns as *I* and *we*) focuses attention on the writer or speaker: *I see a field of fireflies.* **Second person** (*you*) focuses attention on the reader or listener: *You see a shower of sparks.* **Third person** focuses attention on the subject that is being written or talked about: *The physicist sees a cloud of cosmic dust.* All nouns and many pronouns (for example, *he, she, it, they, everyone, no one*) convey third person.

Number refers to one (singular) or more than one (plural) for nouns and pronouns. Shifts of person and number often occur together and cause confusion about the writer's stance toward the subject and the reader.

Confusing	I enjoy reading forecasts of the future, but you never know which ones are going to turn out to be correct and which ones will never happen. One recent prediction claimed that U.S. car buyers will pay twice today's price for a car, but you will get twice the gas mileage. [This short passage shifts from first to second to third person, preventing readers from knowing what the writer wants to say. Is this an informal first-person report? A piece of advice addressed directly to readers? An impersonal piece of informative writing?]
Revised	Although forecasts of the future make enjoyable reading, it is impossible to know which ones will turn out to be correct and which ones will never happen. One recent prediction claimed that U.S. car buyers will pay twice today's price for a car, but they will get twice the gas mileage. [The revisions here make the third-person perspective consistent; revising in other ways would bring other perspectives into focus.]

Avoid shifts from nouns (third person) to the second-person pronoun *you*.

- By the year 2000, most people will live longer, and ~~you~~ they will have to work longer, too.

Avoid shifts between singular and plural in third person.

- The longer ~~a person stays~~ people stay in the workforce, the more competition they will experience from younger job seekers.

! **Alert:** INDEFINITE PRONOUNS (*everyone, someone, anybody,* and others) can cause confusing shifts when writers are trying to avoid sexist language; see **E5.b.**

Staying consistent in subject, voice, and mood   C3.b

Meaning sometimes justifies a shift in SUBJECT within or between sentences. However, a subject shift may occur because writing is drifting out of focus, often as a result of a shift from ACTIVE to PASSIVE VOICE.

Confusing   Most interviewees expect major improvements by the year 2000, but some problems are anticipated.
[The subject shifts from *interviewees* to *problems*; also, the verb voice shifts from active *expect* to passive *are anticipated*.]

Revised   Most interviewees expect major improvements by the year 2000, but they anticipate some problems.

Similarly, avoid unnecessary shifts between statements or questions (INDICATIVE MOOD) and commands (IMPERATIVE MOOD).

Confusing   Interviewees expressed concern about keeping jobs in the United States. Protect the environment, too.
[The first sentence is a statement, but the second sentence shifts unnecessarily to a command.]

Revised   Interviewees expressed concern about keeping jobs in the United States and about protecting the environment.

Staying consistent in verb tense   C3.c

Changes in verb tense are necessary to describe time movement; see **G3.d**. Unnecessary tense shifts, however, can create illogical time sequences.

Confusing   A campaign in the United States to clean up the movies began in the 1920s when civic and religious groups try to ban sex and violence from films.   [The tense shifts from past *began* to present *try*, even though the action of both verbs occurred in the past.]

Revised   A campaign in the United States to clean up the movies began in the 1920s when civic and religious groups tried to ban sex and violence from films.

• Producers and distributors created a film Production Code in the 1930s. At first, violating its guidelines carried no penalty. In time, however, failing to get the board's Seal of Approval ~~dooms~~ doomed a film to poor distribution.

[The illogical tense shift here occurs between sentences.]

C3.d Staying consistent in indirect and direct discourse

Indirect discourse reports someone's words and is not enclosed in quotation marks. Direct discourse repeats someone's words exactly, and the quoted words are enclosed in quotation marks. Also, the grammatical patterns of indirect and direct discourse differ.

Inaccurate Merging of Indirect and Direct Discourse

- He asked did we enjoy the movie.   [This incorrect version has the verb that direct discourse would use, but it lacks quotation punctuation, and the PRONOUN *we* is wrong for direct discourse.]

Accurate Direct Discourse

- He asked, "Did you enjoy the movie?"   [This good version repeats the spoken words exactly and encloses them in quotation marks. It ends correctly with a question mark.]

Accurate Indirect Discourse

- He asked whether we had enjoyed the movie.   [This good version reports someone's words, using the pronoun *we* to clarify who spoke and who was spoken to. Also, the verb *had enjoyed* clarifies the time relationship between the enjoyment and the asking. The statement ends correctly with a period.]

C3.e Revising mixed sentences

Avoiding Scrambled Sentences

In a scrambled sentence, a DEPENDENT CLAUSE or a PHRASE fails to mesh with the INDEPENDENT CLAUSE, derailing meaning.

No   Because television's first transmissions in the 1920s included news programs became popular with the public.   [The opening dependent clause starts off on one track, but the independent clause goes off in another direction. What does the writer want to emphasize—the first transmissions or the popularity of news programs?]

Yes   Television's first transmissions in the 1920s included news programming, which became popular with the public. [Dropping *Because* and adding *which* solves the problem and emphasizes the first transmissions.]

Yes   Because television's first transmissions in the 1920s included news programs, television quickly became popular with the public.   [Putting the first transmissions information into a dependent clause deemphasizes it and emphasizes the idea about popularity in the main clause.]

No By doubling the time allotment for network news to thirty minutes increased the prestige of network news programs. [A PREPOSITIONAL PHRASE, such as *By doubling the time allotment . . .* , cannot be the SUBJECT of a sentence.]

Yes Doubling the time allotment for network news to thirty minutes increased the prestige of network news programs. [Dropping the preposition *by* clears up the problem.]

Yes By doubling the time allotment for network news to thirty minutes, network executives increased the prestige of network news programs. [Inserting a logical subject, *network executives*, clears up the problem by creating an independent clause preceded by a modifying prepositional phrase.]

Avoiding Faulty Predication

When predication is faulty, a subject and PREDICATE do not make sense together; one part or the other needs to be revised.

No The purpose of television was invented to entertain. [The subject, *purpose*, and the predicate, *was invented to entertain*, do not make sense together.]

Yes Television was invented to entertain. [This revision refocuses the subject and keeps the original predicate.]

Yes The purpose of television was to entertain. [This revision refocuses the predicate.]

No Walter Cronkite's outstanding characteristic as a newscaster was believable. [*Believable* could describe *Walter Cronkite*, but the subject of the sentence is *characteristic*, not *Walter Cronkite*.]

Yes Walter Cronkite's outstanding characteristic as a newscaster was believability. [This revision provides a noun, *believability*, to act as a COMPLEMENT renaming *outstanding characteristic*.]

Yes Walter Cronkite had an outstanding characteristic as a newscaster: He was believable. [*Believable* can describe *Walter Cronkite*, who is referred to by the pronoun subject *He*.]

Avoiding *is where*, *is when*, and *reason . . . is because*

Constructions using *is where*, *is when*, or *reason . . . is because* are grammatically flawed.

- ~~A disaster is when~~ television news shows get some of their highest ratings during a disaster.

   [A disaster is not a time, although the word *when* implies that it is.]

- The reason is ~~because~~ *that* many people are gripped by real-life drama.

  [*Because* means "the reason that," so the unrevised sentence says, in effect, "The reason is the reason that many people. . . ."]

Even when *reason* and *is because* are widely separated, the problem still exists.

- ~~One reason that~~ *T*elevision news captured our attention ~~is because~~ *when* its cameras covered the Vietnam War from the battlefield.

  [The best revision may remove *reason . . . is* completely.]

C3.f Using care with elliptical constructions and comparisons

An **elliptical construction** deliberately leaves out, rather than repeats, one or more words that appear elsewhere in a sentence. *I have my book and Joan's* is an elliptical—and acceptable—way to express *I have my book and Joan's book.* An elliptical construction is correct only when the sentence contains exactly what the elliptical structure omits.

- In 1920s Chicago, cornetist Manuel Perez ~~was leading~~ *led* one outstanding jazz group, Tommy and Jimmy Dorsey another.

  [The singular verb *was leading* cannot take the place of *were leading,* which the plural subject *Tommy and Jimmy Dorsey* requires. *Led* works because it goes with both singular and plural subjects.]

- The period of the big jazz dance bands began *in* and lasted through World War II. [*Began* must be followed by *in,* not *through,* as implied.]

In writing a comparison, include all words needed to make clear the relationship between the compared items.

- High achievers make better business executives. *than risk takers do*

  [*Better* implies a comparison, but none was stated.]

- Most stockholders value high achievers more than *they value* risk takers.

  [Who values whom most? The revised sentence reflects one clear meaning. Another clear revision, with a different meaning, is *Most stockholders value high achievers more than risk takers do.*]

from that of a high achiever

- A risk taker's ability to manage long-term growth is very different ˄.

[Different from what? Both items being compared must be expressed.]

Completing *as much as* and Similar Phrases

In *as . . . as . . . than* comparisons (for example, *as pretty as, if not prettier than*), be sure to state the second *as.*

- High achievers value success as much˄, if not more than, high salary.

as

Alert: Proofread carefully for omitted short words.

!

- A high salary may not motivate ˄risk taker as much as the chance ˄

a   *to*

rescue ˄company from financial danger.

a

C4 Misplaced and Dangling Modifiers

A **modifier** is a word, PHRASE, or CLAUSE that describes or limits other words, phrases, or clauses. Place modifiers carefully to prevent your intended meaning from becoming fuzzy or disappearing completely.

Avoiding ambiguous placements

C4.a

Taking Care with *only*

A word such as *only, just, almost, hardly, scarcely,* or *simply* limits the word it precedes. To see this effect, notice how various placements of the word *only* affect the meaning of the sentence *Professional coaches say that high salaries motivate players.*

- **Only** professional coaches say that high salaries motivate players. [No one else says that.]

- Professional coaches **only** say that high salaries motivate players. [The coaches don't believe it.]

- Professional coaches say that **only** high salaries motivate players. [The coaches think nothing else works.]

- Professional coaches say that high salaries motivate **only** players. [No one else is motivated by high salaries.]

When you use *only* in your writing, be sure to position it so that it conveys the exact meaning you intend.

- Auto pioneers Karl Benz and Gottlieb Daimler did not know each other even though they ~~only~~ lived ^only^ 60 miles apart.

  [*Only* needs to modify 60 *miles*, not *lived*.]

Avoiding Squinting Modifiers

A modifier can sometimes "squint," making sense with what comes before it as well as what comes after it. Revise so that your meaning is clear to your readers.

- While Karl Benz watched, the vehicle he had built jerked forward ~~loudly~~ announcing its arrival ^loudly^.

  [Before the revision, the car seems to be both loudly jerking forward and loudly announcing its arrival.]

C4.b Avoiding wrong placements ▮

Usually, the right placement for a modifier is next to the word it is meant to modify.

No   Nicholas Cugnot built the first self-propelled vehicle, determined to travel without horses or carts.   [The modifier *determined to travel without horses or carts* describes *Nicholas Cugnot*, not *vehicle*, and this wrong placement garbles meaning.]

Yes   Determined to travel without horses or carts, Nicholas Cugnot built the first self-propelled vehicle.

C4.c Avoiding split infinitives and other awkward ▮ placements

A **split infinitive** occurs when a modifier separates *to* and a VERB: *to originally plan*. In general, place modifiers before or after infinitives, not directly after the word *to*.

No   Orson Welles's radio drama "War of the Worlds" managed to, on October 30, 1938, convince listeners that they were hearing an invasion by Martians.

Yes   On October 30, 1938, Orson Welles's radio drama "War of the Worlds" managed to convince listeners that they were hearing an invasion by Martians.

Sometimes a modifier seems awkward in any position except between *to* and the verb. Many readers are not distracted by split infinitives like this one:

- Welles wanted to realistically portray a Martian invasion for the radio audience.

If you think your readers prefer that infinitives never be split, you can usually revise the sentence to avoid the split·

- Welles wanted his "Martian invasion" to sound realistic for the radio audience.

Interruptions of SUBJECTS and verbs by highly complex PHRASES or CLAUSES disturb the smooth flow of a sentence.

- ~~The origins of the automobile,~~ if we consider the complete history of many inventors working independently in different countries, *the origins of the automobile* should probably be credited to Nicholas Cugnot in 1769.

Interruptions of a **verb phrase** (a verb using more than one word: *was kissed, had been kissed*) make a sentence lurch instead of flow.

- Karl Benz has~~, by most automobile historians,~~ been given credit *by most automobile historians* for the invention of the automobile.

Alert: Limiting words such as *just, only,* and *never* that modify a MAIN VERB usually should be positioned within the verb phrase: *could never have lifted* [not *could have never lifted*], *had just arrived* [not *just had arrived*]. **!**

Avoiding dangling modifiers   C4.d

A **dangling modifier** confuses meaning because whatever the writer meant it to refer to is in the wrong place, in the wrong grammatical form, or missing from the sentence.

Introductory phrases attach their meaning to the first NOUN after the phrase. They dangle helplessly if that noun is not the modifier's intended subject.

No   When courting Emily, the townspeople gossiped about her.
[The *townspeople* were not courting Emily.]

Yes   When Homer Baron was courting Emily, the townspeople gossiped about her.

C CORRECT SENTENCES

No   Reading Faulkner's short story "A Rose for Emily," the ending surprised us.   [The *ending* did not read the story.]

Yes   Having read Faulkner's short story "A Rose for Emily," we were surprised by the ending.

Yes   We read Faulkner's short story "A Rose for Emily" and were surprised by the ending.

Effective Sentences and Words

jargon

variety

PARALLELISM

wordy

gender neutral

mixed metaphor

pretentious

emphasis

concrete

levels of formality

specific

CONNOTATION

combining sentences

denotation

strong verbs

E EFFECTIVE SENTENCES AND WORDS

E1 Conciseness

Conciseness refers to direct, to-the-point writing. Wordy writing, in contrast, forces readers to clear away excess words before sentences can deliver their messages.

Eliminating unneeded words   E1.a

Padded writing contains deadwood, the empty words and phrases that increase word count but lack meaning. Prune your sentences of deadwood.

- ~~In fact, the~~ ^{The local} television station ~~which was situated in the local area~~ had won ~~a great~~ many awards ^{for} ~~as a result of~~ its ~~having been involved in the~~ coverage of ~~all kinds of~~ controversial issues.

QA Box 38, below, shows some of the most common deadwood phrases and strategies for getting rid of them.

ELIMINATING UNNEEDED WORDS		QA Box 38
Empty Words	**Wordy Examples Revised**	
as a matter of fact	~~As a matter of fact,~~ ^Sstatistics show that many marriages end in divorce.	
at the present time	The bill is being debated ^{now.} ~~at the present time.~~	
because of the fact that, in light of the fact that, due to the fact that	Because ~~of the fact that~~ a special exhibit is scheduled, the museum is open late.	
by means of	We traveled by ~~means of~~ cars.	
factor	The project's final cost was an essential ^{consideration.} ~~factor to consider.~~	
exist	The crime rate ~~that exists~~ is unacceptable.	
for the purpose of	A work crew arrived ~~for the purpose of~~ ^{to} fixing the pothole.	
have a tendency to	The mixture had ~~a tendency~~ ^{tended} to evaporate.	

Continued on next page

QA Box 38, continued from previous page

in a very real sense	~~In a very real sense,~~ *D* drainage problems caused the house to flood.
in the case of	~~In the case of~~ *T* the proposed tax *angered* ~~were angry,~~ residents.
in the final analysis	~~In the final analysis,~~ *N* no observer described the apparent thief accurately.
in the event that	~~In the event that~~ *If* you are late, I will buy our tickets.
in the process of	We are ~~in the process of~~ reviewing six sites.
it seems that	~~It seems that~~ *T* the union struck over wages.
manner	Most people looked at the snake ~~in a fearful manner,~~ *fearfully.*
nature	The review was ~~of a sarcastic. nature,~~
the point I am trying to make	~~The point I am trying to make is that~~ *N* news reporters should not invade people's privacy.
type of	Gordon took a relaxing ~~type of~~ vacation.
what I mean to say	~~What I mean to say is that~~ I expect a bonus.

E1.b Avoiding redundancies

Planned repetition can create a powerful rhythmic effect. Unplanned and purposeless repetition, on the other hand, can irritate readers with its dull drone. Similarly, redundancies deliver the same message more than once, but in different words.

- ~~People~~ *A* anesthetized ~~for surgery~~ *people* can remain semiconscious during surgery but may still feel no pain.

  [*Surgery* is used twice, but it is implied in *anesthetized*. The revision is concise.]

- ~~Bringing~~ *Completing* the project ~~to final completion~~ three weeks early, the new manager earned our ~~respectful regard,~~ *respect.*

  [*Completion* implies *final*, and *regard* implies *respect*. The concise revisions eliminate redundancy.]

rectangular
- The ⌃package, ~~rectangular in shape~~⌃ lay on the counter.

  [*Rectangular* is a *shape*. The concise revision eliminates redundancy.]

Eliminating wordy sentence structures　　E1.c

Revising Unnecessary Expletive Constructions

An **expletive** construction is one that uses *it* or *there* plus a form of the VERB *be* before the sentence SUBJECT. Removing the expletive and revising can sometimes make the sentence more direct.

　　　　　　　　S　　must
- ~~It is necessary for~~ ⌃students ~~to~~⌃ fill out both registration forms.

　　　　　　　　　　　　　T　　　　offers three majors
- ~~There are three majors offered by~~ ⌃the computer science department⌃.

Revising from Passive to Active Constructions

The **passive voice** focuses on the receiver of the verb's action: *Oxygen was discovered by Joseph Priestley*. The **active voice** focuses on the doer of the action: *Joseph Priestley discovered oxygen*. The active voice is often livelier and more concise than the passive. One way to revise an unnecessary passive is to make the doer of the action the subject of the sentence. Another way is to use a verb that makes the sentence subject the doer of the action.

Passive	Volunteer work was done by the students for credit in sociology.　[This passive is unnecessary. The students are the ones doing the action, so *students*, not *volunteer work*, should be the subject of the sentence.]
Active	The students did volunteer work for credit in sociology.
Active	Volunteer work earned the students credit in sociology. [Here, *volunteer work* can serve as the subject because it performs the action of the verb *earned*.]

Be particularly alert for the passive voice that misleads readers by hiding information about who acts: *Cracks in the foundation of the structure had been found, but they were not considered serious*. Left out of the sentence is information that may be important about who found cracks and who decided that they were not serious.

Reducing sentences　　E1.d

When you revise, look at your writing to see if you can improve it by combining sentences and simplifying CLAUSES and PHRASES.

Combining Sentences

During revision, look at sentences as sets. Try to reduce the information in one sentence to a group of words for inclusion in another
sentence.

- ~~The Titanic was discovered~~ ^{S} seventy-three years after being sunk by
  an iceberg$_{\odot}$, ~~The wreck~~ the Titanic was located in the Atlantic by a team of
  French and American scientists.

Reducing Clauses

Try reducing a clause to a phrase by dropping some words. Sometimes you can reduce a clause to a single word.

- The Titanic, ~~which was~~ a huge ocean liner, sank in 1912.
- The scientists held a memorial service for the dead passengers and
  crew members, ~~who had died~~.

Reducing Phrases

- ~~Loaded with luxuries, the~~ The luxury liner was thought to be unsinkable.

E1.e Using strong verbs and avoiding nouns formed from verbs

Strong VERBS directly convey an action. *Be* and *have*, both weak verbs,
tend to create wordy structures.

Weak verb   The plan before the city council has to do with tax
                 rebates.

Strong verb The plan before the city council proposes tax rebates.

! Alert: When you revise, look carefully for verbs with the pattern *be*
+ ADJECTIVE + *of* (such as *be aware of, be capable of*). Many of these
phrases can be replaced with one-word verbs: *I envy* [not *am envious
of*] *your ability as a public speaker.* Use *appreciate*, not *be appreciative of;*
illustrate, not *be illustrative of;* and *support*, not *be supportive of.*

When you revise, also look for NOUNS derived from verbs (usually
ending with *-ance, -ment,* and *-tion*) that can be turned into verbs. Such
revisions make sentences more concise and usually replace a weak
verb with a stronger verb.

No   The accumulation of paper went on for more than 30 years.

Yes   The paper accumulated for more than 30 years.

E2 Coordination and Subordination

COORDINATION and SUBORDINATION help writers communicate relationships between ideas.

Two ideas	The sky turned brighter.
	The wind calmed down.
Coordinated version	The sky turned brighter, and the wind calmed down.
Subordinated versions	As the sky turned brighter, the wind calmed down. [The *wind* is the focus.]
	As the wind calmed down, the sky turned brighter. [The *sky* is the focus.]

Using coordination to show relationships of equivalent ideas   E2.a

Coordination uses grammatical equivalency to communicate balance or sequence in ideas. A **coordinate** (or **compound**) **sentence** contains grammatically equivalent INDEPENDENT CLAUSES joined either by a semicolon or by a coordinating conjunction (*and, but, for, or, nor, yet, so*).

- The sky turned brighter, and the wind calmed down.
- The sky turned brighter; the wind calmed down.

Alert: Use a comma before a coordinating conjunction that joins two independent clauses; see **P2.a**. **!**

Avoiding coordination problems   E2.b

Illogical coordination occurs when coordinated ideas are either unrelated or nonequivalent.

No	Computers came into common use in the 1970s, and they sometimes make costly errors. [The statement in each INDEPENDENT CLAUSE is true, but the ideas are not logically connected and therefore should not be coordinated.]
Yes	Computers came into common use in the 1970s, and now they are indispensable business tools.

Overused coordination reads as if the words simply tumbled out of the writer's head.

No	Dinosaurs could have disappeared for many reasons, and one theory holds that the climate suddenly became cold, and another suggests that a sudden shower of meteors and asteroids hit the earth, so the impact created a huge dust cloud that caused a false winter. The winter lasted for years, and the dinosaurs died.
Yes	Dinosaurs could have disappeared for many reasons. One theory holds that the climate suddenly became cold, and another suggests that a sudden shower of meteors and asteroids hit the earth. The impact created a huge dust cloud that caused a false winter. The winter lasted for years, killing the dinosaurs.

E2.c Using subordination to show relationships of nonequivalent ideas

In sentences, subordination helps you to express the relative importance of ideas. You can emphasize an idea by presenting it in an INDEPENDENT CLAUSE and deemphasize it by presenting it in a DEPENDENT CLAUSE. What information you choose to subordinate within a sentence depends on the meaning you want to deliver.

Unclear Relationships

- In 1888, two cowboys had to fight a dangerous Colorado snowstorm. They were looking for cattle. They came to a canyon. They saw outlines of buildings through the snow. Survival then seemed certain.

Clear Relationships

- In 1888, two cowboys had to fight a dangerous Colorado snowstorm while they were looking for cattle. When they came to a canyon, they saw outlines of buildings through the snow. Survival then seemed certain.

A subordinating word at the start of a clause makes the clause dependent. SUBORDINATING CONJUNCTIONS, listed in **QA Box 24**, start grammatically dependent ADVERB CLAUSES. RELATIVE PRONOUNS (*who, which, that*) and RELATIVE ADVERBS (such as *where* or *why*) start grammatically dependent ADJECTIVE CLAUSES. Patterns of subordination with adverb clauses and adjective clauses are shown in **QA Box 39**, on the next page.

SUBORDINATION

QA
Box
39

SENTENCES WITH ADVERB CLAUSES

- **Adverb clause,** independent clause.
  - **After the sky grew dark,** the wind died suddenly.
- Independent clause, **adverb clause.**
  - Birds stopped singing, **as they do during an eclipse.**
- Independent clause, **adverb clause.**
  - The stores closed **before the storm began.**

SENTENCES WITH ADJECTIVE CLAUSES

- Independent clause **restrictive (essential)* adjective clause.**
  - Weather forecasts warned of a storm **that might bring a thirty-inch snowfall.**
- Independent clause, **nonrestrictive (nonessential)* adjective clause.**
  - Spring is the season for tornadoes, **which may have wind speeds over 220 miles an hour.**
- Beginning of independent clause **restrictive (essential)* adjective clause** end of independent clause.
  - Anyone **who lives through a tornado** remembers the experience.
- Beginning of independent clause, **nonrestrictive (nonessential)* adjective clause,** end of independent clause.
  - The sky, **which had been clear,** turned greenish black.

*For an explanation of restrictive and nonrestrictive elements, see **P2.e.**

Avoiding subordination problems

E2.d

Illogical subordination occurs when the SUBORDINATING CONJUNCTION does not show the proper relationship between the INDEPENDENT CLAUSE and the DEPENDENT CLAUSE (see **QA Box 24** on page 52).

No Because Beethoven was deaf when he wrote them, his final symphonies were masterpieces.   [*Because* is illogical. It conveys that the masterpieces resulted from the deafness.]

Yes Although Beethoven was deaf when he wrote them, his final symphonies were masterpieces.   [*Although* is logical. It conveys that Beethoven wrote masterpieces despite being deaf.]

Overused subordination crowds too many images or ideas together, making readers lose track of the message. If you have used more than two dependent clauses in a sentence, check carefully to see whether the meaning of the sentence is clear.

No   A new technique for eye surgery, which is supposed to correct nearsightedness, which previously could be corrected only by glasses, has been developed, although many doctors do not approve of the new technique because it can create unstable vision.

Yes   A new technique for eye surgery, which is supposed to correct nearsightedness, has been developed. Previously, nearsightedness could be corrected only by glasses. Many doctors do not approve of the new technique, however, because it can create unstable vision.   [In the revision, one long sentence is broken into three sentences, making the material easier to read and the relationships among ideas clearer.]

E3 Sentence Style

You gain the pleasure of expressing yourself with clarity and grace as you develop sentence style. Experimenting with techniques described in this chapter—parallelism, variety, and emphasis—can help you find your unique writing style.

E3.a Using parallelism for balance and rhythm ▮

Parallelism is the use of equivalent grammatical forms to express equivalent ideas. An equivalent grammatical form is a word or group of words that matches—that is, is parallel to—the structure of a corresponding word or group of words. When you are expressing similar information or ideas, parallel sentence structures echo that fact and also provide balance and rhythm to help deliver meaning.

Using Parallel Words, Phrases, and Clauses

Parallel words   Recommended exercise includes running, swimming, and cycling.

Parallel phrases

Exercise helps people to maintain healthy bodies and to handle mental pressures.

Parallel clauses

Many people exercise because they want to look healthy, because they need to increase stamina, and because they hope to live longer.

To avoid faulty parallelism, be sure that words, PHRASES, or CLAUSES occur in the same grammatical form.

No	The strikers had tried shouting, threats, and pleading.
Yes	The strikers had tried shouting, threatening, and pleading.
Yes	The strikers had tried shouts, threats, and pleas.
No	The committee members read the petition, were discussing its arguments, and the unanimous decision was to ignore it.
Yes	The committee members read the petition, discussed its arguments, and decided unanimously to ignore it.

Using Parallel Structures with Conjunctions

Words, phrases, or clauses joined with COORDINATING CONJUNCTIONS (*and, but, for, or, nor, yet, so*) usually deliver their message most clearly and concisely when put in parallel form.

- You come to understand what to expect when you tease a cat, or toss a pebble in a pool, or touch a hot stove.
  —Ann E. Berthoff, *Forming, Thinking, and Writing*

Parallel forms are also usually called for when you link elements of a sentence with CORRELATIVE CONJUNCTIONS (such as *either . . . or* and *not only . . . but also*).

- Differing expectations for marriage can lead not only to disappointment but also to anger.
  —Norman DuBois, student

Alert: A VERB or a PREPOSITION immediately preceding the first correlative conjunction in a pair carries its meaning to both pairs: *Look in **both** the encyclopedia **and** the dictionary.* That same verb or preposition positioned *after* the first conjunction must be repeated—or another verb or preposition used—after the second conjunction in the pair: Look **both in** *the encyclopedia* **and in** *the dictionary.*

Using Parallel Structures and Repetition

Deliberate repetition of word forms, word groups, and sounds creates a rhythm that intensifies a sentence's message, a highly effective technique if not overused.

- You can fool some of the people all of the time, and all of the people some of the time, but you cannot fool all of the people all of the time.

—Abraham Lincoln

Balanced sentences use parallel structures to enhance the message of ideas that are compared or contrasted.

- By night, the litter and desperation disappeared as the city's glittering lights came on; by day, the filth and despair reappeared as the sun rose.

—Jennifer Kirk, student

E3.b Using a variety of sentence lengths

When you use a variety of sentence lengths, you communicate clear distinctions among ideas, helping your readers understand the focus of your material. Also, you avoid the unbroken rhythm of monotonous sentence length that can lull a reader into inattention.

Revising Strings of Short Sentences

Unplanned strings of many short sentences rarely establish relationships and levels of importance among ideas. Try to make clear distinctions between the major and minor points in your essay.

No   There is a problem. It is widely known as sick-building syndrome. It is really indoor air pollution. It causes office workers to suffer. They have trouble breathing. They have painful rashes. Their heads ache. Their eyes burn.

Yes   Widely known as sick-building syndrome, indoor air pollution causes office workers to suffer. They have trouble breathing. They have painful rashes. Their heads ache. Their eyes burn.   [Many revisions are possible; this one uses a long sentence to introduce the idea of indoor air pollution and its victims and then uses a series of short sentences to emphasize each problem it causes. The revised version is also more concise (**E1**), reducing 38 words to 28.]

Revising Overcompounded Sentences

The compounding of a sentence must be justified by its meaning. If you string sentences together only with COORDINATING CONJUNCTIONS (such as *and, but,* and *so*), revise them to make the relationships among ideas clear.

No Science fiction writers are often thinkers, and they are often dreamers, so they let their imaginations wander. Jules Verne was such a writer, and he predicted space ships and atomic submarines, but most people did not believe airplanes were possible.

Yes Science fiction writers are often thinkers and dreamers who let their imaginations wander. Jules Verne was one such writer. He predicted space ships and atomic submarines before most people believed airplanes were possible.

Revising for a Mix of Sentence Lengths

To emphasize one idea among many others, you can express it in a sentence noticeably different in length or structure from the sentences surrounding it.

- Today is one of those excellent January partly cloudies in which light chooses an unexpected landscape to trick out in gilt, and then shadow sweeps it away. **You know you are alive.** You take huge steps, trying to feel the planet's roundness arc between your feet.

- Kazantzakis says that when he was young he had a canary and a globe. When he freed the canary, it would perch on the globe and sing. All his life, wandering the earth, he felt as though he had a canary on top of his mind, singing.
  —Annie Dillard, *Pilgrim at Tinker Creek*

Choosing sentence subjects for emphasis E3.c

The sᴜʙᴊᴇᴄᴛ of a sentence establishes the focus for that sentence. The subject should correspond to the emphasis you want to communicate to your reader. The following sentences all contain the same information. Notice how changes of subject (and vᴇʀʙ) influence meaning and impact.

- Our study showed that 25 percent of college students' time is spent eating or sleeping. [Focus is on the study.]

- College students eat or sleep 25 percent of the time, according to our study. [Focus is on the students.]

- Eating or sleeping occupies 25 percent of college students' time, according to our study. [Focus is on eating and sleeping.]

- Twenty-five percent of college students' time is spent in eating or sleeping, according to our study. [Focus is on the percentage of time.]

E3.d Adding modifiers to basic sentences for variety and emphasis

You can achieve a rich variety of sentence patterns when you add MODIFIERS to basic sentences. Also, beginning a sentence with a modifier can effectively vary the "start-with-the-SUBJECT" pattern of most English sentences.

Your decision to expand a basic sentence will depend on the focus of each sentence and the way it works with surrounding sentences to deliver its intended meaning. Position modifiers precisely so that your focus is clear; see **C4**.

Basic sentence	The river rose.
Adjective	The **swollen** river rose.
Adverb	The river rose **dangerously**.
Prepositional phrase	**In April**, the river rose **above its banks**.
Participial phrase	**Swelled by melting snow,** the river rose, **flooding the farmland.**
Absolute phrase	**Trees swirling away in the current**, the river rose.
Adverb clause	**Because the snows had been heavy that winter**, the river rose.
Adjective clause	The river, **which runs through vital farmland**, rose.

E3.e Inverting standard word order for variety and emphasis

Standard word order in English sentences places the SUBJECT before the VERB: *The mayor* [subject] *walked* [verb] *into the room*. Because this pattern is so common, any variation from it creates emphasis. Inverted word order places the verb before the subject: *Into the room walked* [verb] *the mayor* [subject]. Used sparingly, inverted word order can be very effective.

E4 Word Meanings and Word Impact

E4.a Learning about words and their meanings

You might be surprised at how much information a good dictionary has about the meaning and the use of words. Three fine dictionaries are *Webster's New World Dictionary, Webster's New Collegiate Dictionary,* and *American Heritage Dictionary of the English Language.* Here is an annotated entry for the word *contrary* from *Webster's New World Dictionary,* Third College Edition, showing many of the kinds of information you can expect to find.

A dictionary's introductory pages describe the types of information found in word entries.

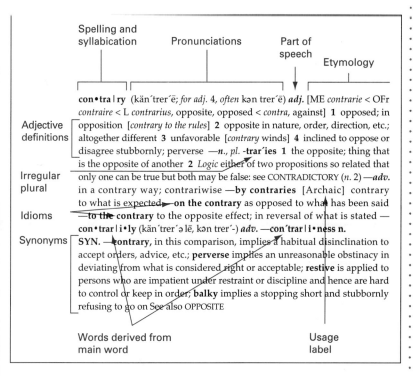

Spelling and syllabication | Pronunciations | Part of speech | Etymology

con•tra l ry (kän´trer´ē; *for adj.* 4, *often* kən trer´ē) *adj.* [ME *contrarie* < OFr *contraire* < L *contrarius,* opposite, opposed < *contra,* against] **1** opposed; in opposition [*contrary to the rules*] **2** opposite in nature, order, direction, etc.; altogether different **3** unfavorable [*contrary* winds] **4** inclined to oppose or disagree stubbornly; perverse —*n., pl.* **-trar´ies 1** the opposite; thing that is the opposite of another **2** *Logic* either of two propositions so related that only one can be true but both may be false: see CONTRADICTORY (*n.* 2) —*adv.* in a contrary way; contrariwise —**by contraries** [Archaic] contrary to what is expected —**on the contrary** as opposed to what has been said —**to the contrary** to the opposite effect; in reversal of what is stated — **con•trar l i•ly** (kän´trer´ə lē, kən trer´-) *adv.* —**con´trar l i•ness n.**

SYN. —**contrary,** in this comparison, implies a habitual disinclination to accept orders, advice, etc.; **perverse** implies an unreasonable obstinacy in deviating from what is considered right or acceptable; **restive** is applied to persons who are impatient under restraint or discipline and hence are hard to control or keep in order; **balky** implies a stopping short and stubbornly refusing to go on See also OPPOSITE

Adjective definitions
Irregular plural
Idioms
Synonyms

Words derived from main word | Usage label

Choosing exact words   E4.b

Diction—choice of words—affects the clarity and impact of your messages.

Understanding Denotation and Connotation

Denotation is a word's explicit dictionary meaning—its definition. Readers expect writers to use words according to established meanings.

Be aware that subtle shades of meaning differentiate words with the same general definitions. For example, it is wrong to describe a person famous for praiseworthy achievements as *notorious.* Although *notorious* means "well-known" and "publicly discussed," *notorious* also carries the meaning "unfavorably known or talked about." George Washington is famous; Al Capone is notorious.

Connotation refers to ideas that a word implies. Connotations convey associations such as emotional overtones beyond a word's direct, explicit definition. For example, the word *home* evokes in many people more emotion than does its denotation, "a dwelling place," or its synonym *house*. *Home* may connote warmth, security, and the love of family. Or *home* may connote painful sights and sounds of institutionalized old or disabled people. As you write, be aware of the additional layer of meaning that connotations deliver.

Using Specific and Concrete Language

Specific words identify individual items in a group (*Oldsmobile, Honda*). **General words** relate to an overall group (*car*). **Concrete words** identify persons and things that can be perceived by the senses—seen, heard, tasted, felt, smelled (*black padded vinyl dashboard*). **Abstract words** denote qualities, concepts, relationships, acts, conditions, and ideas (*transportation*).

Specific and concrete words can bring life to general and abstract words. Always supply enough specific, concrete details and examples to illustrate generalizations and abstractions, keeping in mind your writing purpose and your readers; see **W1.a.**

Specific language is not always preferable to general language, and concrete language is not always preferable to abstract language. Effective writing usually balances them.

- GENERAL   SPECIFIC   SPECIFIC   SPECIFIC
  My car, a 220-horsepower Trans Am, accelerates from 0 to 50
  SPECIFIC   SPECIFIC
  miles per hour in 6 seconds but gets only 18 miles per gallon.

- SPECIFIC   ABSTRACT   GENERAL
  In contrast, the Dodge Lancer gets very good gas mileage; about
  SPECIFIC   GENERAL   SPECIFIC   SPECIFIC   ABSTRACT
  35 mpg in highway driving and 30 mpg in stop-and-go traffic.

E4.c   Increasing your vocabulary

Increasing your vocabulary will help you read faster, understand more of what you read, and write with greater precision and impact.

CHOOSING WHAT WORDS TO LEARN

- In reading materials you own, mark unfamiliar words and then define them in the margin so that you can study the meaning in context.
- Use context clues to figure out definitions, or look the words up in a dictionary.
- Listen closely to learn how speakers use the language. When you hear or see new words, write them down to look up later.

STUDYING NEW VOCABULARY WORDS

- Write each new word and its meaning on an index card or in a notebook.
- Select eight to ten words to study each week.
- Set aside time each day to study your selected words, and carry your cards or notebook to study in spare moments.
- Use mnemonics—memory-jogging techniques—to help you memorize words.
- Use the new words in your writing and, when possible, in conversation.

Understanding Word Roots, Prefixes, and Suffixes

Becoming aware of word parts can help expand your awareness of word meanings. **Prefixes** are syllables in front of a root word that modify its meaning. *Ante-* (*before*) before the root *bellum* (*war*) gives *antebellum*, which means "before the war." In American English, antebellum refers to the time before the Civil War.

Suffixes are syllables added to the end of a root word that modify its meaning. For example, *excite* plus *-able* means "able to be excited" and *excite* plus *-ment* means "the state of being excited."

Some unabridged dictionaries list prefixes and suffixes with their meanings, and many college dictionaries define word parts in the alphabetical entries. Also, the etymology (word history) in a dictionary entry gives information about the word's roots.

Using appropriate language E4.d

As words communicate meaning, they affect readers and listeners. Sometimes word choices are clearly either right or wrong. Often, however, the choices are more subtle. As a writer, you want to choose words that communicate your meaning as clearly and effectively as possible to deliver the meaning you intend.

Understanding Levels of Formality

TONE in writing is conveyed mostly by the level of formality and the attitude toward the reader that your language communicates.

Informal word choices, including slang, colloquialisms, and regionalisms, create an informal tone. Informal tone also results from SENTENCE FRAGMENTS, contractions, and other forms that approximate casual speech. Medium language level uses general English—not too casual, not too formal. This level uses standard vocabulary (for example, *learn* instead of *wise up*), conventional sentence structure, and few or no contractions. A highly formal language level uses a Latinate vocabulary (*edify* for *learn*) and, often, dramatic stylistic flourishes.

Academic writing should range from medium to somewhat formal levels of language.

Informal	Ya know stars? They're a gas!
Medium	Gas clouds slowly changed into stars.
Highly formal	The condensations of gas spun their slow gravitational pirouettes, slowly transmogrifying gas cloud into star.

—Carl Sagan, "Starfolk: A Fable"

Using Edited American English

The language standards you are expected to use in academic writing are those of edited American English—the written language of a book like this one. Such language conforms to widely established rules of grammar, sentence structure, punctuation, and spelling. Readers often encounter English that varies from the standard, as in many advertisements. As a writer, do not let published departures from edited American English influence you into believing they are acceptable in academic writing.

You may find that early drafts of your academic writing contain language that departs from edited American English. Worry not. First get your ideas onto paper. Then revise your early drafts so that your final drafts are in edited American English.

Understanding When to Avoid Slang and Colloquial or Regional Language

Slang consists of new words (*yuppie*) or existing words that have new meanings (*wired* meaning "nervous"). Slang is appropriate only in very informal situations. **Colloquial language** is characteristic of casual conversation and informal writing: *The student flunked* [instead of *failed*] *chemistry*. **Regional** (also called **dialectal**) **language** is specific to a particular geographic area: *They have nary a cent*. Slang, colloquial, and regional language are not substandard or illiterate, but they are usually not appropriate for academic writing.

E4.e Using figurative language ▌

In **figurative language**, words are used for more than their literal meaning. There are various types of figurative language.

■ *Analogy*: a comparison of similar traits between dissimilar things. An analogy can be developed in one, several, or many sentences.

  ● A cheetah sprinting across the dry plains after its prey, the base runner dashed for home plate, his cleats kicking up dust.

- *Irony:* the use of words to suggest the opposite of their usual sense.
  - Told that the repair would cost $2,000 and take two weeks, she said, "Oh, wonderful."

- *Metaphor:* a comparison of otherwise dissimilar things that does not use the words *like* or *as* to draw the comparison. (The section following this list can help you avoid the error of a mixed metaphor.)
  - The rush-hour traffic bled out of the city's major arteries.

- *Overstatement* (also called *hyperbole*): deliberate exaggeration for emphasis.
  - If this paper is late, the professor will kill me.

- *Personification:* the assignment of a human trait to something not human.
  - The book begged to be read.

- *Simile:* a direct comparison between otherwise dissimilar things that uses the words *like* or *as*.
  - Langston Hughes says that a deferred dream dries up "like a raisin in the sun."

- *Understatement*: deliberate restraint for emphasis.
  - It is warm when the temperature reaches 105 degrees.

Avoiding Mixed Metaphors

Mixed metaphors confuse readers by combining images that do not work together: *Milking the workers for all they were worth, the supervisor barked orders at them.* The first image is of taking milk from a cow, but the final image of barking suggests a dog.

Avoiding clichés   E4.f

A cliché is an overused, worn-out expression. Many once-clever phrases have grown trite: *dead as a doornail, gentle as a lamb, straight as an arrow.* If you have read such an expression over and over again, so has your reader. Rephrase a cliché, or delete it.

No   Needing to travel 500 miles before dark, we left at the crack of dawn.

Yes   Needing to travel 500 miles before dark, we left at dawn.

Using precise language   E4.g

Avoid spending time looking for long, fancy words to explain a point. Instead, make what you write exact, accessible, and still engaging.

Extremely complex ideas or subject areas may require complex terms or phrases to explain them, but in general the simpler the language, the more likely it is to be understood.

Avoiding Slanted Language

When you feel strongly about a topic, slipping into biased or emotionally loaded language can be all too easy. Such slanted language usually does not convince a careful reader to agree with your point. Rather, it compromises your credibility in the reader's mind. For example, suppose you are arguing against the use of animals in medical experimentation. If you refer to "laboratory Frankensteins" who "maim helpless puppies and kittens," you are using slanted language. Less loaded language might refer to "laboratory technicians who experiment on animals."

Avoiding Pretentious Language

Pretentious language draws attention to itself with overly complex sentences and words of many syllables. Academic writing does not call for big words used for their own sake. Overblown words may obscure your message and damage your credibility with your reader.

No The raison d'être for my matriculation in this institution of higher learning is the acquisition of a better education.

Yes My reason for being in college is to get a better education.

Avoiding Unnecessary Jargon

Jargon—specialized vocabulary of a particular group—evolves in every field: professions, academic disciplines, commerce, and even hobbies. Specialized language can aid communication. Using jargon unnecessarily, however, shuts readers out. If you need to use jargon for a general audience, be sure to explain the specialized meanings.

   • Eutrophic changes (or eutrophication) is the nutritional
     enrichment of the water, promoting the growth of aquatic
     plants.

                              —David and Solomon, *The World of Biology*

Avoiding Euphemisms

Euphemisms attempt to avoid unpleasant truths with the use of "tactful" words. Euphemisms may sometimes be properly tactful in social situations (as in using *passed away* instead of *died* when offering condolences). Most of the time, however, euphemisms drain meaning and clarity from writing. When the truth is "My cousin lies," you should usually write that rather than "My cousin has a wonderfully vivid imagination."

E5 Gender-Neutral Language

Understanding gender in the English language E5.a

Unlike English, most other languages assign gender (masculine, feminine, or neuter) to all NOUNS, and a few languages assign gender to almost all words. Although English does not assign gender to words, some English words have gender-specific meanings, such as *he, she, it, him, her, his, hers, its, man, boy, woman, girl, heiress*. When you use one of these words, you deliver gender information along with whatever other message you deliver.

Using gender-neutral language E5.b

Sexist language assigns roles or characteristics to people on the basis of gender. Most people feel that sexist language unfairly discriminates against both sexes. It inaccurately assumes that all nurses and homemakers are female (always calling them "she") and all physicians and car mechanics are male (always calling them "he").

You can make gender-neutral word choices that avoid unnecessary—and often untrue—sexist assumptions underlying some gender-specific words: for example, *police officer* instead of *policeman, people* or *humans* instead of *mankind, representative* instead of *congressman, salesperson* instead of *salesman* or *saleswoman.*

One of the most common occurrences of sexist language is the use of masculine pronouns in gender-neutral cases: *No one wants to lose his job.* Women as well as men hold jobs, and neither group wants to lose them. When *his* is used with *job*, the females disappear. Although tradition holds that masculine pronouns are correct in such situations, using them to represent all the people in a group that contains both women and men distorts reality.

Many writers have begun to use a *he or she* construction rather than only *he* or only *she*. If you use it, remember that *he or she* acts as a singular pronoun. As a subject of a sentence, therefore, *he or she* calls for a singular verb. For the sake of your writing style, try to avoid using *he or she* more than once in a sentence or in consecutive sentences. Revising into the plural may be a better solution.

In addition to word choice, demeaning stereotypes such as "Women are bad drivers" or "Men can't cook" use language in a sexist fashion. Similarly, sexism arises when language fails to treat both sexes equally. For example, if you describe a woman by her looks, clothes, age, or marital status, describe a man the same way in the same context. If you use the first name of one person in a partnership, use the first name of the other; if you use a title for one, such as *Mr.*, *Dr.*, or *Mrs.*, use a title for both.

No   Mr. Miller and his wife, Jeannette, live in Idaho.

Yes   Phil and Jeannette Miller live in Idaho.

Yes   Mr. and Mrs. Miller live in Idaho.

QA Box 40, below, shows specific ways to avoid sexist language by revising into gender-neutral language.

QA Box 40

AVOIDING SEXIST LANGUAGE

■ **Avoid using the masculine pronoun to refer both to males and to females.**

Use a pair of pronouns.	● A doctor has little time to read outside his ⟨*or her*⟩ specialty.
Use the plural	● A successful doctor knows that ⟨*they have*⟩ ~~he has~~ to work hard.
Omit the gender-specific pronoun.	● Everyone hopes ~~that he will~~ ⟨*to*⟩ win the scholarship.

■ **Avoid stereotyping jobs and roles by gender.**
  ● supervisor [*not* foreman]
  ● businessperson, business executive [*not* businessman]
  ● poet, actor [*not* poetess, actress]

■ **Avoid expressions that exclude one sex.**
  ● person [*not* man]
  ● humanity, people [*not* mankind]
  ● the average person [*not* the common man]
  ● superstition [*not* old wives' tale]

■ **Avoid demeaning and patronizing labels.**
  ● nurse [*not* male nurse]
  ● professional, executive, manager [*not* career girl]
  ● My ~~girl~~ ⟨*assistant*⟩ will help you. [*Or* Ida Morea will help you.]

Punctuation

comma, semicolon, colon

*

independent clauses, quotation marks

TWO HOUR TIME LIMIT

5¢ 10¢

CITY CHICAGO

RED FLAG
INDICATES VIOLATION
INSTRUCTIONS
1-INSERT COIN IN CORRECT SLOT.
2-TURN HANDLE TO RIGHT AS FAR
AS POSSIBLE AFTER EACH COIN.

apostrophe

?

coordinate adjectives

P PUNCTUATION

P1 End Punctuation

Using a period after statements, mild commands, and indirect questions   P1.a

Statement	Mountain climbers enjoy the outdoors.
Mild command	Pack warm clothes for the high elevations.
Indirect question	I asked if they wanted to climb Mt. Everest.
	[A direct question would end with a question mark: *I asked, "Do you want to climb Mt. Everest?"*]

For information on using periods in abbreviations, see **S5.a**.

Using a question mark after a direct question   P1.b

A **direct question** asks a question outright and ends with a question mark. In contrast, an **indirect question** reports an asked question and ends with a period; see **P1.a**. A directly quoted question also ends with a question mark.

- Have you ever thought about climbing Mt. Everest?
- I asked, "Do you want to climb Mt. Everest?"

Questions in a series can each be followed by a question mark, whether or not each question is a complete sentence.

- After the storm had passed, the mountain climbers debated what to do. Turn back? Move on? Rest for a while?

Alert: When questions in a series are not complete sentences, you can choose whether to capitalize the first letter of each, but be consistent in each piece of writing.   **!**

When a polite request is phrased as a question, using a period emphasizes the request: *Would you please send me a copy.* Using a question mark emphasizes the politeness: *Would you please send me a copy?*

Use words, not a question mark within parentheses (?), to communicate irony or sarcasm.

No	Having the flu is a pleasant (?) experience.
Yes	Having the flu is as pleasant as a near-drowning experience.

Using an exclamation point for a strong command or an emphatic declaration   P1.c

A **strong command** gives a very firm order: *Look out behind you!* An **emphatic declaration** makes a shocking or surprising statement: *Those cars are going to crash!*

Avoid overusing exclamation points. Instead, choose words that communicate the strength of your message. Reserve exclamation points for dialogue or—very rarely—for a short declaration within a longer passage.

No   Each day in Nepal, we tried to see Mt. Everest! Each day we
            failed to see it! The summit stayed shrouded! Clouds defeated
            us!

Yes   Each day in Nepal, we tried to see Mt. Everest. Each day we
            failed to see it. The summit stayed shrouded. Clouds
            defeated us!

Use words, not an exclamation point in parentheses (!), to communicate amazement or sarcasm.

No   At 29,141 feet (!), Mt. Everest is the world's highest
            mountain.

Yes   At a staggering 29,141 feet, Mt. Everest is the world's highest
            mountain.

P2 Comma Use

The comma separates and groups sentence parts, thereby helping a writer to create clarity for readers. As you are DRAFTING and REVISING, if you are in doubt about a comma, insert and circle it clearly so that you can find it when you are editing and decide whether it is correct.

Two practices can help you prevent certain comma problems: (1) As you are writing, do not insert a comma simply because you happen to pause to think before moving on. (2) As you reread your writing, do not insert commas according to your personal habits of pausing. Although a comma communicates a slight pause, pausing is not a reliable guide for writers because breathing rhythms, accents, and thinking spans vary greatly.

QA Box 41 shows patterns and examples of comma uses, as well as references to sections where each use is fully explained. For many of your editing questions about commas, you may be able to check the box for a sentence like the one you want to punctuate, and then follow its comma pattern.

COMMA PATTERNS

COMMAS WITH COORDINATING CONJUNCTIONS LINKING INDEPENDENT CLAUSES (P2.a)

Independent clause, $\begin{cases} and \\ but \\ for \\ or \\ nor \\ so \\ yet \end{cases}$ independent clause.

- Postcards are ideal for brief greetings, **and** they can also be miniature works of art.

COMMAS WITH INTRODUCTORY ELEMENTS (P2.b)

Introductory clause, independent clause.

- **Although most postcards cost only a dime,** one recently sold for thousands of dollars.

Introductory phrase, independent clause.

- **On postcard racks,** several designs are usually available.

Introductory word, independent clause.

- **However,** most cards show local landmarks.

COMMAS WITH ITEMS IN SERIES (P2.c)

item, item, item

- **Places, paintings, people** appear on postcards.

item, item, and item

- **Places, paintings, and people** appear on postcards.

COMMAS WITH COORDINATE ADJECTIVES (P2.d)

coordinate adjective, coordinate adjective noun

- Some postcards feature **appealing, dramatic scenes.**

NO COMMAS WITH CUMULATIVE ADJECTIVES (P2.d)

adjective adjective noun

- Other postcards feature **famous historical scenes.**

COMMAS WITH NONRESTRICTIVE ELEMENTS (P2.e)

Nonrestrictive element, independent clause.

- **Four years after the first postcard appeared,** the U.S. government began to issue stamped postcards.

Continued on next page

QA Box 41, continued from previous page

Beginning of independent clause, nonrestrictive element, end of independent clause.

- The Golden Age of postcards, **which lasted from about 1900 to 1929,** yielded many especially valuable cards.

Independent clause, nonrestrictive element.

- Collectors attend postcard shows, **which are similar to baseball-card shows.**

NO COMMAS WITH RESTRICTIVE ELEMENTS (P2.e)
Beginning of independent clause restrictive element end of independent clause.

- Collectors **who attend these shows** may specialize in a particular kind of postcard.

COMMAS WITH QUOTED WORDS (P2.g)
Explanatory words, "Quoted words."

- One collector told me, "Attending a show is like digging for buried treasure."

"Quoted words," explanatory words.

- "I always expect to find a priceless postcard," he said.

"Beginning of quoted words," explanatory words, "end of quoted words."

- "Everyone there," he joked, "believes a million-dollar card is hidden in the next stack."

P2.a Using commas before coordinating conjunctions linking independent clauses

When a coordinating conjunction (*and, but, for, nor, or, so, yet*) links INDEPENDENT CLAUSES, use a comma before the conjunction. Do not put a comma *after* a coordinating conjunction linking independent clauses; see **P3.a**.

- The sky turned black, and the wind stopped.

! Alert: To avoid creating a COMMA SPLICE, do not use a comma between independent clauses unless they are linked by a coordinating conjunction; see **C2.b**.

No Five inches of snow fell in two hours, one inch of ice fell later.

Yes Five inches of snow fell in two hours, **and** one inch of ice fell later.

When independent clauses containing other commas are linked by a coordinating conjunction, separating the clauses with a semicolon may make the sentence easier for your reader to understand.

- Because temperatures stayed below freezing, the snow did not melt; and people wondered, gazing at the white landscape, when they would see grass again.

Using commas to set off introductory clauses, phrases, and words
P2.b

Introductory clauses are usually ADVERB CLAUSES, which start with SUBORDINATING CONJUNCTIONS such as *because, although, when* (for a list, see **QA Box 24**). When an adverb clause precedes an INDEPENDENT CLAUSE, separate the clauses with a comma.

- When the topic is dieting, most people have an opinion.

When a phrase introduces an independent clause, many writers separate phrase and clause with a comma.

- Between 1544 and 1689, sugar refineries appeared in London and New York. [introductory prepositional phrase]
- Beginning in infancy, we develop lifelong tastes for sweet and salty foods. [introductory participial phrase]
- Fondness for sweets being a problem for many adults, consumers were horrified to learn that sugar was added to most commercial baby foods. [introductory absolute phrase]

When an introductory word appears at the beginning of a sentence, many writers follow it with a comma. These words include TRANSITIONAL EXPRESSIONS (such as *for example* and *in addition*) and CONJUNCTIVE ADVERBS (such as *therefore* and *however*); see **QA Box 10** on page 19.

- For example, fructose is fruit sugar.

Interjections are introductory words that convey surprise or other emotions. They are followed by commas or exclamation points: *Oh, you are allergic to cats. Yes! Your sneezing does worry me.*

Using commas with items in series
P2.c

A series within a sentence is a group of three or more words, PHRASES, or CLAUSES that match in grammatical form and in importance.

Words	The earliest clothing fabrics were made from such natural fibers as cotton, silk, linen, wool.
Phrases	Fabric today is made from natural fibers, from synthetic fibers, or from natural and synthetic fiber blends.
Clauses	Natural fibers are durable and absorbent, synthetic fibers resist wrinkling and retain dyes well, and blends offer the advantages of each.

When the items in a series contain commas or other punctuation, or when the items are long and complex, separating them with semicolons instead of commas ensures that your sentence will deliver the meaning you intend.

Some authorities omit the comma when the last two items of a series are separated by a COORDINATING CONJUNCTION, but using the comma may help your reader to understand your meaning more quickly.

Numbered or lettered lists within a sentence are items in a series. Use commas (or semicolons if the items are long) to separate three or more items.

- Three synthetic fibers predominate in clothing manufacture: (1) rayon, (2) polyester, and (3) acrylic.

! Alert: Do not use a comma before the first item or after the last item in a series unless a different rule makes it necessary.

P2.d Using commas between coordinate adjectives

Coordinate adjectives are two or more ADJECTIVES that equally modify a NOUN. Use a comma between coordinate adjectives unless a COORDINATING CONJUNCTION (such as *and* or *but*) links them. Do not use a comma between **cumulative adjectives**, which build up meaning from word to word as they move toward a noun.

| Coordinate adjectives | The large, friendly, restless crowd wanted the concert to start. |
| Cumulative adjectives | The concert featured several familiar backup singers. |

If you are unsure whether adjectives are coordinate or cumulative, use the following test.

TEST FOR COORDINATE AND CUMULATIVE ADJECTIVES

- Can the order of the adjectives be changed without changing the meaning or creating nonsense? If yes, they are coordinate and need commas.
  - The large, restless, friendly crowd wanted the concert to start. [*Friendly, restless,* and *large* can be interchanged, so they are coordinate adjectives and need commas.]
  - The concert featured backup familiar several singers. [*Several familiar backup* cannot be interchanged, so they are cumulative adjectives and do not need commas.]

- Can *and* be inserted between the adjectives? If yes, they are coordinate and need commas.
  - The large and restless and friendly crowd wanted the concert to start. [Coordinate—use commas.]

- The concert featured several and familiar and backup singers. [Cumulative—do not use commas.]

Using commas to set off nonrestrictive (nonessential) elements

Restrictive elements (also called essential elements) and nonrestrictive elements (also called nonessential elements) modify NOUNS or PRONOUNS. Nonrestrictive elements are set off by commas.

A **restrictive element** limits or makes specific the meaning of the word it applies to. A **nonrestrictive element** leaves the meaning of the word general. Some examples can help to make this idea clearer, and **QA Box 62** on page 267 explains more about general and specific meanings of nouns.

- Farmers, **who use chemical fertilizers,** may be damaging the water supply.

In the example above, *who use chemical fertilizers* is marked as a nonrestrictive element by the commas around it. This nonrestrictive modifier leaves the meaning of farmers general, so the sentence means that all farmers may be damaging the water supply and all farmers use chemical fertilizers. If *who use chemical fertilizers* is removed, readers still understand the sentence's essential message: *Farmers may be damaging the water supply.*

Here is another example:

- Farmers **who use chemical fertilizers** may be damaging the water supply.

This time, *who use chemical fertilizers* has no commas around it, so it is restrictive. It limits the noun *farmers* to the specific group of farmers who use chemical fertilizers. This sentence means that only those farmers who use chemical fertilizers (not *all* farmers) may be damaging the water supply. In this sentence, *who use chemical fertilizers* is essential to the sentence's meaning.

You might wonder whether *nonessential* implies that you should delete any nonessential element from a sentence. No. Nonessential in this context describes grammatical form, not content.

Set off nonrestrictive ADJECTIVE CLAUSES with commas. Adjective clauses usually begin with *who, which,* or *that.*

Nonrestrictive	Farming, **which is a major source of food production,** may not always be dependent on the weather. [Farming is not meant to be limited by *which is a major source of food production*—commas needed.]
Restrictive	Much food **that consumers buy canned or frozen** is processed by the same companies

that grow it. [The first restrictive clause limits *food*; the second one limits *companies* to only those that grow the food—no commas.]

Set off nonrestrictive PHRASES with commas.

Nonrestrictive   Farmers, **trying to enhance crop growth,** use pesticides and fertilizers. [*Farmers* is not meant to be limited by *trying to enhance crop growth*—commas needed.]

Restrictive   Farmers **retaining complete control over their land** are uncommon today. [*Farmers* is meant to be limited to only those retaining complete control over their land—no commas.]

An **appositive** renames the noun preceding it. Most appositives are nonrestrictive, but, depending on context, they are occasionally restrictive. Set off nonrestrictive appositives but not restrictive ones.

Nonrestrictive   The agricultural scientist, **a new breed of farmer,** controls the farming environment.

Restrictive   The agricultural scientist **Wendy Singh** has helped develop a new crop rotation system. [The specific agricultural scientist is Wendy Singh—no commas.]

P2.f   Using commas to set off transitional and parenthetical words, contrasts, words of direct address, and tag questions

CONJUNCTIVE ADVERBS (such as *however* and *therefore*) and TRANSITIONAL EXPRESSIONS (such as *for example* and *in addition*) can be introductory (**P2.b**), or they can fall within sentences. They are usually set off with commas. **QA Box 10** on page 19 lists many of these words and phrases.

- Midwestern America, therefore, is the world's breadbasket.
- California and Florida are important food producers, for example.

Parenthetical expressions are "asides," additions to sentences that the writer thinks of as extra. If they are not enclosed in parentheses, they should be set off with commas.

- Most growers, I imagine, hope to export food.

Expressions of contrast describe something by stating what it is not. They are set off with commas.

- Food, not technology, tops the list of U.S. exports.

Words of **direct address** indicate the person or group spoken to. They are set off with commas.

- Maybe the future, all you computer majors, lies in soybeans rather than software.

Tag questions (you know what they are, **don't you?**) are set off with commas.

- Taking a course in agricultural economics doesn't seem so silly now, does it?

Using commas with quoted words

P2.g

Use a comma to set quoted words off from short explanations in the same sentence. This rule holds no matter where the explanatory words are positioned.

- The poet William Blake wrote, "Love seeketh not itself to please." [explanatory words before quoted words]
- "My love is a fever," said William Shakespeare.   [explanatory words after quoted words]
- "I love no love," proclaimed poet Mary Coleridge, "but thee." [explanatory words between quoted words]

Alert: If explanatory words end with *that* immediately before quoted or paraphrased words, do not use a comma after *that*. **!**

- Shakespeare wrote that "love is a fever."
- Shakespeare wrote that his love felt like a fever.

Using commas in dates, names, addresses, and numbers

P2.h

Commas with Dates

Use a comma after the day in month-day-year dates. If a weekday name is included, use a comma after it too.

- July 20, 1969
- Sunday, July 20, 1969

Within a sentence, use commas after the day and the year in a month-day-year date.

- Everyone watched television on July 20, 1969, to see Neil Armstrong walk on the moon.

But if you use day-month-year order for dates, no commas are needed.

- Everyone watched television on 20 July 1969 to see Neil Armstrong walk on the moon.

Do not use a comma between a month and year, a month and day, or a season and year.

- The major news story in July 1969 was the moon landing; news coverage was especially heavy on July 21. I will always remember summer 1969.

Commas with Names, Places, and Addresses

When an abbreviated title (*Jr., M.D., Ph.D.*) comes after a name, use a comma between the name and the title. When a sentence continues after a name and title, use a comma after the title in addition to the comma after the name.

- Rosa Gonzales, M.D., was the principal witness for the defense.

In an inverted name, use a comma between last and first names.

- Troyka, David

Use a comma between a city and state. When a sentence continues after a city and state, also use a comma after the state.

- Philadelphia, Pennsylvania, is home to the Liberty Bell.

When a sentence includes a complete address, separate all the items except the zip code with commas. The zip code follows the state after a space and is not followed by a comma.

- I wrote to Mr. U. Lern, 10-01 Rule Road, Classgate, New Jersey 07632 for the instruction manual.

Commas in Letter Openings and Closings

At the end of the opening of an informal letter, use a comma. (Use a colon after the opening in a formal letter.)

- Dear Betty,

After the closing of a formal or informal letter, use a comma.

- Sincerely yours,   - Love,

Commas with Numbers

Counting from the right, put a comma after every three digits in numbers over four digits.

- 72,867   - 150,567,066

In a four-digit number, a comma is optional for money, distance, amounts, and most other measurements, but be consistent in using or omitting it.

- $1776   - $1,776
- 1776 miles   - 1,776 miles
- 1776 potatoes   - 1,776 potatoes

Do not use commas in street-address numbers, page numbers of four
or more digits, or a four-digit year. (Use a comma in a year of five or
more digits: *25,000* B.C.)

- 12163 Dean Drive
- see page 1338
- 1998

Use a comma to separate related measurements written as words.

- five feet, four inches

Use a comma to separate an act and a scene in plays and to separate
a page reference from a line reference.

- Act ii, scene iv
- page 120, line 6

Using commas to avoid misreadings

P2.i

A comma is sometimes needed to clarify the meaning of a sentence,
even though no other rule calls for one.

- Those who can, practice many hours a day.
- George dressed, and performed for a sellout crowd.

P3 Comma Misuse

Not misusing commas with coordinating conjunctions

P3.a

See **P2.a** for the correct use of commas between **compound independent clauses**—that is, INDEPENDENT CLAUSES linked by a coordinating
conjunction (*and, but, for, nor, or, so, yet*).

But when words, PHRASES, or DEPENDENT CLAUSES are linked by
these same coordinating conjunctions, do not use a comma.

No Habitat for Humanity depends on volunteer labor, and asks for
donations for its construction projects. [Compound phrases, not
independent clauses—a comma should not be used.]

Yes Habitat for Humanity depends on volunteer labor and asks for
donations for its construction projects.

Do not put a comma *after* a coordinating conjunction that joins independent clauses.

No	An old house can be renovated in about two weeks but, an apartment may take a week or less to restore.
Yes	An old house can be renovated in about two weeks, but an apartment may take a week or less to restore.

P3.b Not using commas after subordinating conjunctions and prepositions

No	Although, winds exceeded 50 miles an hour, little damage occurred.
Yes	Although winds exceeded 50 miles an hour, little damage occurred.
No	People expected more damage from, the high winds.
Yes	People expected more damage from the high winds.

P3.c Not misusing commas with items in series

For the correct use of commas in series, see **P2.c**.

Do not use a comma before the first or after the last item in a series, unless another rule makes it necessary.

No	The street lights were decorated with red, white, and blue, ribbons for the Fourth of July.
Yes	The street lights were decorated with red, while, and blue ribbons for the Fourth of July.

Do not use a comma between only two items linked by a COORDINAT-ING CONJUNCTION.

No	Everyone enjoyed the parade, and the concert.
Yes	Everyone enjoyed the parade and the concert.

P3.d Not using commas between cumulative adjectives

For the use of commas with COORDINATE ADJECTIVES and a test for determining whether ADJECTIVES are cumulative or coordinate, see **P2.d**.

No	The concert featured several, new, rock bands.
Yes	The concert featured several new rock bands.

P3.e Not using commas around restrictive (essential) elements

For the correct use of commas with NONRESTRICTIVE (nonessential) elements, see **P2.e**.

No	Vegetables, that have been steamed or stir-fried, stay crisp and flavorful. [The *that* clause is restrictive, limiting vegetables to only those steamed or stir-fried—no comma.]
Yes	Vegetables that have been steamed or stir-fired stay crisp and flavorful.

Not misusing commas with quoted words
P3.f

For the correct use of commas with quoted words, see **P2.g**.

Do not use a comma to set off a quotation introduced by *that*, whether or not the sentence contains directly quoted words.

No	John said that, he likes stir-fried vegetables.
Yes	John said that he likes stir-fried vegetables.
No	He claims, that "ginger-soy sauce makes any vegetable tasty."
Yes	He claims that "ginger-soy sauce makes any vegetable tasty."

Not using commas between certain sentence structures and words
P3.g

As a rule, do not let a comma separate a SUBJECT from its VERB.

No	Orville and Wilbur Wright, made their first successful airplane flights in 1903.
Yes	Orville and Wilbur Wright made their first successful airplane flights in 1903.

As a rule, do not let a comma separate a verb from its OBJECT.

No	These inventors enthusiastically tackled, the problems of powered flight and aerodynamics.
Yes	These inventors enthusiastically tackled the problems of powered flight and aerodynamics.

As a rule, do not let a comma separate a verb from its COMPLEMENT.

No	Flying has become, an important industry and a popular hobby.
Yes	Flying has become an important industry and a popular hobby.

As a rule, do not let a comma separate an ADVERB from the ADJECTIVE it modifies or an adjective from the NOUN it modifies.

No	The Wright brothers once agreed to build an airplane for purely, military, purposes.
Yes	The Wright brothers once agreed to build an airplane for purely military purposes.

As a rule, do not use a comma after *such as*.

No   The Wright brothers were fascinated by other vehicles, such as, bicycles and gliders.

Yes   The Wright brothers were fascinated by other vehicles, such as bicycles and gliders.

As a rule, do not use a comma before *than* in a comparison.

No   The 1903 airplane sustained its flight longer, than any other engine-powered aircraft had.

Yes   The 1903 airplane sustained its flight longer than any other engine-powered aircraft had.

Do not use a comma before an opening parenthesis; when a comma is required, place it after the closing parenthesis.

No   Because aviation enthralls so many of us, (especially some children) hobbyists from all over the world visit Kitty Hawk's flight museum.

Yes   Because aviation enthralls so many of us (especially some children), hobbyists from all over the world visit Kitty Hawk's flight museum.

If advice against using a comma clashes with a rule requiring it, use the comma.

- Kitty Hawk, North Carolina, attracts thousands of tourists each year.   [Although the comma after North Carolina separates the subject and verb, it is required to set off a city-state combination from the rest of the sentence.]

P4 Semicolon Use

P4.a Using a semicolon between closely related independent clauses

When INDEPENDENT CLAUSES are related in meaning, you can separate them with a semicolon instead of a period. A period signals complete separation; a semicolon signals that the clauses are more closely related in meaning.

- This is my husband's second marriage; it's the first for me.
  —Ruth Sidel, "Marion Deluca"

- It is rare for us to leave wild animals alive; when we do, we often do not leave them wild.
  —Brigid Brophy, "The Rights of Animals"

Using a semicolon when a conjunctive adverb or other transitional expression links independent clauses **P4.b**

You can use a semicolon between two INDEPENDENT CLAUSES when the second clause begins with a CONJUNCTIVE ADVERB or other TRANSITIONAL EXPRESSION; for a list, see **QA Box 10** on page 19.

No The average annual rainfall in Death Valley is about two inches, nevertheless, hundreds of species live there.

Yes The average annual rainfall in Death Valley is about two inches; nevertheless, hundreds of species live there.

Alerts: (1) Do not use *only* a comma between independent clauses connected by a conjunctive adverb or other words of transition, or you will create the error called a COMMA SPLICE; see **C2.b**. (2) Usually use a comma *after* a conjunctive adverb or transitional expression that begins an independent clause, although some writers omit the comma after short words such as *then, next, soon.*

Using semicolons for clarity between comma-containing structures **P4.c**

When comma-containing INDEPENDENT CLAUSES are linked by a coordinating conjunction (*and, but, for, nor, or, so, yet*), you may make your message clearer by using a semicolon before the coordinating conjunction.

- When the male peacock has presented his back, the spectator will usually begin to walk around him to get a front view; but the peacock will continue to turn so that no front view is possible.
  —Flannery O'Connor, "The King of the Birds"

When a sentence has a long, comma-containing series of words, PHRASES, or clauses, using semicolons instead of commas to separate items may make your message clearer to readers.

- Functioning as assistant chefs, the students chopped onions, green peppers, and parsley; sliced chicken and duck into strips; and laid out utensils before the executive chef appeared.

Not misusing semicolons **P4.d**

Do not use a semicolon between a DEPENDENT and an INDEPENDENT CLAUSE.

No The new computers arrived; although the computer lab had not been built yet.

Yes The new computers arrived although the computer lab had not been built yet.

Use a colon, not a semicolon, to introduce a list; see **P5.a**.

No The newscast featured three major stories; the President's State
of the Union Address, the introduction of an electric car, and
pictures from the space probe.

Yes The newscast featured three major stories: the President's State
of the Union Address, the introduction of an electric car, and
pictures from the space probe.

P5 Colon Use

P5.a Using a colon when an independent clause introduces a list, an appositive, or a quotation

Use a colon before a list when the words introducing the list are an
INDEPENDENT CLAUSE. The words *the following* and *as follows* usually
signal the need for a colon. Conversely, do not use a colon after *such
as*, *like*, *including*, and similar words.

Listed items The students demanded the following: an
expanded menu in the cafeteria, improved
janitorial services, and more up-to-date
textbooks.

Appositives Museums in New York and Florida own the
best-known works of Louis Comfort Tiffany's
studio: those wonderful stained-glass
windows. [*Stained-glass windows* renames
best-known works.]

Quotations The little boy in *E.T.* did say something
neat: "How do you explain school to a
higher intelligence?"
—George F. Will, "Well, I Don't Love You, E.T."

! **Alert:** If a direct quotation's introductory words are not an independent clause, use a comma, not a colon, between the introductory
words and the quoted words.

P5.b Using a colon between independent clauses when the second clause explains or summarizes the first

- We will never forget the first time we made dinner at home
together: He got food poisoning and was too sick to work for four
days.
—Lisa Baladendrum, student

Alert: You can use a capital or a lowercase letter for the first word of an independent clause following a colon. Whichever you choose, be consistent in each piece of writing. **!**

Understanding conventional uses of colons

P5.c

Between Title and Subtitle

- *Literature: An Introduction to Critical Reading*

Between Hours and Minutes and Between Minutes and Seconds

- The runner passed the halfway point at 1:23:02.

Between Numbers in Ratios

- a proportion of 7:1   • a 3:5 ration

Between Bible Chapters and Verses

- Psalms 23:1–3

After Words in Memo Headings

- To: Dean Kristen Joy
  From: Professor Daniel Black
  Re: Student Work-Study Program

After Formal Letter Salutations

- Dear Ms. Carter:

Not misusing colons

P5.d

A complete INDEPENDENT CLAUSE must precede a colon except in documentation (**M1–M3** and **A1–A4**) and other conventional material (**P5.c**).

When a DIRECT OBJECT consists of a series or list of items, do not use a colon.

No   We bought: eggs, milk, cheese, and bread.

Yes   We bought eggs, milk, cheese, and bread.

Do not let the words *such as, including, like,* and *consists of* lure you into using a colon.

No   The health board discussed several problems, including: water
           quality, sewage treatment, and the lack of an alternate water
           supply.

Yes   The health board discussed several problems, including water
           quality, sewage treatment, and the lack of an alternate water
           supply.

Do not separate a DEPENDENT CLAUSE from an independent clause with a colon.

No   After the drought ended: water restrictions were dropped.

Yes   After the drought ended, water restrictions were dropped.

P6 Apostrophe Use

P6.a Using an apostrophe to show that a noun is possessive

The **possessive case** communicates ownership (*the writer's pen*) or other relationship (*the writer's parent*).

In NOUNS, possession can be communicated by PHRASES beginning with *of* (*a comment of the instructor*) or by an apostrophe in combination with *-s* (*the instructor's comment*).

Adding *-'s* to Nouns Not Ending in *-s*

- She felt a **parent's** joy.   [*Parent* is a singular noun not ending in -s.]
- They care about their **children's** education.   [*Children* is a plural noun not ending in -s.]

Adding *-'s* to Singular Nouns Ending in *-s*

- The **business's** system for handling complaints is inefficient.
- Lee **Jones's** car insurance is expensive.

Adding Only an Apostrophe to Plural Nouns Ending in *-s*

- The **boys'** statements were printed in the newspaper.
- Three **months'** maternity leave is in the workers' contract.

Adding *-'s* to the Last Word in Compound Words and Phrases

- His **mother-in-law's** company manufactures scuba gear.

Adding *-'s* to Each Noun in Individual Possession

- **Olga's and Joanne's houses** are next to each other.   [Olga and Joanne each own a house; they do not own the houses jointly.]

Adding *-'s* to Only the Last Noun in Joint or Group Possession

- **Brina and Avram's house** has a screened porch.   [Brina and Avram own one house.]
- **Kareem and Chaka's houses** are usually rented.   [Kareem and Chaka jointly own more than one house.]

Using -'s to show that an indefinite pronoun is possessive

Indefinite pronouns refer to general or nonspecific persons or things: *somebody, anything, no one* (**G4.d**). Do not use apostrophes with POSSESSIVE PRONOUNS, such as *its, hers, theirs*; see **P6.e**.

- **Anybody's** help would be welcome.
- Are **everyone else's** notes complete?

Using an apostrophe to signal omissions in contractions

In choosing whether to use a contraction or a full form, consider that many college instructors think contractions are appropriate only in informal writing. Also, avoid contracted forms for years in all academic writing (for example, use *1999*, not *'99*).

- It's still snowing. Don't you miss spring?   [informal]

Using -'s to show plurals of letters, numerals, symbols, and words used as terms

- Printing *w*'s is hard for Billie.
- The address includes six 2's.
- A line of &'s onscreen may mean the keyboard is jammed.
- All the *for*'s were misspelled *four*.

Alert: Letters as letters and words as words should be either under-lined (or printed in italic type) or enclosed in quotation marks. **!**

For the plural form of decade years, two styles are acceptable: with an apostrophe (*1870's*) or without (*1870s*). This book uses the form without an apostrophe. Whichever form you prefer, be consistent in each piece of writing.

Not misusing apostrophes

Do not use an apostrophe with a PRESENT-TENSE VERB.

No   Cholesterol plays' a key role in longevity.
Yes   Cholesterol plays a key role in longevity.

Do not add an apostrophe at the end of a nonpossessive NOUN ending in *s*.

No   Heart disease can cause a medical crisis'.
Yes   Heart disease can cause a medical crisis.

Do not place the apostrophe before the -*s* in POSSESSIVE plural nouns; place it after the -*s*.

No   Everyone is interested in those scientist's findings.

Yes   Everyone is interested in those scientists' findings.

Do not use an apostrophe in a nonpossessive plural.

No   Team's of doctors are researching the effects of cholesterol.

Yes   Teams of doctors are researching the effects of cholesterol.

Do not use an apostrophe with a possessive PRONOUN. Be especially careful not to confuse *its* with the contraction for *it is*: *it's*.

No   Because cholesterol has been widely publicized, it's role in heart disease is well known.

Yes   Because cholesterol has been widely publicized, its role in heart disease is well known.

No   Scientists who's work is respected get research grants.

Yes   Scientists **whose** work is respected get research grants.

P7 Quotation Marks

P7.a Using quotation marks accurately with direct quotations of prose, poetry, and speech

Direct quotations are exact words copied from a print source or transcribed from a nonprint source; they are placed in quotation marks. INDIRECT QUOTATIONS and PARAPHRASES are not enclosed in quotation marks.

Using Quotation Marks for Short Quotations of Prose or Poetry

A "short" quotation of prose is one that is no longer than four handwritten or typed lines (MLA STYLE) or forty words (APA STYLE). A short quotation of poetry is no more than three lines of a poem. Enclose short quotations in quotation marks, but do not otherwise set them off from your words.

- Edward T. Hall explains the practicality of close conversational distances: "If you are interested in something, your pupils dilate; if I say something you don't like, they tend to contract" (47). Some cultures prefer arm's length for all but the most intimate conversations.

- As W. H. Auden wittily defined personal space, "Some thirty inches from my nose / The frontier of my person goes" (539).

Alert: Use a slash with a space on either side to signal the end of one line and the start of another in short quotations of poetry. Capitalize and punctuate quotations of poetry exactly as in the original. **!**

Setting Long Quotations of Prose or Poetry Off from Your Words

A "long" quotation of prose is one that is more than four typed or handwritten lines (MLA style) or more than forty words (APA style). A "long" quotation of poetry is more than three lines of a poem. Set long quotations off from your words by starting them on a new line and by indenting each line. If you are following MLA guidelines and are preparing your paper on a computer, indent each line of the quotation 1 inch (one tab); if you are using a typewriter, indent each line ten spaces. If you are following APA guidelines, indent each line of the quotation five spaces.

Do not enclose a set-off quotation in quotation marks. Use quotation marks only around words you are quoting that are enclosed in quotation marks in the original source. In the example below, the words "wrist distance" are in double quotation marks in the source by Desmond Morris, so they are in double quotation marks in the set-off quotation as well.

For advice about preparing a paper, including long quotations, see **M3.a** for MLA format and **A1.a** and **A1.e** for APA format.

- As Desmond Morris explains, personal space varies among cultures:

      When you are talking to someone in the street or in any open space, reach out with your arm and see where the nearest point on his body comes. If you hail from western Europe, you will find that he is at roughly fingertip distance from you. In other words, as you reach out, your fingertips will just about make contact with his shoulder. If you come from eastern Europe you will find you are standing at "wrist distance." If you come from the Mediterranean region you will find that you are much closer to your companion. (23)

  Obviously, encroaching on a stranger's personal space would be easy.

Using Quotation Marks for Spoken Words (Direct Discourse)

When you quote spoken words (DIRECT DISCOURSE) or want to show dialogue, use quotation marks to enclose each speaker's words. Start a new paragraph each time the speaker changes.

- "I don't know how you can see to drive," she said.
- "Maybe you should put on your glasses."
- "Putting on my glasses would help you to see?"
- "Not me; you," Macon said. "You're focused on the windshield instead of the road."

—Anne Tyler, *The Accidental Tourist*

When one speaker's words continue for more than one paragraph, use quotation marks at the start of each paragraph but at the end of only the last paragraph of the speech.

Do not enclose INDIRECT DISCOURSE in quotation marks.

- The mayor said that he was tired. [The direct-discourse version is *The mayor said, "I am tired."*]

P7.b Knowing when to use single quotation marks

If quotation marks occur in words you have enclosed in double quotation marks (" "), replace the original source's double quotation marks with single quotation marks (' ').

Original Source

- Personal space ... has been likened to a snail shell, a soap bubble, an aura, and "breathing room."

—Robert Sommer, *Personal Space: The Behavioral Basis of Design*, page 26

Single Quotation Marks Within Double Quotation Marks

- Robert Sommer, an environmental psychologist, compares personal space to "a snail shell, a soap bubble, an aura, and 'breathing room'" (26).

P7.c Using quotation marks for some titles

QA Box 46 (S4.a) shows when to use quotation marks, italics or underlining, or neither for most names and titles. In general, use quotation marks around the titles of short published works: poems; short stories; essays; articles from periodicals; pamphlets; brochures; song titles; and individual episodes of television or radio series.

P7.d Using quotation marks accurately for special treatment of words, letters, and numerals

Technical terms and words used as terms can either be enclosed in quotation marks or italicized or underlined (see S4.a). Whichever style you choose, be consistent in each piece of writing.

Technical terms	"Plagiarism"—the unacknowledged use of another person's words or ideas—is a serious offense. Plagiarism can result in expulsion. [Once the term has been introduced—and usually defined—it needs no special treatment.]
Words as terms	Many people confuse "affect" and "effect."
Translations	My grandfather usually ended arguments with *de gustibus non disputandum est* ("there is no arguing about tastes"). [Italicize (or underline) the words being translated.]
Ironic words	The proposed tax "reform" is actually a tax increase.

Not misusing quotation marks   P7.e

Do not use quotation marks around language you sense is tired or inappropriate. Revise for accurate, appropriate, fresh words.

Stale	They "eat like birds" in public and "stuff their faces" in private.
Revised	They nibble and graze in public and gorge themselves in private.

Do not enclose a word in quotation marks merely to call attention to it.

No	Remember, "plagiarism" can result in expulsion.
Yes	Remember, plagiarism can result in expulsion.

Do not enclose indirect quotations or paraphrases in quotation marks.

No	The Code of Conduct points out that "plagiarism can result in expulsion." [The original words in the Code of Conduct are "Grounds for expulsion include plagiarism."]
Yes	The Code of Conduct points out that plagiarism can result in expulsion.

Do not use quotation marks to enclose the title of your own paper at the top of the page or on a title page or if you refer to the title within your paper. If the title of your paper refers to another title, use quotation marks or italics (or underlining) around the other title, as appropriate; see **QA Box 46** in **S4.a**.

No	"The Elderly in Nursing Homes: A Case Study"
Yes	The Elderly in Nursing Homes: A Case Study

| No | Character Development in Shirley Jackson's The Lottery |
| Yes | Character Development in Shirley Jackson's "The Lottery" |

P7.f Using other punctuation accurately with quotation marks

Placing Commas and Periods Inside Closing Quotation Marks

- Having enjoyed F. Scott Fitzgerald's "The Freshest Boy," we were eager to read his longer works.
- Edward T. Hall coined the word "proxemics."

Placing Colons and Semicolons Outside Closing Quotation Marks

- We try to discover "how close is too close": We do not want to invade others' personal space.
- Anne Agnastos claims that the current job market "offers opportunities that never existed before"; others disagree.

Positioning Question Marks, Exclamation Points, and Dashes

If a question mark, exclamation point, or dash punctuates the words enclosed in quotation marks, put it inside the closing quotation mark.

- "Did I Hear You Call My Name?" was the winning song.
- They shouted, "We won the lottery!"

If a question mark, exclamation point, or dash punctuates words that are not included in quotation marks, put it outside the closing quotation mark.

- Have you read Nikki Giovanni's poem "Knoxville, Tennessee"?
- Edward T. Hall's coined word "proxemics"—which is related to "proximity"—can now be found in the dictionary.

P8 Other Punctuation Marks

P8.a Knowing when to use the dash

Dashes let you interrupt a sentence's structure to add information. Use dashes sparingly—if you do use them—so that their impact is not diluted by overexposure.

Dashes have a few conventional uses. They can indicate interrupted or broken-off speech: *"Watch out for the—too late."*

In typed papers, make a dash by hitting the hyphen key twice (--). Do not put a space before, between, or after the hyphens. In handwritten papers, make a dash slightly longer than a hyphen, using one unbroken line (—).

Adding Information with Dashes

Dashes emphasize added information, such as examples, definitions, appositives, contrasts, and asides.

- The care-takers—those who are helpers, nurturers, teachers, mothers—are still systematically devalued.
  —Ellen Goodman, "Just Woman's Work"

- Although the emphasis at the school was mainly language— speaking, reading, writing—the lessons always began with an exercise in politeness.
  —Elizabeth Wong, *Fifth Chinese Daughter*

- Two of the strongest animals in the jungle are vegetarians—the elephant and the gorilla.
  —Dick Gregory, *The Shadow That Scares Me*

- Tampering with time brought most of the house tumbling down, and it was this that made Einstein's work so important—and controversial.
  —Banesh Hoffmann, "My Friend, Albert Einstein"

- I live on an income well below the poverty line—although it does not seem like poverty when the redbud and dogwood are in bloom together—and when I travel I have to be careful about expenses.
  —Sue Hubbell, *Beekeeper*

Alerts: (1) If the words within a pair of dashes would take a question mark or an exclamation point as a separate sentence, use that punctuation before the second dash: *A first love—do you remember?— stays in the memory forever.* (2) Do not use commas, semicolons, or periods next to dashes. Revise to avoid such a possibility.

Knowing when to use parentheses   P8.b

Like dashes (**P8.a**), parentheses let you interrupt a sentence's structure to add information. Dashes tend to call attention to whatever they set off; parentheses tend to deemphasize whatever they enclose.

Parentheses have a few conventional uses. They can be used to enclose numbers or letters of listed items: *The two topics to be discussed are (1) whether membership dues should be raised and (2) the fund-raising campaign.* Especially in business writing, parentheses are sometimes used to enclose a numeric version of a spelled-out number: *The order of fifteen (15) cartons was shipped yesterday.*

Adding Information in Parentheses

Parentheses can be used to enclose the same kind of material that dashes set apart (amplifications such as explanations, definitions, examples, contrasts, and asides).

- In division (also known as partition) a subject commonly thought of as a single unit is reduced to its separate parts.
  —David Skwire, *Writing with a Thesis*

- Though other cities (Dresden, for instance) had been utterly destroyed in World War II, never before had a single weapon been responsible for such destruction.
  —Lawrence Behrens and Leonard J. Rosen,
  Writing and Reading Across the Curriculum

- The sheer decibel level of the noise around us is not enough to make us cranky, irritable, or aggressive. (It can, however, affect our mental and physical health, which is another matter.)
  —Carol Tavris, *Anger: The Misunderstood Emotion*

Using Other Punctuation with Parentheses

Do not put a comma before an opening parenthesis, even if what precedes the parenthetical material requires a comma; put the comma after the closing parenthesis.

No   Although different from the first film we watched, (*The Wizard of Oz*) *Gone with the Wind* is also worth studying.

Yes   Although different from the first film we watched (*The Wizard of Oz*), *Gone with the Wind* is also worth studying.

When a complete sentence in parentheses occurs within another sentence, do not use a period to signal the end of the parenthetical sentence. Do, however, use a question mark or exclamation point if either is called for. (Capitalize the first word only if it is a proper noun.)

No   Looking for his car keys (he had left them in the kitchen.) wasted an hour.

Yes   Looking for his car keys (he had left them in the kitchen) wasted an hour.

A parenthetical sentence that stands alone starts with a capital and ends with a period (or question mark or exclamation point) inside the closing parenthesis.

Yes   Looking for his car keys wasted an hour. (He had left them in the kitchen.)

Knowing when to use brackets   P8.c

Brackets enclose words you insert into quotations. For example, to fit quoted words smoothly into the structure of your own sentence, you may have to change a word or two in the quotation; such changes belong in brackets.

Original source	Surprisingly, this trend is almost reversed in Italy, where males interact closer and display significantly more contact than do male/female dyads and female couples. —Robert Shuter, "A Field Study of Nonverbal Communication in Germany, Italy, and the United States," page 305
Quotation	Although German and American men stand farthest apart and touch each other the least, Shuter reported "this trend [to be] almost reversed in Italy" (305).

Use brackets to enclose any explanatory or clarifying words you have written within the quoted material to help your reader understand the quote.

Original source	This sort of information seems trivial, but it does affect international understanding. —Charles G. Morris, *Psychology: An Introduction*, page 516
Quotation	"This sort of information [about personal space] seems trivial, but it does affect international understanding" (Morris 516).

If you find a mistake in something you want to quote—a wrong date, an error of fact—do not change the original words. To show that you see the error, insert the Latin word *sic* in brackets right after the error. Meaning "so" or "thus," the [sic] says to a reader, "It is thus in the original." If you are using MLA STYLE for your paper, use regular (roman) type, not italic or underlined, for the word and the brackets.

* The report mentions an unintended consequence of doubling the floor space: "With extra room per person, the tenets [sic] would sublet."

Knowing when to use the ellipsis   P8.d

An **ellipsis** is a set of three spaced periods. Its most important function is to show that a quotation omits some of the original writer's words.

Original   For over a century twins have been used to study how genes make people what they are. Because they share precisely the same genes but live in different surroundings under different influences, identical twins reared apart are helping science sort out which qualities of body and mind are shaped by our genes, and which by upbringing. Researchers needn't worry about running out of subjects: according to the Twins Foundation, there are approximately 4.5 million twin individuals in the United States alone, and about 70,000 more are born each year.

—Sharon Begley, "Twins," page 84

Quotation Omitting Words from a Sentence

- Begley says, ". . . identical twins reared apart are helping science sort out which qualities of body and mind are shaped by our genes, and which by upbringing" (84).   [First words of quoted sentence omitted]

- Begley says, "Because they share precisely the same genes . . . identical twins reared apart are helping science sort out which qualities of body and mind are shaped by our genes, and which by upbringing" (84).   [Words within quoted sentence omitted]

- Begley says, "Because they share precisely the same genes but live in different surroundings under different influences, identical twins reared apart are helping science . . ." (84).   [Last words of quoted sentence omitted and MLA or APA parenthetical reference used]

The third example above shows how to handle a sentence-ending ellipsis when a parenthetical reference in MLA or APA style comes at the end. Here is the same example without a parenthetical reference, using four dots, the first one for the sentence-ending period, and then three spaced dots for the ellipsis.

- Begley says, "Because they share precisely the same genes but live in different surroundings under different influences, identical twins reared apart are helping science. . . ."   [Last words of quoted sentence omitted]

Quotation with One or More Sentences Omitted

- Begley says, "For over a century twins have been used to study how genes make people what they are. . . . Researchers needn't worry about running out of subjects" (84).

To show omissions from short quotations of poetry—that is, quotations of three lines or less—use ellipses as shown in the prose quotations above. To show an omission of one or more lines from a set-off quotation of poetry, use a full line of spaced periods; make the line of periods as long as the line of poetry above it. Use an ellipsis for any omission of less than a line in a set-off quotation of poetry.

Original Source

- Fear no more the heat o' the sun
  Nor the furious winter's rages;
  Thou thy worldly task hast done,
  Home art gone, and ta'en thy wages;
  Golden lads and girls all must,
  As chimney-sweepers, come to dust.

  —William Shakespeare, from *Cymbeline*

Quotation Omitting Lines

- Fear no more the heat o' the sun,
  Nor the furious winter's rages;

  . . . .

  Golden lads and girls all must,
  As chimney-sweepers, come to dust.

Knowing when to use the slash   P8.e

To quote three lines or less of poetry, enclose the lines in quotation marks, with a slash to divide one line of poetry from the next. Leave a space on each side of the slash. (For setting off four or more lines of quoted poetry, see **P7.a**.)

- Consider the beginning of Anne Sexton's poem "Words": "Be careful of words, / even the miraculous ones."

If you have to type numerical fractions that are not on your keyboard, use the slash to separate the numerator and denominator. Use a hyphen to join a whole number to its fraction.

- 1/16
- 1-2/3

Try to avoid word combinations like *and/or* when writing in the humanities. In those academic disciplines where the use of word combinations is acceptable, separate the words with a slash, leaving no space before or after it.

Spelling
and Mechanics

homonyms

plurals

italics

numerals

spelled-out numbers

hyphens

proper adjectives

names and terms

abbreviations

S SPELLING AND MECHANICS

S1 Spelling

You might be surprised to know this about good spellers: They do not always remember how to spell every word they write, but they sense when to check a word's spelling. Try not to ignore your inner voice that questions a spelling; look the word up.

How do you look a word up when you do not know how to spell it? If you know the first few letters, find them and then browse for the word. If you do not know them, try to find the word in a thesaurus under a synonym. When writing on a computer, use a spell-check, but also proofread. That is the only way to discover words that may be correctly spelled but are not the words you intended (for example, *whole* for *hole*).

Knowing rules for spelling plurals, adding suffixes, and spelling *ie*, *ei* words   S1.a

Spelling Plurals

- **Adding -*s* or -*es*:** Plurals of most words are formed by adding -*s*, including words that end in "hard" -*ch* (sounding like *k*): *leg, legs; shoe, shoes; stomach, stomachs.* For words ending in -*s*, -*sh*, -*x*, -*z*, or "soft" -*ch* (as in *beach*), add -*es* to the singular: *lens, lenses; beach, beaches; tax, taxes; coach, coaches.*

- **Words Ending in -*o*:** Add -*s* if the -*o* is preceded by a vowel (*radio, radios; cameo, cameos*). Add -*es* if the -*o* is preceded by a consonant (*potato, potatoes*). A few words can be made plural either way: *cargo, volcano, tornado, zero.*

- **Words Ending in -*f* or -*fe*:** Some -*f* and -*fe* words are made plural by adding -*s*: *belief, beliefs.* Others require changing -*f* or -*fe* to -*ves*: *life, lives; leaf, leaves.* Words ending in -*ff* or -*ffe* simply add -*s*: *staff, staffs; giraffe, giraffes.*

- **Compound Words:** For most compound words, add -*s* or -*es* at the end of the last word: *checkbooks, player-coaches.* For a few, the word to make plural is not the last one: *sister-in-law, sisters-in-law; mile per hour, miles per hour.* (For hyphenating compound words, see **S2.b**.)

- **Internal Changes and Endings Other Than -*s*:** A few words change internally or add endings other than -*s* to become plural: *foot, feet; man, men; mouse, mice; crisis, crises; child, children.*

- **Foreign Words:** Plurals other than -*s* or -*es* are listed in good dictionaries. In general, for many Latin words ending in -*um*, form plurals by changing -*um* to -*a*: *curriculum, curricula;*

datum, data; medium, media; stratum, strata. For Latin words that end in *-us,* the plural is often *-i: alumnus, alumni; syllabus, syllabi.* For Greek *-on* words, the plural is often *-a: criterion, criteria; phenomenon, phenomena.*

- **One-Form Words:** A few spellings are the same for the singular and plural: *deer, elk, fish, quail.* The differences are conveyed by adding words, not endings: *one deer, nine deer; rice, bowls of rice.*

Spelling Suffixes

A suffix is an ending added to a word to change that word's meaning or its grammatical function: *depend, dependable.*

- **-y Words:** If the letter before the final *y* is a consonant, change the *y* to *i* unless the suffix begins with an *i* (for example, *-ing*): *fry, fried, frying.* If the letter before the *-y* is a vowel, keep the final *y: employ, employed, employing.* These rules do not apply to irregular verbs (see **QA Box 32** on pages 63–64).

- **-e Words:** Drop a final *e* when the suffix begins with a vowel unless doing so would cause confusion (for example, *be + ing* does not become *bing*): *require, requiring; like, liking.* Keep the final *e* when the suffix begins with a consonant: *require, requirement; like, likely.* Exceptions include *argument, judgment,* and *truly.*

- **Words That Double a Final Letter:** If the final letter is a consonant, double it only if it passes all three of these tests: (1) its last two letters are a vowel followed by a consonant; and (2) it has one syllable or is accented on the last syllable; and (3) the suffix begins with a vowel: *drop, dropped; begin, beginning; forget, forgetful, forgettable.*

- **-cede, -ceed, -sede Words:** Only one word ends in *-sede: supersede.* Three words end in *-ceed: exceed, proceed, succeed.* All other words whose endings sound like "seed" end in *-cede: concede, intercede, precede.*

- **-ally and -ly Words:** The suffixes *-ally* and *-ly* turn words into adverbs. For words ending in *-ic,* add *-ally: logically, statistically.* Otherwise, add *-ly: quickly, sharply.*

Using the *ie, ei* Rule

The old rhyme for *ie* and *ei* is usually true:

- "*I* before *e* [*believe, field, grief*],
  Except after *c* [*ceiling, conceit*],
  Or when sounded like 'ay'
  As in *neighbor* and *weigh*." [*eight, vein*]

Here are major exceptions (sorry!) to memorize.

- *ie* conscience, financier, science, species
- *ei* either, neither, leisure, seize, counterfeit, foreign, forfeit, sleigh, sleight (as in slight-of-hand), weird

Spelling homonyms and other commonly confused words

Words that sound exactly like others (*morning, mourning; to, too, two*) are called **homonyms**. They, as well as words that sound almost alike, can be confusing. **QA Box 42**, below, gives a comprehensive list.

Another source of confusion is "swallowed" pronunciation: not pronouncing a letter or letters at the end of a word. For example, as verbs expressing past time, *use to* and *prejudice* may be what a writer hears—and writes—but only *used to* and *prejudiced* are correct.

Also confusing are expressions that should always be written as two words, such as *all right* (not *alright*) and *a lot* (not *alot*).

HOMONYMS AND OTHER COMMONLY CONFUSED WORDS

QA
Box
42

accept	to receive
except	with the exclusion of
advice	recommendation
advise	to recommend
affect	to influence [VERB]; emotion [NOUN]
effect	result [NOUN]; to bring about or cause [VERB]
aisle	space between rows
isle	island
allude	to make indirect reference to
elude	to avoid
allusion	indirect reference
illusion	false idea, misleading appearance
already	by this time
all ready	fully prepared
altar	sacred platform or place
alter	to change
altogether	thoroughly
all together	everyone or everything in one place
are	PLURAL form of *to be*
hour	sixty minutes
our	PLURAL form of *my*

Continued on next page

➤ *QA Box 42, continued from previous page*

ascent	the act of rising or climbing
assent	consent [NOUN]; to consent
assistance	help
assistants	helpers
bare	nude, unadorned
bear	to carry; an animal
board	piece of wood
bored	uninterested
brake	device for stopping
break	to destroy, make into pieces
breath	air taken in
breathe	to take in air
buy	to purchase
by	next to, through the agency of
capital	major city
capitol	government building
choose	to pick
chose	PAST TENSE of *to chose*
cite	to point out
sight	vision
site	a place
clothes	garments
cloths	pieces of fabric
coarse	rough
course	path; series of lectures
complement	something that completes
compliment	praise, flattery
conscience	sense of morality
conscious	awake, aware
council	governing body
counsel	advice
dairy	place associated with milk production
diary	personal journal
descent	downward movement
dissent	disagreement
dessert	final, sweet course in a meal
desert	to abandon; dry, usually sandy area
device	a plan; an implement
devise	to create

Continued on next page

QA Box 42, continued from previous page

die	to lose life (*dying*); one of a pair of dice
dye	to change the color of something (*dyeing*)
dominant	commanding, controlling
dominate	to control
elicit	to draw out
illicit	illegal
eminent	prominent
immanent	living within; inherent
imminent	about to happen
envelop	to surround
envelope	container for a letter or other papers
fair	light-skinned; just, honest
fare	money for transportation; food
formally	conventionally, with ceremony
formerly	previously
forth	forward
fourth	number four
gorilla	animal in ape family
guerrilla	soldier conducting surprise attacks
hear	to sense sound by ear
here	in this place
hole	opening
whole	complete; an entire thing
human	relating to the species *Homo sapiens*
humane	compassionate
insure	buy or give insurance
ensure	guarantee, protect
its	POSSESSIVE form of *it*
it's	contraction for *it is*
know	to comprehend
no	negative
later	after a time
latter	second one of two things
lead	heavy metal substance; to guide
led	PAST TENSE of *to lead*
lightning	storm-related electricity
lightening	making lighter
loose	unbound, not tightly fastened
lose	to misplace

Continued on next page

➤ QA Box 42, continued from previous page

maybe	perhaps [ADVERB]
may be	might be [VERB]
meat	animal flesh
meet	to encounter
miner	a person who works in a mine
minor	under-age
moral	distinguishing right from wrong; the lesson of a fable, story, or event
morale	attitude or outlook, usually of a group
of	PREPOSITION indicating origin
off	away from
passed	PAST TENSE of *to pass*
past	at a previous time
patience	forbearance
patients	people under medical care
peace	absence of fighting
piece	part of a whole; musical arrangement
personal	intimate
personnel	employees
plain	simple, unadorned
plane	to shave wood; aircraft
precede	to come before
proceed	to continue
presence	being at hand; attendance at a place or in something
presents	gifts
principal	foremost [ADJECTIVE]; school head [NOUN]
principle	moral conviction, basic truth
quiet	silent, calm
quite	very
rain	water drops falling to earth; to fall like rain
reign	to rule
rein	strap to guide or control an animal [NOUN]; to guide or control [VERB]
raise	to lift up
raze	to tear down
respectfully	with respect
respectively	in that order

Continued on next page

QA Box 42, continued from previous page

right	correct; opposite of *left*
rite	ritual
write	to put words on paper
road	path
rode	PAST TENSE of *to ride*
scene	place of an action; segment of a play
seen	viewed
sense	perception, understanding
since	measurement of past time; because
stationary	standing still
stationery	writing paper
than	in comparison with; besides
then	at that time; next; therefore
their	POSSESSIVE form of *they*
there	in that place
they're	contraction for *they are*
through	finished; into and out of
threw	PAST TENSE of *to throw*
thorough	complete
to	toward
too	also; indicates degree (*too much*)
two	number following one
waist	midsection of the body
waste	discarded material; to squander, to fail to use up
weak	not strong
week	seven days
weather	climatic condition
whether	if
where	in which place
were	PAST TENSE of *to be*
which	one of a group
witch	female sorcerer
whose	POSSESSIVE form of *who*
who's	contraction for *who is*
your	POSSESSIVE form of *you*
you're	contraction for *you are*
yore	long past

S2 Hyphens

S2.a Knowing how to hyphenate at the end of a line

QA Box 43

END-OF-LINE HYPHENATION

- **Do not divide very short words, one-syllable words, or words pronounced as one syllable.**

  wealth   envy   screamed
  - we-alth   • en-vy   • scream-ed

- **Do not leave or carry over only one or two letters.**

  alive   open   covered
  - a-live   • o-pen   • cover-ed

- **Divide words only between syllables.***

  pro-cess
  - proc-ess

- **Divide between consonants, keeping pronunciation in mind.**

  full-ness   omit-ting   as-phalt
  - ful-lness   • omitt-ing   • asp-halt

- **If possible, divide a hyphenated word only at the hyphen, and divide a closed compound word only between complete words.**

  self-conscious   master-piece
  - self-con-scious   • mas-terpiece

  sister-in-law   stomach-ache
  - sis-ter-in-law   • stom-achache

  *To check how to divide a word into syllables, look the word up in a dictionary.

S2.b Knowing when to hyphenate prefixes, suffixes, compound words, and numbers

Prefixes and **suffixes** are syllables attached to words, prefixes at the beginning and suffixes at the end. **Compound words** are two or more words combined to express one concept. Some prefixes and suffixes are hyphenated; others are not. Compound words can be written as separate words (*night shift*), hyphenated words (*tractor-trailer*), or one word (*handbook*). **QA Box 44,** on the next page, explains hyphenation of prefixes, suffixes, compound words, and numbers.

HYPHENATING PREFIXES, SUFFIXES, COMPOUND WORDS, AND NUMBERS

Prefixes and Suffixes

- **Use hyphens after the prefixes** *all-*, *ex-*, *quasi-*, **and** *self-*.
  - all-inclusive
  - self-reliant

- **Do not use a hyphen when** *self* **is a root word rather than a prefix.**
  - selfishness
  - selfless
  - selfhood

- **Use a hyphen to avoid a distracting string of letters.**
  - anti-intellectual
  - bell-like

- **Use a hyphen before the suffix** *-elect*.
  - president-elect

- **Use a hyphen when a prefix comes before a number or before a word that starts with a capital letter.**
  - post-1950
  - pro-American

- **Use a hyphen between a prefix and a compound word.**
  - anti-gun control

- **Use a hyphen to prevent confusion in meaning or pronunciation.**
  - re-dress ("dress again")
  - un-ionize ("remove the ions")
  - redress ("set right")
  - unionize ("form a union")

- **Use a hyphen when two or more prefixes apply to one root word.**
  - two-, three-, or four-year program
  - pre- and postwar eras

Compound Words

- **Use a hyphen for most compound modifiers that precede the noun. Do not use a hyphen for most compound modifiers** *after* **the noun.**
  - well-researched report
  - two-inch clearance
  - report is well researched
  - clearance of two inches

- **Use a hyphen between compound nouns joining two units of measure.**
  - light-year
  - kilowatt-hour
  - foot-pound

- **Do not use a hyphen when a compound modifier starts with an** *-ly* **adverb.**
  - happily married couple

Continued on next page

➤ QA Box 44, continued from previous page

- **Do not use a hyphen when a compound modifier is in the comparative or superlative form.**
  - better fitting shoe
  - least welcome guest
  - most significant factor

- **Do not use a hyphen when a compound modifier is a foreign phrase.**
  - post hoc fallacies

- **Do not use a hyphen with a possessive compound modifier.**
  - a full week's work
  - eight hours' pay

Spelled-Out Numbers*

- **Use a hyphen between two-word numbers from twenty-one through ninety-nine.**
  - thirty-five
  - two hundred thirty-five

- **Use a hyphen in a compound-word modifier formed from a number and a word.**
  - fifty-minute class [*also* 50-minute class]
  - three-to-one odds [*also* 3-to-1 odds]

- **Use a hyphen between the numerator and the denominator of two-word fractions.**
  - one-half
  - two-fifths
  - seven-tenths

*For information about when to use numerals and when to use words for numbers, see **S6**.

! **Alert:** Use figures rather than words for any fraction that is expressed in more than two words. If you cannot use figures (for example, if a sentence starts with a multiword fraction and you cannot rearrange it, use hyphens between the words of the numerator's number and the words of the denominator's number but not between the numerator and the denominator: *two one-hundredths* (2/100), *thirty-three ten-thousandths* (33/10,000).

S3 Capitals

S3.a Capitalizing at the start of a sentence and other sentencelike structures

Capitalize the first word in a sentence.

- Four inches of snow fell last winter.

After a Colon

When the words after a colon are not a complete sentence, do not capitalize. When a complete sentence follows a colon, you can begin with a capital or a lowercase letter, but be consistent in each piece of writing.

- Only one solution occurred to her: She picked up the ice cream and pushed it back into the cone.

- Only one solution occurred to her: she picked up the ice cream and pushed it back into the cone.

A Series of Questions

When questions in a series are not complete sentences, you can begin each question with a capital or a lowercase letter; be consistent within each piece of writing.

- What facial feature would most people like to change? Eyes? Ears? Nose?

- What facial feature would most people like to change? eyes? ears? nose?

Listed Items

When listed items are complete sentences, capitalize them, whether the items are run in—as in the next example—or each starts a new line.

- Three problems caused the shortage: (1) Bad weather delayed delivery. (2) Poor scheduling created slowdowns. (3) Inadequate maintenance caused equipment breakdowns.

Do not capitalize listed items that are not complete sentences.

- The delays resulted from (1) bad weather, (2) poor scheduling, and (3) equipment breakdowns.

Inside Parentheses

A complete sentence enclosed in parentheses sometimes stands alone and sometimes falls within the structure of another sentence. Those that stand alone start with a capital letter and end with a period, question mark, or exclamation point. A complete sentence in parentheses that falls within the structure of another sentence does not start with a capital letter and does not end with a period. Examples are at the top of the next page. (However, if the parenthetical sentence is a question, end it with a question mark, and if it is an exclamation, end it with an exclamation point.)

- I didn't know till years later that they called it the Cuban Missile Crisis. But I remember Castro. (We called him Castor Oil and were awed by his beard—beards were rare in those days.) We might not have worried so much (what would the Communists want with our small New Hampshire town?) except that we lived 10 miles from an air base.

  —Joyce Maynard, *An 18-Year-Old Looks Back on Life*

S3.b Knowing when to capitalize the first letter of a quotation

If your words in a sentence serve only to introduce quoted words, capitalize the first quoted word.

- Encouraging students to visit other countries and learn new languages, Mrs. Velez says, "You will absorb a good accent with the food."

When you interrupt quoted words with your own explanatory words, do not capitalize the continued part of the quoted words.

- "You will absorb a good accent," says Mrs. Velez, "with the food."

If you make quoted words part of the structure of your own sentence, do not capitalize the first quoted word, unless it is a P<small>ROPER</small> N<small>OUN</small>. Often, a phrase such as *writes that*, *thinks that*, or *says that* signals the kind of integrated quotation that does not begin with a capital letter.

- Mrs. Velez believes that "you will absorb a good accent with the food" if you visit a country whose language you want to learn.

Capitalize a quotation of poetry the way the original is capitalized. For more information on quotations, see **P7**.

S3.c Capitalizing proper nouns and proper adjectives

Capitalize P<small>ROPER</small> N<small>OUNS</small> (*Mexico, Arthur*) and P<small>ROPER</small> A<small>DJECTIVES</small> (*a Mexican diplomat, the Arthurian legend*).

! **Alert:** (1) Do not capitalize D<small>ETERMINERS</small> and other words just because they accompany proper nouns or proper adjectives: *Here is a Canadian penny* [not *A Canadian penny*], for example. (2) A proper noun or proper adjective that becomes very common may lose its capital letter: *french fries, italics, pasteurized.*

Certain COMMON NOUNS are capitalized when specific names or titles are added to them: *We visit a lake every summer. This summer we went to Lake Ontario.*

Knowing when to capitalize names and terms   S3.d

CAPITALIZATION

QA
Rnx
45

	Capitals	Lowercase Letters
Names and titles	Mother Teresa [a name]	my mother [relationship]
	President Lincoln	a president
	the President [now in office]	
	Democrat [a party member]	democrat [a believer in democracy]
	Senator Barbara Mikulski	the senator
	Professor Roberts	the professor
Groups of humanity	Caucasian [race]	white [*also* White]
	Negro [race]	black [*also* Black]
	Oriental [race]	
	Muslim	
	Jewish	
Organizations	Congress	a congressional hearing
	the Ohio State Supreme Court	the state supreme court
	the Republican Party	the party
	Amgen Corporation	the corporation
Places	Dallas	a city
	India	a country
	the South [a region]	turn south [a direction]
	Main Street	the street
	Atlantic Ocean	the ocean
Buildings	Lee High School	the high school
	China West Café	the restaurant
	the Capitol [the building in Washington, D.C.]	the state capitol
Scientific terms	Earth [the planet]	the earth [where we live]
		the moon, the sun
	the Milky Way	the galaxy
	Staphylococcus aureus	a staphylococcal infection
	Newton's law	the theory of gravity
Languages, Nationalities	Spanish	
	Chinese	

Continued on next page

➤ QA Box 45, continued from previous page

	Capitals	**Lowercase Letters**
School courses	Chemistry 342 my English class	a chemistry course my literature course
Names of things	the *Los Angeles Times* *Time* Purdue University Heinz Ketchup	the newspaper the magazine the university ketchup
Seasons and time names	Friday August	spring, summer, fall, autumn, winter
Historical periods	World War II the Great Depression [in the 1930s] the Reformation	the war the depression [any economic downturn] an era, an age the eighteenth century the civil rights movement
Religious terms	God Buddhism the Koran the Bible	a god, a divinity
Letter parts	Dear Ms. Tauber: Sincerely yours,	
Titles of works*	"Trifles" *The Grapes of Wrath*	the play the novel
Compound words	post-Victorian Italian American Indo-European	
Acronyms and initialisms	IRS IBM	

*For capitalizing the title fo your own papers, see **M3.a** (MLA style) or **A1.e** (APA style).

S4 Italics or Underlining

In printed material, **roman type** is standard. Type that slants to the right is called **italic type**. In typewritten or handwritten material, underlining stands for italics. Italic type is available in many word-processing programs; if it is not available in yours, use underlining. If it is available, use whichever style your instructors prefer.

Handwritten and underlined	<u>Catch 22</u>
Typed and underlined	<u>Catch 22</u>
Italic type	*Catch 22*

Knowing when to use italics (or underlining)   S4.a

QA Box 46

ITALICIZING OR UNDERLINING

	Italicize	Do Not Italicize
Titles and names	*The Bell Jar* [a novel]	
	Death of a Salesman [a play]	
	Collected Works of O. Henry [a book]	"The Last Leaf" [a story in the book]
	Simon & Schuster Handbook for Writers [a book]	"Agreement" [a chapter in the book]
	The Prose Reader [a collection of essays]	"Putting In a Good Word for Guilt" [one essay]
	The Iliad [a book-length poem]	"Nothing Gold Can Stay" [a short poem]
	Liar, Liar [a film]	
	the *Los Angeles Times** [a newspaper]	
	Scientific American [a magazine]	"The Molecules of Life" [an article in a magazine]
	Aida [an opera]	
	Symphonie Fantastique [a long musical work]	Concerto in B-flat Minor [a musical work identified by form, number, and key—neither quotation marks nor underlining]
	Twilight Zone [a television series]	"Terror at 30,000 Feet" [an episode of a television series]
	The Best of Bob Dylan [a recording]	"Mr. Tambourine Man" [one song]
	the U.S.S. *Intrepid* [a ship; note that U.S.S. is not italic]	aircraft carrier [a general class of ship]
	Voyager 2 [specific aircraft, spacecraft, satellites]	Boeing 787 [general names shared by classes of aircraft, spacecraft, or satellites]

Continued on next page

> ➤ QA Box 46, continued from previous page

	Italicize	**Do Not Italicize**
Other words	*joie de vivre* [words in a language other than English]	burrito, chutzpah [widely understood non-English words]
	What does *our* imply? [a word referred to as such]	
	the *abc*'s; confusing *3*'s and *8*'s [letters and numerals referred to as such]	

*Even if *The* is part of the title printed on a newspaper, do not capitalize it and do not underline it in the body of your paper. In MLA documentation, omit the word *The*.

S4.b Using italics (or underlining) for emphasis ▌

Underline (or use italics) sparingly for emphasis. As a rule, rely on your choice of words and sentence structures to convey emphasis in academic writing.

- The pain from my injury was <u>severe</u>.
- The pain from my injury was so severe that I could not breathe.

S5 Abbreviations

The abbreviation guidelines here hold for general writing and for writing in the humanities. Some of them change for other disciplines.

❗ Alert: (1) A college dictionary shows how to format abbreviations, including capitalization, periods, and spacing. (2) When the period of an abbreviation falls at the end of a sentence, it serves also as a sentence-ending period. When a question mark or exclamation point ends a sentence, place it after the abbreviation's period.

S5.a Knowing when and how to use abbreviations ▌

Abbreviating Specific Times, Measurements, and Amounts

Use the abbreviations *a.m.* (or *A.M.*) and *p.m.* (or *P.M.*) with exact times.

❗ Alert: You can use capital or lowercase letters for *a.m.* and *p.m.*; whichever style you choose, use it consistently in one piece of writing.

- 7:15 a.m.
- 7:15 A.M.
- 3:47 p.m.
- 3:47 P.M.

With specific years, *A.D.* (or *C.E.*, for "common era") precedes the year and *B.C.* (or *B.C.E.*) follows it.

- A.D. 934
- C.E. 934
- 1200 B.C.
- 1200 B.C.E.

With specific dollar-and-cent amounts expressed in figures, use $. In combinations of figures and words for large dollar amounts, also use $.

- $4.95
- $34 million

As a rule, avoid symbols in the body of your paper, even if you use them in a table, graph, or other illustration. However, let common sense and clarity for your readers guide you. If you mention temperatures once or twice in a paper, spell them out: *ninety degrees, minus twenty-six degrees.* If you mention temperatures throughout a paper, use figures and symbols: *90°, −26°.*

In tables, but not in the body of your paper, you can abbreviate measurements and amounts (such as *in., mi., cm., km., gal., ml., lb., kg.*) with specific numbers, as well as days and months (such as *Mon., Jan., Aug.*).

Abbreviating Titles

Commonly abbreviated titles of address include *Dr., Mr., Mrs.,* and *Ms.* You can use them with full names or with last names only.

- Dr. Anna Freud
- Dr. Freud
- Mr. Daljit Singh
- Mr. Singh

Only full names follow other commonly abbreviated titles; some of the more familiar ones are in the left-hand column below. When you want to use these titles with a last name only, do not abbreviate them; see the right-hand column.

Use with Full Name	Use with Last Name Only
Col. [Col. Lee Potts]	Colonel [Colonel Potts]
Gen.	General
Gov.	Governor
Rep.	Representative
Rev.	Reverend
Sen.	Senator

Abbreviations of academic and professional degrees (such as *Ph.D.* for Doctors of Philosophy and *M.D.* for physicians) follow the names: *Betty Sun, M.D.* Do not use both a title of address before a name and an abbreviated degree after a name: *Seth Reichlin, Ph.D.* or *Dr. Seth Reichlin* (not *Dr. Seth Reichlin, Ph.D.*).

Abbreviations related to family generations, such as *Jr., Sr., II,* and

III, are considered part of the names they follow, so you can use them with other abbreviations, such as those for titles before names and for academic and professional degrees after names.

- Mrs. Kenneth Huizinga, Jr.
- Roy J. Modugno Sr., D.D.S.

! **Alert:** (1) Use a comma between a name and most abbreviations following it. Some people omit the comma for the generation designations *II*, *III*, and so on (*Fred D. Fumia II*) but not for *Jr.* and *Sr.* (*Andrew Watson, Jr.*). (2) Use a comma between abbreviations following a name: *Fred D. Fumia II, M.D.*

Abbreviating Names and Terms

You can use common and widely recognized abbreviated names of companies, organizations, and even countries, such as *FBI, UN, NBC,* and *USA.*

! **Alert:** Use the abbreviation *U.S.* (or *US*) as an ADJECTIVE form for *United States* (*the U.S. ski team*), but not as a NOUN form: *The United States* [not *The U.S.*] *has many different climates.*

If you want to use an abbreviated form of a long name (of an organization but not of a person) throughout a paper, spell out the full name when you first use it, and follow the name with the abbreviation in parentheses. Then you can use the abbreviation alone.

- Spain voted to continue as a member of the **North Atlantic Treaty Organization (NATO)**, to the surprise of other **NATO** members.

Abbreviating Addresses

For addresses in correspondence, you can use such abbreviations as *St., Ave., Blvd., Apt., NE, SW,* and the two-letter postal abbreviations for state names.

If you include a full address—street, city, and state—in the body of a paper, you can abbreviate the state name. Spell out any other combination of a city and a state, and spell out a state by itself.

- I wrote to Mr. U. Lern, 10-01 Rule Road, **Classgate, NJ** 07632 for the instruction manual. He had moved to **Falstaff, Arizona,** before my letter arrived.

! **Alert:** When you use city-state combination within a sentence, use a comma between the city and state names and after the state name unless it is the last word in the sentence.

- The Centers for Disease Control in Atlanta, ~~GA~~ *Georgia,* sometimes quarantines livestock.

Knowing when to use *etc.* and other Latin abbreviations — S5.b

The abbreviation *etc.* is from Latin *et cetera*, which means "and the rest." Do not use *etc.* in the body of a paper you are writing in the humanities. Acceptable substitutes are *and the like, and so on,* and *and so forth.* Latin abbreviations, including *etc.,* are used in various documentation systems; see **M1–M3** and **A1–A4**.

S6 Numbers

Knowing when to use spelled-out numbers — S6.a

If you mention numbers only a few times in a paper, spell out numbers that can be expressed in one or two words—unless communicating exact quantities to your readers is an important consideration.

- Iceland's population increases by more than ~~1~~ one percent a year, but that gain translates into fewer than ~~3,000~~ three thousand individuals.

Alert: Use a hyphen between spelled-out, two-word numbers from *twenty-one* through *ninety-nine*. **!**

If numbers occur fairly frequently in your paper, spell out those from *one* through *nine* and use figures for all others. If a sentence starts with a number, spell it out; do not use a figure.

- ~~$375~~ Three hundred seventy-five dollars per credit is the tuition rate for nonresidents.

In practice, you can usually revise a sentence so that the number does not come first: *The tuition rate for nonresidents is $375 per credit.*

Do not mix spelled-out numbers and figures that refer to the same thing. Use figures. In the following example, all numbers referring to volunteers should be figures, and *four* should be spelled out because it refers to a different quantity—days.

- In the past ~~4~~ four days, our volunteers increased from ~~five~~ 5 to ~~eight~~ 8 to ~~seventeen~~ 17 to 233. On Saturday, ~~thirty-seven~~ 37 people who usually volunteer on weekdays joined the usual Saturday staff of ~~forty-one~~ 41 volunteers.

S6.b Knowing when to use numerals

USING NUMERALS

Dates	August 6, 1941
	1732–1845
	34 B.C. to A.D. 230
Addresses	237 North 8th Street
	Export Falls, MN 92025
Times	8:09 a.m.
	4:00 p.m. [*but* four o'clock, *not* 4 o'clock; 4 p.m. *or* four in the afternoon, *not* four p.m. *or* 4 in the afternoon]
Decimals and fractions	5.55
	98.6
	3.1416
	7/8
	12-1/4
	3/4 [*or* three-quarters, *not* 3-quarters]
Chapters and pages	Chapter 27, page 245
Act, scene, and line numbers	act II, scene ii, lines 75–79 [or act 2, scene 2)
Scores and statistics	a 6-0 score
	a 5 to 3 ratio
	29 percent
Identification numbers	93.9 on the FM dial
	call 1-212-555-3930
Measurements	2 feet
	67.8 miles per hour
	1.5 gallons, 3 liters
	8-1/2″ x 11″ paper [*or* 8-1/2 x 11-inch]
Temperatures	43° F
	4° Celsius
Money	$1.2 billion
	$3.41
	25 cents [*or* 25¢, *but not* twenty-five ¢]

Research Writing

R RESEARCH WRITING

R1 Starting a Research Project

A research project involves three processes: conducting research, understanding the results of your research, and writing the paper based on that understanding. Every research project has as its goal answering a question. Although research assignments are not usually phrased as questions, all assignments imply that you need to search for answers. To attempt to find these answers, you must track down information from varied sources.

Attempt is an important word in relation to research. Some research questions can lead to a final, definitive answer. Others cannot, especially when a subject is currently evolving or when an assignment requires you to investigate a debatable topic and then argue your opinion in your paper.

Scheduling for research writing R1.a

If you feel overwhelmed by the prospect of research writing, you are not alone. If you break down research writing into a series of steps, however, the project can seem far less intimidating. Research writing takes time, so plan ahead and budget your time realistically. **QA Box 48** shows a sample schedule that you can adapt to your individual needs.

RESEARCH WRITING SCHEDULE	QA Box 48

Assignment received (date) ____ /____ /____

1 Prepare to conduct research. (**R1.a**)
2 Keep a research log. (**R1.b**)
3 Choose a suitable topic. (**R1.c**)
4 Review how to evaluate sources. (**R2.b**)
5 Determine documentation style (**R2.c**) and make bibliographic cards (**R2.d**).
6 Locate sources. (**R2**)
7 Compile a working list of sources. (**R2.a**)
8 Take notes. (**R2.e**)
9 Draft a thesis statement. (**W1.f**)
10 Draft the paper. (**R4**)
11 Document correctly. (**R3, M1–M3** and **A1–A4**)
12 Revise the paper. (**R4**)
13 Edit and proofread the paper. (**W3, R4**)

Assignment due (date) ____ /____ /____

R1.b Keeping a research log

A **research log** is a focused journal or diary. Use your research log to record the history of your search for information. Also use it to record the ideas that occur to you during your research process. The log keeps you from having to retrace your steps or reconstruct your thoughts unnecessarily. Although much of your log will not find its way into your paper, its entries provide valuable help as you decide on your next research step and on when to move from gathering material to organizing it to writing the paper.

R1.c Choosing a topic for research

Your first step in the process of research writing is to choose your topic (unless you are assigned a specific topic). Whether you are expected to choose a topic of your own or to narrow an assigned subject into a researchable topic, be systematic. If you begin to experience "research topic block," stay calm and trust that ideas will occur to you as you follow the suggestions below, which can help you begin to get an overview of your area of interest.

- Decide on an area of interest to you. Think back on subjects you have read about, studied, or experienced.
- Browse through a few textbooks in your area of interest. Read the table of contents and major headings. Scan the text for material that catches your interest. As you narrow your focus, note names of important books and experts, often mentioned in reference lists at the end of chapters or at the back of the book.
- Talk briefly with a professor in your area of interest. Ask for the names of major books and authorities on the subject that interests you and for advice about subcategories within it.
- Read an encyclopedia article about your area of interest and its subcategories. Do not, however, stop with the encyclopedia—college-level research demands a thorough search of a variety of sources.
- Go online and browse. A Web browser like Netscape provides several Web search engines, like Yahoo or Excite. When you "search on" a word or phrase, the search engine lists all the websites it finds that include your search term. Some of these websites may be of interest.
- Consult the vertical file in your college library. It contains materials, too short or informal to be listed in the library's catalog, that may suggest timely subcategories of the subject that interests you.

Once you have an overview of your subject and its subcategories, you are ready to choose a topic, following the guidelines in **QA Box 49**.

CHOOSING A RESEARCH TOPIC

QA
Box
49

1 Think through various topics before making a final choice. Avoid rushing. Keep your mind open to flashes of insight and alternative ideas, but do not allow indecision to take up too much time.

2 Be practical. Work within the established time limit and paper length, and be sure that sufficient resources on your topic are available.

3 Choose a sufficiently narrow topic. Avoid topics that are too broad, such as communication, or nonverbal communication, or even personal space and its messages. A well-narrowed topic would be Cultural Differences in Acceptable Distances for Personal Space.

4 Choose a topic worth researching. Avoid trivial topics, because they prevent you from doing what is expected of a student researcher: investigating related ideas; analyzing them critically; and creating a synthesis of complex, sometimes conflicting concepts.

5 Try to select a topic that interests you. Your topic will be a companion for quite a while, perhaps most of a semester.

R2 Finding and Evaluating Sources

Many sources are available in libraries: books, articles, and media such as videotapes. Also, you can access electronic sources via computer (your school's or your own system). Additional source material can result from doing field research: your own interviews, observations, and experiments.

Using a search strategy   R2.a

A search strategy is an organized procedure for locating and assembling sources of information for your research. A search strategy takes time, so plan accordingly. You usually need to locate and evaluate many more sources than you eventually use in your paper.

Undertaking Field Research

If you intend to do field research, which usually happens away from a library, plan ahead carefully. When you undertake field research, you have to gather primary (original) data or information as well as analyze and synthesize information from all your sources. Ways of gathering primary data include interviews, surveys, and observations.

Allow extra time if you want to interview an expert on your topic. First, schedule an appointment at the convenience of the person you want to interview. Then write, reflect on, and perhaps revise the questions you plan to ask so that you can feel confident about getting the information you seek.

If you want to survey a group of people on an issue related to your topic, write the questions for your questionnaire. Then test the questionnaire on a few people who are not in the group you intend to survey. Revise any questions that do not work well.

If you intend to observe an event such as a concert or a play, get tickets right away. If you need to visit a museum, decide on a date to visit, check that the museum will be open that day, and allow enough leeway in your calendar for a follow-up visit.

Researching in the Library

Get to know the physical layout of your college library. Locate and read any written guides to the library's resources. Become aware of the breadth and depth of its collection of books, periodicals, reference works, indexes to periodicals, and specialized works. When you do library research, don't hesitate to ask a reference librarian how best to locate information you have tried unsuccessfully to find.

The way that research is done is changing rapidly. Whereas once card catalogs listed a library's holding on index cards organized by title, subject, and author and stored in rows of long, narrow drawers, now it is more common to find electronic card catalogs. Much information once collected in large books now exists in online indexes and databases for nearly every discipline.

Technology in any library is designed to ease your search for and access to sources. Learn how to use the technologies available to you *before* you start your actual search. If you are confident about how to access information electronically, you will feel that you are in control of your research project. Many electronic systems provide extensive help at the touch of a key, as well as screen-by-screen guidance and instructions. Still, don't hesitate to ask people for help when technology is new to you; soon your skills will be comfortably sharp.

For both print and online resources, a crucial part of your search strategy is to narrow your focus continually so that you can search efficiently. You may find help in the Library of Congress Subject Headings (LCSH); it lists the terms many catalogs (both card and online) use to index subjects.

To access and retrieve some computerized information, you need to figure out key words related to your topic so that the system can search for the topic in a database. Try out various possibilities as key words. Online systems can search entire articles for the appearance of particular words or phrases, and they can do narrower searches for key words in the titles of the articles in their databases.

In addition to the electronic information systems that may organize your library, you may have access to the Internet and the World Wide Web. Many books can help you learn about the resources available to you through the Internet, as well as about the ways to access these resources.

Online systems can flood you with potential sources, making it difficult to know which ones to use. The more specific your topic, the easier it becomes to read abstracts of articles to learn whether you should read the full article. In general, use the most current sources available as long as you are sure that the authors are credible.

Evaluating sources   R2.b

Whether information comes from a library source, from field research, or from electronic sources, it always requires your careful evaluation. First, decide whether the information relates to your topic in more than a vague, general sense. Next, use the criteria in **QA Box 50** to evaluate the source.

CRITERIA FOR EVALUATING SOURCES AND INFORMATION

QA
Box
50

Authoritative: Check encyclopedias, textbooks, and articles in academic journals, and ask experts. If a person or a specific work is mentioned often, that source is probably recognized as authoritative on your topic.

Reliable: Check different sources. If the same information appears, it is likely to be reliable. Check the reliability of information from field research—an interview, for example—against at least one authoritative library or electronic source.

Well supported: Check that each source supports assertions or information with sufficient evidence; see **T2.c.** Be wary of a source that offers little to back up a position.

Balanced tone: Approach a source critically. If the source's tone is unbiased and the reasoning logical, the source is likely to be balanced; see **T2.e–f.**

Current: Check that information is up-to-date. Long-accepted information is sometimes replaced or modified by new research. Check the library's catalogs and indexes to journals; the most recent information in any field first appears in that field's academic journals.

R2.c Determining your documentation style ▌

The term **documentation style** refers to a system for providing information about each source you have used in a research paper. Documentation styles vary among academic disciplines. Never mix documentation styles; use only one style in each piece of writing. Modern Language Association (MLA) style is often used in the humanities; see **M1–M3**. American Psychological Association (APA) style is often used in the social sciences; see **A1–A2**. Chicago Manual style (CM) is used in various disciplines in the humanities, including English and history; see **A3**. Council of Biology Editors (CBE) style is used in biological and other sciences; see **A4**.

R2.d Creating a working bibliography ▌

Before you start to consult sources, check with your course instructor to find out what documentation style to use. When you decide to take notes on a source, the first step is to record for that source all the bibliographic information you will need to fulfill the requirements of that particular documentation style. In addition, for each library source, record the library call number, being careful to copy it exactly. For each online source, record the electronic "address" and the date you access the source. Write the information either on a bibliographic card—only one source per card—or in a notebook, or create a computer file for bibliographic information about your sources. Cards have the advantage of being easy to arrange in correct order when the time comes to compile a list of sources.

R2.e Taking useful notes ▌

Taking good notes is essential for using source materials well in your research paper. Note-taking is a decision-making process. For library sources, including electronic ones, use the following list to make sure that your notes provide you with the information you will need when it is time to write and document your research paper.

You can take notes on notecards or in a computer file. Notecards have the advantage of portability.

NOTE-TAKING DECISIONS FOR LIBRARY AND ELECTRONIC RESEARCH

■ Using the Criteria for Evaluating Sources and Information (**QA Box 50**), decide whether the source is a good one and whether to take notes on it. On every notecard, or in every note you write in a computer file, either copy a quotation (always being sure to enclose it in quotation marks—see **R3.c**) or paraphrase (**R3.d**) or summarize (**R3.e**) the material in your own words. Record the page number(s) of the source material covered by each note. Even if a source does not appear to be useful, record its title and location in your research log, along with a message to yourself about why you rejected it. What seems useless now might have potential if you revise your focus or narrow your topic.

- Decide what to put in your notes. Knowing how to select material for notes comes with experience. Sort major information from minor information as it relates to your topic, leaving out unimportant details but not overlooking important material. When you begin, if you have only a general sense of your topic, read and take notes widely. Stay alert for ways to narrow the topic. Of course, once you have narrowed your topic, you can focus your note-taking however you choose.

- Decide how you are going to differentiate your sources' ideas—recorded in the quotations, paraphrases, and summaries in your notes—from your own ideas and opinions as you read actively and critically (**T1.c**) and think critically (**T2**). Ideas tend to pop in and out of mind during research, so catch them on paper right away. You can use your research log to keep track of your thoughts about the direction and progress of your research. You might record your "response notes" in a different color ink, or you might put them on the back of the relevant notecard, or, if using a computer, you can use boldface type for your response notes.

- Decide how to take notes to avoid plagiarizing your sources. You must use procedures that prevent plagiarism. This matter is so important that **R3** is devoted to it.

Use the following list to make decisions about note-taking for field research.

NOTE-TAKING DECISIONS FOR FIELD RESEARCH

- Decide how you are going to take notes. Ask permission to record an interview; then you can take notes later from the recording. If permission is not granted, take notes as fully as possible without distracting the person. Immediately after the interview, go over your notes to fill in details. For an observation, ask for permission to videotape the event if you have (or can borrow) the equipment, then take notes later from the video. More likely, you will need to take down notes while you observe. If conditions make it impossible to do that (for example, darkness in a performance hall), as soon as you have an opportunity, find a quiet place and write detailed notes.

- Decide what is important in your notes. Because field research conditions can make selective note-taking difficult, go over your notes while your memory is fresh to highlight major categories of information. Again, take the opportunity to fill in details.

- Decide what you must document. Check with your instructor for guidelines. Although your observations, questionnaires, or surveys produce primary data, your instructor may have special requirements. For example, you may be asked to submit your data (such as filled-out questionnaires) with your research paper. Guidelines for documenting performances and interviews appear in **M2**, **A2**, and **A3**.

R3 Using Sources and Avoiding Plagiarism

R3.a Avoiding plagiarism

To **plagiarize** is to present another person's words or ideas as if they were your own. Plagiarism is like stealing. It is a serious offense that can be grounds for failure of a course or expulsion from a college. Plagiarism can be intentional, when you deliberately incorporate other people's work in your own writing without mentioning and documenting the source, or it can be unintentional—but no less serious an offense—if you are unaware of what must be acknowledged and how to document it. All college students are expected to know what plagiarism is and how to avoid it.

What do you *not* have to document? When you write a paper that draws on outside sources, you are not expected to document common knowledge or your own thinking. **Common knowledge** is information that most educated people know, although they might need to remind themselves of certain facts by looking information up in a reference book.

What should you document? Everything that you get from an outside source. Expressing the words or ideas of others in your own words does not release you from the obligation to document.

Your own thinking is what you learn by building on what you already know. You are expected to think about the new material, formulate a thesis, and organize a paper.

You are plagiarizing if you put a source's ideas into your words and pass them off as yours. Similarly, you are plagiarizing if you combine the main ideas of several sources, put them into your own words, and pass that off as yours. Here are practices to help you avoid plagiarism.

- Record complete documentation information. Become thoroughly familiar with the documentation style you are using; see **M1–M2** and **A1–A4**. Make a master list of the documentation facts required for each source, and write down all the facts you need as you go along.

- Use a consistent note-taking system. Always use different colors of ink or a code system to keep three things separate: (1) quotations from a source; (2) material paraphrased or summarized from a source; and (3) your own thoughts triggered by what you are reading. For quotations, always write clear, perhaps oversize, quotation marks that you cannot miss later.

Integrating sources into your writing   R3.b

Analysis and Synthesis

Before trying to integrate sources into your writing, you need both to analyze and to synthesize your material; for a detailed discussion of these important processes, see **T1–T3**. Analysis requires you to break ideas down into their component parts so that you can think them through separately. Do this while reading and reviewing your notes. Synthesis requires you to make connections among different ideas, seeking relationships and connections that tie them together.

Your research paper can be successful only if it reflects your synthesis of the ideas that you are dealing with. To offer a mere recitation of separate ideas is to miss the major requirement of demonstrating your ability to think well. As you quote (**R3.c**), paraphrase (**R3.d**), and summarize (**R3.e**) to integrate sources, remember that these three techniques are not ends in themselves; they are the means of presenting your synthesis of the material.

Using quotations effectively   R3.c

A **quotation** is the exact words of a source enclosed in quotation marks; for more about uses of quotation marks and about setting off quotations, see **P7**.

Conflicting demands confront you when you use quotations in your writing. Although they are useful in providing support, if you use too many quotations, you lose coherence and control of your paper. You want your writing to be coherent and readable, so use quotations sparingly. Generally, if more than a quarter of your paper consists of quotations, you have written what some people call a "scotch tape special." Having too many quotations may give readers—including instructors—the impression that you have not developed your own thinking and are letting other people do your talking.

QA Box 51

GUIDELINES FOR USING QUOTATIONS

1 Use quotations from authorities on your subject to support what you say, not to present your thesis or main points.

2 Select quotations that fit your message.

3 Choose a quotation only if

■ its language is particularly appropriate or distinctive

■ its idea is particularly hard to paraphrase accurately

■ the authority of the source is especially important to support your thesis or main point

■ the source's words are open to interpretation

4 Do not use quotations in more than a quarter of your paper; rely mostly on paraphrase (**R3.d**) and summary (**R3.e**).

5 Quote accurately; always check each quotation against the original source—and then recheck.

6 Mesh quotations smoothly into your writing.

7 Avoid plagiarism; see **R3.a**.

8 Document carefully. Set quotations off with quotation marks (or see **P7.a** for long quotations)—otherwise, you will be plagiarizing.

Making Quotations Mesh with Your Sentences

The greatest risk you take when you use quotations is that you will end up with choppy, incoherent sentences. Such problems arise when the quoted parts do not mesh with the style, grammar, or logic of your prose. Read the material aloud and try to hear whether the language flows smoothly and gracefully.

If you have to add a word or two to a quotation so that it fits with your prose, put the added words in brackets; see **P8.c**. Make sure, however, that your additions do not distort the meaning of the quotation. Similarly, if for the sake of conciseness and focus you delete part of a quotation, indicate the omission with an ellipsis; see **P8.d**. Make sure that the remaining words accurately reflect the source's meaning and that the sentence structure is still correct.

Incoherent	Sommer says personal space for people, "like the porcupines in Schopenhauer's fable, people like to be close enough to obtain warmth and comradeship but far enough away to avoid pricking one another" (26).
Revised	Sommer says people, "like the porcupines in Schopenhauer's fable, . . . like to be close enough to obtain warmth and comradeship but far enough away to avoid pricking one another" (26). [The revision corrects a grammar problem. The ellipsis shows an omission from Sommer's words—in this case, the word *people*—to make a smooth fit between the introductory words and Sommer's words.]

Integrating Author Names and Source Titles

You can make sure that your reader is prepared for a quotation by mentioning the name of the person you are quoting as you introduce a quotation. You might also give the title of the work you are quoting from, if doing so does not seriously interrupt the flow of language. Moreover, if the source is a noteworthy figure, you can give additional authority to your material if you refer to his or her credentials. Here are examples that use author names and source titles effectively.

Source	Binkley, Sue. *The Clockwork Sparrow: Time, Clocks, and Calendars in Biological Organisms.* Englewood Cliffs: Prentice, 1990. [This source information is arranged in MLA documentation style.]
Original material	Artificial lighting, jet travel, and space exploration permit sudden disruptions of natural temporal sequences (4). [These are Binkley's words as written on page 4 in *The Clockwork Sparrow*.]

Integrating Author's Name with the Quotation

* Sue Binkley explains that "artificial lighting, jet travel, and space exploration permit sudden disruptions of natural temporal sequences" (4).

Integrating Author's Name and Title of Source

* Sue Binkley explains in The Clockwork Sparrow that "artificial lighting, jet travel, and space exploration permit sudden disruptions of natural temporal sequences" (4).

Integrating Author's Name, Credentials, and Title of Source

- Sue Binkley, who has researched circadian rhythms for twenty years, explains in <u>The Clockwork Sparrow</u> that "artificial lighting, jet travel, and space exploration permit sudden disruptions of natural temporal sequences" (4).

Integrating Author's Name with an Introductory Analysis

- Sue Binkley, a leading researcher in circadian rhythms who has found our modern life causes many dislocations of biological clocks, explains that "artificial lighting, jet travel, and space exploration permit sudden disruptions of natural temporal sequences" (4).

R3.d Paraphrasing accurately

A paraphrase precisely restates in your words the written or spoken words of someone else.

**QA
Box
52**

GUIDELINES FOR WRITING PARAPHRASES

1 Say what the source says, but no more.

2 Reproduce the source's order of ideas and emphases.

3 Use your own words, phrasing, and sentence structure to restate the message. If some words have only awkward synonyms, quote the original's words—but very sparingly. You can use technical terms used in the original (such as *circadian rhythms*).

4 Read your sentences over to make sure that they do not distort the source's meaning.

5 Expect your material to be as long as, and possibly longer than, the original.

6 Avoid plagiarism; see **R3.a**.

7 Document carefully. You are required to give the source of any paraphrase, just as you do for quotations (**R3.c**) and summaries (**R3.e**).

Select for paraphrase only the passages that carry ideas you need to reproduce in detail. Because paraphrasing calls for a very close approximation of a source, avoid trying to paraphrase whole chapters—or even a whole page.

Source   Morris, Desmond. *Manwatching.* New York: Abrams, 1977: 131. [This source information is arranged in MLA documentation style.]

Original material

Unfortunately, different countries have different ideas about exactly how close is close. It is easy enough to test your own "space reaction": when you are talking to someone in the street or in any open space, reach out with your arm and see where the nearest point on his body comes. If you hail from western Europe, you will find that he is at roughly fingertip distance from you. In other words, as you reach out, your fingertips will just about make contact with his shoulder. If you come from eastern Europe, you will find you are standing at "wrist distance." If you come from the Mediterranean region, you will find that you are much closer to your companion, at little more than "elbow distance."

Unacceptable Paraphrase

- Regrettably, different nations think differently about exactly how close is close. Test yourself: when you are talking to someone in the street or in any open space, stretch your arm out to measure how close that person is to you. If you are from western Europe, you will find that your fingertips will just about make contact with the person's shoulder. If you are from eastern Europe, your wrist will reach the person's shoulder. If you are from the Mediterranean region, you will find that you are much closer to your companion, when your elbow will reach that person's shoulder (Morris 131). [The spotlighted words are plagiarized.]

Acceptable Paraphrase

- People from different nations think that being close means different things. You can easily see what your reaction is to how close to you people stand by reaching out the length of your arm to measure how close someone is as the two of you talk. When people from western Europe stand on the street and talk together, the space between them is the distance it would take one person's fingertips to reach to the other person's shoulder. People from eastern Europe converse at a wrist-to-shoulder distance. People from the Mediterranean, however, prefer an elbow-to-shoulder distance (Morris 131).

The first attempt to paraphrase is not acceptable. All that the writer has done is simply change a few words. What remains is plagiarized because the passage keeps most of the original's language, has the same sentence structure, and uses no quotation marks. The documentation is correct, but its accuracy does not make up for the unacceptable paraphrasing.

The second paraphrase is acceptable. It captures the essence of the original in the student's own words.

In the unacceptable paraphrase below, see if you can find and underline the plagiarized words and phrases before you read the acceptable paraphrase.

Source   Weiss, R. "Safety Gets Short Shrift on Long Night Shift."
                    Science News 21 Jan. 1989: 37.   [This source information
                    is arranged in MLA documentation style.]

Original   In a pilot study of 28 medical interns, Czeisler says he
material   was surprised to find that during the past year more
                    than one-quarter of them had fallen asleep while talking
                    on the telephone. Thirty-four percent reported at least
                    one actual or near-miss automobile accident during the
                    year because of sleepiness—more than triple the
                    percentage they reported in the year before their
                    internship.   [These are Weiss's words as written in "Safety
                    Gets Short Shrift."]

Unacceptable Paraphrase

- Czeisler says he was surprised to find in a
  research project involving 28 medical interns
  during a one-year period over one-quarter had fallen
  asleep talking on the phone, and 34 percent became
  so sleepy that they had or almost had car accidents
  (Weiss 37).

Acceptable Paraphrase

- In a study by Czeisler of 28 medical interns
  observed during late night shifts over a one-year
  period, 25 percent admitted to falling asleep while
  talking on the phone, and 34 percent had at least
  one accident or near accident during that period
  (Weiss 37).

R3.e Summarizing accurately

Summaries differ from paraphrases in one important way: A paraphrase restates the original material completely (**R3.d**), but a summary provides only the main point of the original source and is much shorter. Summarizing is the technique you will probably use most frequently, both for taking notes and for incorporating into your own writing what you have learned from sources.

QA
Box
53

GUIDELINES FOR WRITING SUMMARIES

1 Identify the main points and condense them without losing the essence of the material.

2 Use your own words to condense the message.

3 Keep your summary short.

4 Avoid plagiarizing; see **R3.a**.

5 Document carefully. You are required to give the source of any summary, just as you do for quotations (**R3.c**) and paraphrases (**R3.d**).

Do not be tempted to interpret something the author says or to make some judgment about the value of the argument as you write a summarizing note. Your own opinions do not belong in a summary, but if opinions and other ideas do occur to you, jot them down immediately; see **R2.e** for ideas about how to differentiate your own ideas and opinions from your notes summarizing a source.

Source Coleman, Richard. *Wide Awake at 3:00 A.M.: By Choice or By Chance?* New York: Freeman, 1986: 69.   [This source information is arranged in MLA documentation style.]

Original material An important variable in determining the degree of jet lag is the direction of travel, not whether the flight is outgoing or home-coming. When traveling in a westbound direction, New York to Los Angeles, for example, we must set our wristwatches and biological clocks back by 3 hours because our day has been extended. (If you normally keep to a bedtime of 11:00 P.M. to 7:00 A.M. and upon arrival in Los Angeles you also stay up till 11:00 P.M. local time, you will experience a 27-hour day. Traveling eastbound, Los Angeles to New York, requires setting your watch ahead by 3 hours, or shortening the day to 21 hours.)

Because our internal biological clock naturally gravitates to a 25-hour day, it makes sense that we can more easily adjust to westbound travel, which extends the day. In a series of studies of jet lag, volunteers have been flown back and forth between Europe and the United States (six time zones) to measure cognitive-motor performance, body temperature, and fatigue ratings. When performance before and after the six-time-zone flight was assessed, it was found that the travelers reached their peak performance within two to four days following westbound flight, but required nine days following eastbound travel.

Unacceptable Summary

- The degree of jet lag is related to the direction of travel, westbound travel lengthening the day, which is easier for biological clocks to adjust to, and eastbound travel shortening it, which is harder on biological clocks (Coleman 69).   [The spotlighted words are plagiarized.]

Acceptable Summary

- Eastbound travelers find it harder than westbound travelers to adjust, because traveling east forces people to go to bed before their biological clocks are ready for them to do so (Coleman 69).

! Alert: Be sure not to confuse summarizing with synthesizing; the differences are explained in **T3**. In writing a research paper, you want to use summaries of your sources' ideas and information, but your summaries are only the foundation on which to build your synthesis. A research paper that merely offers summaries does not demonstrate the ability to make the connections among ideas that synthesis demands.

R3.f Using verbs to mesh source material with your sentences

As you work quotations, paraphrases, and summaries into your writing, do so effectively by using verbs from **QA Box 54**, below.

QA Box 54

VERBS USEFUL FOR INTEGRATING QUOTATIONS, PARAPHRASES, AND SUMMARIES

agree	complain	emphasize	note	see
analyze	concede	explain	observe	show
argue	conclude	find	offer	speculate
ask	consider	grant	point out	state
assert	contend	illustrate	refute	suggest
believe	declare	imply	report	suppose
claim	deny	insist	reveal	think
comment	describe	maintain	say	write

R4 Drafting and Revising a Research Paper

DRAFTING and REVISING a research paper have much in common with the writing processes for writing any type of paper. But more is demanded.

- You must demonstrate that you have conducted your research thoroughly.
- You must demonstrate your understanding of the information you have located.
- You must organize for effective presentation.
- You must integrate sources into your writing without PLAGIARIZING, by SYNTHESIZING and by properly using the techniques of quoting, PARAPHRASING, and summarizing; see **R3**.
- You must document your sources; see **M1–M3** and **A1–A4**.

These special demands take extra time for drafting, thinking, redrafting, and rethinking.

Expect to write a number of drafts of your research paper. Successive drafts help you to gain authority over the information you learn from your research. The first draft is your initial chance to discover new insights and fresh connections. Only the act of writing makes such discovery possible.

A first draft is a rough draft, a prelude to your later work of revising, editing, and proofreading. Some researchers work with their notes in front of them. They organize piles of notecards and then use the cards for drafting a thesis statement (see **W1.f**) and for outlining (see **W1.g**). Other researchers quickly write a partial first draft, without using their notes, to get a broad view of their material. They then go back and write a complete first draft with their notes at hand, correcting and inserting information and adding documentation (see **M1–M3** and **A1–A4**).

A second draft results from reading the first draft critically and then revising it. Try to get some distance from your material by taking a break of a few days. Then reread your draft and think how it can be improved. You might also ask other people to read and react to it.

As you work, pay attention to any uneasy feelings you have that hint at the need to rethink or rework your material. Experienced writers expect to revise; they know that writing is really rewriting. As you revise, consult the revision checklists in **QA Box 6** on pages 12–13 to remind yourself of general principles of writing. Also, consult **QA Box 55**, below, the special checklist for revising a research paper.

QA Box 55

REVISION CHECKLIST FOR A RESEARCH PAPER

If the answer to each question is not "yes," you need to revise. The references in parentheses tell you where to find useful information.

1 Does the introductory paragraph lead effectively into the material? **(W4.a)**

2 Are you fulfilling the promise of the thesis statement?

3 Do the ideas follow from one another?

4 Do you stay on the topic?

5 Are important questions answered?

6 Do you avoid bogging the paper down with irrelevant or insignificant information?

7 Do you avoid leaving gaps in information?

8 Have you integrated source material without plagiarizing? **(R3.a)**

9 Have you used quotations, paraphrases, and summaries well? **(R3.c–e)**

10 Does the concluding paragraph end the material effectively? **(W4.g)**

A final draft shows that you have revised well. It shows also that you have edited and proofread for correct grammar, spelling, and punctuation; see **W3**. No amount of careful research and good writing can make up for a sloppy manuscript. If any page is messy with corrections, redo it.

For a sample student research paper in MLA documentation style, see **M3.b**. For guidelines on preparing a typed copy of a research paper using MLA documentation style, see **M3.a**.

MLA
Documentation

Print
Sources

Parenthetical references

In-text
citations

Works Cited list

Electronic sources

BOOKS

M MLA DOCUMENTATION

M1 MLA In-Text Citations

One of the documentation styles frequently used in the humanities was developed by the Modern Language Association (MLA). In MLA style, you are expected to document your sources in two separate, equally important ways:

1 Within the body of the paper, use in-text citations, as described in this chapter.

2 At the end of the paper, provide a list of sources titled Works Cited; as described in **M2**.

Citing sources in the body of a paper in MLA style M1.a

In-text citations are information that is included in the sentences or in parenthetical references within the paper, both to signal material used from outside sources and to enable readers to locate the original sources. In-text citations function with Works Cited, an alphabetical list at the end of the paper containing full information about the sources that have been quoted from (see **R3.c**), paraphrased (see **R3.d**), or summarized (see **R3.e**).

In most in-text citations, a name or a title usually identifies a source, and page numbers usually show the exact location in that source. In general, put page number information in parentheses at the end of a quotation or paraphrase. Try to introduce names of authors and titles of sources in your own sentences, where they become part of the flow of your writing.

Citations of Paraphrases

- People from the Mediterranean prefer an elbow-to-shoulder distance from each other (Morris 131).   [Name and page numbers cited in parentheses]

- Desmond Morris notes that people from the Mediterranean prefer an elbow-to-shoulder distance from each other (131). [Name cited in text, page number cited in parentheses]

Also see **R3.c** on incorporating names, titles, and other information in your sentences to establish the authority of your sources.

A parenthetical reference belongs at the end of the material it refers to, usually at the end of a sentence. If you are citing a quotation enclosed in quotation marks, place the parentheses after the closing quotation mark but before sentence-ending punctuation.

- Binkley claims that artificial light reduced SAD-related "depression in 87 percent of patients . . . within a few days; relapses followed" (203–04) when light treatment ended.

- Research shows that "the number, rate, and direction of time-zone changes are the critical factors in determining the extent and degree of jet lag symptoms" (Coleman 67).

Place a parenthetical reference for a long quotation (one that you set off from your own sentences with indentation—see **P7.a**) outside the punctuation ending the last sentence; for an example, see a student's research paper in **M3.b**.

M1.b Citing specific sources in MLA style

The examples in this section show how to handle various types of citations in the body of your paper. Many of these examples show parenthetical citations so that you will know how to do them, but remember that you usually can—and should—give names and titles in your own sentences.

One Author—MLA

All the examples in **M1.a** showed citations of works by one author. Notice that no punctuation separates the author's name from the page number in parenthetical citations.

Two or Three Authors—MLA

Give authors' names (order and spelling) as they appear on the book (title page) or article. Spell out the word *and*.

- As children get older, they become more aware of standards for personal space (Worchel and Cooper 536).

More Than Three Authors—MLA

For a book by more than three authors, you can name all authors, or you can use the first author's name only, followed by *et al.*, either in a parenthetical reference or in your sentence.

- Fisher et al. have found that personal space gets larger or smaller depending on the circumstances of the social interaction (158).

- Personal space gets larger or smaller depending on the circumstances of the social interaction (Fisher et al. 158).

More Than One Source by an Author—MLA

When you use two or more sources by the same author, include the relevant title in each citation. In parenthetical citations, use a shortened version of the title. For a paper using as sources Edward T. Hall's *The Hidden Dimension* and "Learning the Arabs' Silent Language," parenthetical citations would be *Hidden* and "Learning." Shorten the titles as much as you can without making them ambiguous to readers, and start with the word by which the work is alphabetized in Works Cited. Separate the name and title with a comma, but do not use punctuation between the title and page number.

- Most people are unaware that interpersonal distances exist and contribute to people's reactions to one another (Hall, Hidden 109).

- Arabs know the practicality of close conversational distances (Hall, "Learning" 41).

When you incorporate the title into your own sentences, you can omit a subtitle but do not shorten more than that.

Two or More Authors with the Same Last Name—MLA

Use each author's first initial and full last name in each parenthical citation. In your sentences you can use either the first initial or full first name. If both authors have the same first initial, use the full name in all instances.

- According to British zoologist Desmond Morris, conversational distances vary between people from different countries (131). If an American backs away from an Arab, the American is considered cold, the Arab pushy (C. Morris 516).

Group or Corporate Author—MLA

When a corporation or other group is named as the author of a source you want to cite, use the corporate name just as you would an individual's name.

- In a five-year study, the Boston Women's Health Collective reported that these tests are usually unreliable (11).

- A five-year study shows that these tests are usually unreliable (Boston Women's Health Collective 11).

Work Cited by Title—MLA

If no author is named, use the title in citations; shorten it for parenthetical citations but always make the first word the one by which you alphabetize it. The following citation is to an article titled "Are You a Day or Night Person?"

- The "morning lark" and "night owl" connotations typically are used to categorize the human extremes ("Are You" 11).

Multivolume Work—MLA

If you use more than one volume of a multivolume work, include the relevant volume number in each citation. Separate the volume number and page number with a colon followed by a space.

- Although Amazon forest dwellers had been exposed to these viruses by 1900 (<u>Rand</u> 3: 202), Borneo forest dwellers escaped them until the 1960s (<u>Rand</u> 1: 543).

Novel, Play, Poem—MLA

Often when you cite literary works, you can give location information that is more useful than page numbers. Unlike page numbers, part, chapter, act, scene, canto, stanza, or line numbers do not change no matter where the work appears. Unless your instructor tells you not to, use arabic numerals for these references, even if the literary work uses roman numerals (except for lowercase roman numerals used for pages of a preface or other front matter in a book).

If a novel has parts and/or chapters, give these after the page numbers. Use a semicolon after the page number but a comma to separate a part from a chapter.

- Flannery O'Connor describes one character in <u>The Violent Bear It Away</u> as "[seeing] himself divided in two--a violent and a rational self" (139; pt. 2, ch. 6).

For plays, give act, scene, and/or line numbers if they are used. Use periods between these numbers.

- Among the most quoted of Shakespeare's lines is Hamlet's soliloquy beginning "To be, or not to be: that is the question" (3.1.56).

For poems and plays, give canto, stanza, and/or line numbers. Use periods between these numbers.

- In "To Autumn," Keats's most melancholy image occurs in the lines "Then in a wailful choir the small gnats mourn / Among the river swallows" (3.27–28).

Work in an Anthology or Other Collection—MLA

You may want to cite a work you have read in a book that contains many works by various authors and that was compiled, written, or edited by someone other than the person you are citing. For example, suppose you want to cite "When in Rome" by Mari Evans, which you have read in a literature text by Pamela Annas and Robert Rosen. Use Evans's name and the title of her work in the in-text citation and as the first information for the entry in the Works Cited list.

> ◆ In "When in Rome," Mari Evans uses parentheses to enclose lines expressing the houseworker's thoughts as her employer offers lunch, as in the first stanza's "(an egg / or soup / . . . there ain't no meat)" (688–89).

Indirect Source—MLA

When you want to quote words that you found quoted in someone else's work, put the name of the person whose words you are quoting into your own sentence. Indicate the work where you found the quotation either in your sentence or in a parenthetical citation beginning with "qtd. in."

> • Martin Scorsese acknowledges the link between himself and his films: "I realize that all my life, I've been an outsider. I splatter bits of myself all over the screen" (qtd. in Giannetti and Eyman 397).
>
> • Giannetti and Eyman quote Martin Scorsese as acknowledging the link between himself and his films: "I realize that all my life, I've been an outsider. I splatter bits of myself all over the screen" (397).

Two or More Sources in One Reference—MLA

If more than one source has contributed to an idea, opinion, or fact in your paper, cite them all. In a parenthetical citation, separate each block of information with a semicolon. You can also use a footnote or an endnote to cite several sources; see **M1.c.**

> • Once researchers agreed that these cultural "distance zones" existed, their next step was to try to measure or define them (Hall 110–20; Henley 32–33; Fisher, Bell, and Baum 153).

An Entire Work—MLA

References to an entire work usually fit best into your own sentences.

> • In <u>The Clockwork Sparrow</u>, Sue Binkley analyzes studies of circadian rhythms undertaken between 1967 and 1989.

An Electronic Source with a Name or Title and Page Numbers—MLA

The principles that govern in-text citations of electronic sources are exactly the same as the ones that apply to books, articles, letters, interviews, or any other information source. When an electronically accessed source identifies its author, use the author's name for in-text citations. If no author is named, use the title of the source for in-text citations and for the first block of information in that source's Works Cited entry. When an electronic source has page numbers, use them exactly as you would the page numbers of a print source.

An Electronic Source with Paragraph Numbers—MLA

When an electronic source has numbered paragraphs instead of page numbers, use them for in-text references as you would page numbers, with two differences: (1) Use a comma followed by one space after the name (or title); and (2) use the abbreviation *par.* for a reference to one paragraph or *pars.* for a reference to more than one paragraph, followed by the paragraph number(s).

- Coleman worried that psychoanalysis might destroy his musical creativity (Francis, pars. 3–7).

An Electronic Source Without Page or Paragraph Numbers—MLA

Many online sources do not number pages or paragraphs. In the Works Cited entry for such a source, include the abbreviation *n. pag.* ("no pagination"). This abbreviation serves to explain to readers why in-text references to this source do not cite page numbers.

- From March to April in 1997, violations of this important environmental regulation increased 123 percent (Procope).

M1.c Using content or bibliographic notes in MLA style

In MLA style, footnotes or endnotes serve two specific purposes: (1) You can use them for commentary that does not fit into your paper but is still worth relating; and (2) you can use them for extensive bibliographic information that would intrude if you were to include it in your text.

Text of Paper

- Eudora Welty's literary biography, <u>One Writer's Beginnings</u>, shows us how both the inner world of self and the outer world of family and place form a writer's imagination.[1]

Commentary Endnote

- [1]Welty, who values her privacy, has resisted
  investigation of her life. However, at the age of
  74, she chose to present her own autobiographical
  reflections in a series of lectures at Harvard
  University.

Text of Paper

- Barbara Randolph believes that enthusiasm
  is contagious (65).[1] Many psychologists have
  found that panic, fear, and rage spread more
  quickly in crowds than positive emotions do,
  however.

Bibliographic Endnote

- [1] Others agree with Randolph. See Thurman 21, 84,
  155; Kelley 421–25; and Brookes 65–76.

See **M3.a** for advice about formatting notes.

M2 MLA Documentation for a Works Cited List

In MLA documentation, in-text citations work together with a list of
all the sources you have referred to in your paper. In this Works Cited
list, include only the sources from which you quote or paraphrase or
summarize. Do not include sources that you have consulted but do
not refer to in the paper. **QA Box 56** on pages 200–202 gives general
information about a Works Cited list, and the rest of this chapter gives
models of specific kinds of Works Cited entries.

M2.a Understanding details about a Works Cited list

QA Box 56

Compiling a Works Cited list in MLA style

TITLE

Works Cited

PLACEMENT OF LIST

Start a new page, numbered sequentially after Notes pages, if any.

CONTENTS AND FORMAT

Include all sources quoted from, paraphrased, or summarized in your paper. Start each entry on a new line at the regular left margin. If the entry uses more than one line, indent all the other lines five spaces or one-half inch from the left margin. Double-space all lines.

SPACING AFTER PUNCTUATION

Examples in the 1995 (fourth) edition of the *MLA Handbook* show only one space after a period ending an information unit, a change from the two spaces called for in earlier editions. Do not leave space after a period within an abbreviation (for example, *n.d.*). Put one space after a colon, semicolon, or comma.

ARRANGEMENT OF ENTRIES

Alphabetize by author's last name. If no author is named, alphabetize by the title's first significant word (not *A*, *An*, or *The*).

AUTHORS' NAMES

Use first names and middle initials, if any, as well as last names. For one author or for the first-named author in multiauthor works, reverse the name. Use the word *and* with two or more authors. Give names in the order used on the title page. Use a comma between the first author's last and first names and after each complete author name except the last. After the last author name, use a period.

CAPITALIZATION OF TITLES

Capitalize all major words in titles. Also see the Capitalization Alert in M3.a.

SPECIAL TREATMENT OF TITLES

Use quotation marks around titles of poems, short stories, essays, articles. Underline titles of books and names of newspapers or journals. Use either <u>an unbroken line</u> or <u>a broken line</u>, <u>like this</u>, but not both styles.

When a book title includes the title of another work that is usually underlined (such as a novel, play, or long poem), do not underline the incorporated title. If the incorporated title is usually enclosed in quotation marks (such as a short story or short poem), keep the quotation marks and underline the complete title of the book.

Drop *A*, *An*, or *The* as the first word of a periodical title.

Continued on next page

➤ QA Box 56, continued from previous page

PLACE OF PUBLICATION
If several cities are listed for the place of publication, give only the first. If a state name is needed because the U.S. city name alone would be ambiguous, use the state's two-letter postal abbreviation. For an unfamiliar city outside the United States, include an abbreviated country name or an abbreviated Canadian province name.

PUBLISHER
Use shortened names as long as they are clear: *Prentice* for *Prentice Hall*, *Simon* for *Simon & Schuster*. Use *UP* for *University Press: Oxford UP* for *Oxford University Press; U of Chicago P* for *University of Chicago Press*.

PUBLICATION MONTH ABBREVIATIONS
Abbreviate all publication months except May, June, and July. Use the first three letters followed by a period: *Dec., Feb., Sep.* (or *Sept.*)

INCLUSIVE PAGE NUMBERS
Inclusive page numbers give the starting page number and the ending page number of any print source that is part of a longer work (for example, a chapter in a book, an article in a journal). Inclusive page numbers signal that the cited work is on those pages and all pages in between. If that is not the case, use the style shown below for discontinuous page numbers. In either case, give numerals only, without the words *page* or *pages* or the abbreviations *p.* or *pp.*

Use the full second number through 99. Then use only the last two digits for the second number unless unclear: *103–04* is clear, but *567–602* requires full numbers.

DISCONTINUOUS PAGES
Use the starting page number followed by a plus sign (+): *32+.*

PARAGRAPH NUMBERS IN ELECTRONIC SOURCES
For electronic sources that number paragraphs instead of pages, give the total number of paragraphs followed by the abbreviation *pars.: 77 pars.*

WORKS CITED ENTRIES: BOOKS
Citations for books have three main parts: author, title, and publication information (place of publication, publisher, and date of publication).

AUTHOR	TITLE	PUBLICATION INFORMATION

Didion, Joan. <u>A Book of Common Prayer</u>. New York: Simon,

1983.

WORKS CITED ENTRIES: ARTICLES
Citations for periodical articles contain three major parts: author, title of article, and publication information (usually the periodical title, volume number, year of publication, and inclusive page numbers).

Continued on next page

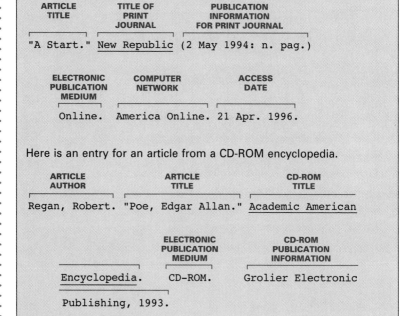

➤ QA Box 56, continued from previous page

AUTHOR   TITLE

Shuter, Robert. "A Field Study of Nonverbal Communication

in Germany, Italy, and the United States."

PUBLICATION INFORMATION

Communication Monographs 44(1977): 298–305.

WORKS CITED ENTRIES: ELECTRONIC SOURCES

Citations for electronic sources in databases contain at least six major parts: author, publication information, title of database, publication medium, name of vendor or computer service, electronic publication date or access date. Electronic versions of sources that also appear in print start with information about the print version. Here is an entry for a journal article with a print version, accessed through America Online. For other online sources, see pages 214-15 and 358.

ARTICLE TITLE	TITLE OF PRINT JOURNAL	PUBLICATION INFORMATION FOR PRINT JOURNAL

"A Start." New Republic (2 May 1994: n. pag.)

ELECTRONIC PUBLICATION MEDIUM	COMPUTER NETWORK	ACCESS DATE

Online. America Online. 21 Apr. 1996.

Here is an entry for an article from a CD-ROM encyclopedia.

ARTICLE AUTHOR	ARTICLE TITLE	CD-ROM TITLE

Regan, Robert. "Poe, Edgar Allan." Academic American

	ELECTRONIC PUBLICATION MEDIUM	CD-ROM PUBLICATION INFORMATION

Encyclopedia. CD-ROM. Grolier Electronic

Publishing, 1993.

M2.b Using sample Works Cited models in MLA style █

The directory on the following page is a numbered list corresponding to the examples that follow the directory. Not every possible documentation model is here. You may find that you have to combine features of models to document a particular source. You will also find information in *MLA Handbook for Writers of Research Papers*, 4th Edition, by Joseph Gibaldi, and at <http://www.mla.org/set_stl.htm>.

DIRECTORY—MLA WORKS CITED

Nonprint Sources

Electronic Sources

Print Sources

1 Book by One Author—MLA

Welty, Eudora. <u>One Writer's Beginnings</u>. Cambridge: Harvard
UP, 1984.

2 Book by Two or Three Authors—MLA

Leghorn, Lisa, and Katherine Parker. <u>Woman's Worth</u>.
Boston: Routledge, 1981.

Kelly, Alfred H., Winfred A. Harbison, and Herman Belz.
<u>The American Constitution: Its Origins and
Development</u>. New York: Norton, 1983.

3 Book by More Than Three Authors—MLA

Moore, Mark H., et al. <u>Dangerous Offenders: The Elusive
Target of Justice</u>. Cambridge: Harvard UP, 1984.

Give only the first author's name, followed by a comma and the
phrase *et al.* ("and others").

4 Two or More Works by the Same Author(s)—MLA

Morris, Desmond. <u>Manwatching: A Field Guide to Human Behavior</u>. New York: Abrams, 1977.

---, ed. <u>Primate Ethology</u>. London: Wiedenfeld, 1967.

Give author name(s) in the first entry only. In the second and subsequent entries, use three hyphens and a period to stand for exactly the same name(s). If the person served as editor or translator, put a comma and the appropriate abbreviation (*ed.* or *trans.*) following the three hyphens. Arrange the works in alphabetical (not chronological) order according to book title, ignoring labels such as *ed.* or *trans.*

5 Book by Group or Corporate Author—MLA

The Boston Women's Health Collective. <u>Our Bodies, Ourselves</u>. New York: Simon, 1986.

American Psychological Association. <u>Publication Manual of the American Psychological Association</u>. 4th ed. Washington: APA, 1994.

Cite the full name of the corporate author first. When a corporate author is also the publisher, use a shortened form of the corporate name at the publisher position.

6 Book with No Author Named—MLA

<u>The Chicago Manual of Style</u>. 14th ed. Chicago: U of Chicago P, 1993.

If there is no author's name on the title page, begin the citation with the title. Alphabetize the entry according to the first significant word of the title (*Chicago*, not *The*).

7 Book with an Author and an Editor—MLA

If your paper refers to the work of the book's author, put the author's name first. If your paper refers to the work of the editor, put the editor's name first.

Brontë, Emily. <u>Wuthering Heights</u>. Ed. David Daiches. London: Penguin, 1985.

David Daiches, ed. <u>Wuthering Heights</u>. By Emily Brontë. London: Penguin, 1985.

8 Translation—MLA

Freire, Paulo. <u>Pedagogy of the Oppressed</u>. Trans. Myra Bergman Ramos. New York: Seabury, 1970.

9 Work in Several Volumes or Parts—MLA

Jones, Ernest. <u>The Last Phase</u>. New York: Basic, 1957. Vol.
    3 of The Life and Work of Sigmund Freud. 3 vols.

If you are citing only one volume, put the volume number before the publication information. If you wish, you can give the total number of volumes at the end of the entry.

Randall, John Herman, Jr. <u>The Career of Philosophy</u>. Vol.
    1. New York: Columbia UP, 1962. 2 vols.

MLA recommends using arabic numerals, even if the source uses roman numerals (*Vol. 6* for *Vol. VI*).

10 One Selection from an Anthology or an Edited Book—MLA

Galarza, Ernest. "The Roots of Migration." <u>Aztlan: An</u>
    <u>Anthology of Mexican American Literature</u>. Ed. Luis
    Valdez and Stan Steiner. New York: Knopf, 1972.
    127–132.

Give the author and title of the selection first and then the full title of the anthology. Information about the editor starts with *Ed.* (for "Edited by," so do not use *Eds.* when there is more than one editor). Give the name(s) of the editor(s) in normal order rather than reversing first and last name.

11 More Than One Selection from the Same Anthology or Edited Book—MLA

Gilbert, Sandra M., and Susan Gubar, eds. <u>The Norton</u>
    <u>Anthology of Literature by Women</u>. New York: Norton,
    1985.

Kingston, Maxine Hong. "No Name Woman." Gilbert and Gubar
    2337–47.

If you cite more than one selection from the same anthology, you can list the anthology as a separate entry with all the publication information. Then, list each selection from the anthology by author and title of the selection, but give only the name of the editor(s) of the anthology and the page number(s) of the selection. Here *ed.* stands for "editor," so use *eds.* if more than one editor is named.

12 Signed Article in a Reference Book—MLA

Holt, Robert R. "Freud, Sigmund." <u>International</u>
    <u>Encyclopedia of the Social Sciences</u>. Ed. David L.
    Sills. 18 vols. New York: Macmillan, 1968.

If the articles in the book are alphabetically arranged, omit volume and page numbers. If the reference book is frequently revised, give only the edition and year of publication.

13 Unsigned Article in a Reference Book—MLA

"Ireland." <u>Encyclopaedia Britannica</u>. 1974 ed.

If you are citing a widely used reference work, do not give full publication information. Instead, give only the edition and year of publication.

14 Edition—MLA

Gibaldi, Joseph, and Walter S. Achtert. <u>MLA Handbook for
    Writers of Research Papers</u>. 3rd ed. New York: MLA,
    1988.

If a book is not a first edition, the edition number is on the title page. Place the abbreviated information (*2nd ed., 3rd ed.*, etc.) between the title and the publication information. Give only the latest copyright date for the edition you are using.

15 Anthology or Edited Book—MLA

Valdez, Luis, and Stan Steiner, eds. <u>Aztlan: An Anthology
    of Mexican American Literature</u>. New York: Knopf,
    1972.

Unlike item 10, *ed.* stands for "editor" here, so use *eds.* when more than one editor is named; also see items 10 and 11.

16 Introduction, Preface, Foreword, or Afterword—MLA

Angeli, Primo. Foreword. <u>Shopping Bag Design 2: Creative
    Promotional Graphics</u>. By Judi Radice. New York:
    Library of Applied Design-PBC International, Inc.,
    1991. 8.

Give first the name of the writer of the part you are citing, then the name of the cited part, capitalized but not underlined or in quotation marks. If the author of the book is someone different from the writer of the cited material, after the book title put *By* and the book author's name. After the publication information, give inclusive page numbers for the cited part, using roman or arabic numerals as the source does.

17 Unpublished Dissertation or Essay—MLA

Geissinger, Shirley Burry. "Openness versus Secrecy in
    Adoptive Parenthood." Diss. U. of North Carolina at
    Greensboro, 1984.

State the author's name first, then the title in quotation marks (not underlined), then a descriptive label (such as *Diss.* or *Unpublished essay*), then the degree-granting institution (for dissertations), and finally the date.

18 Reprint of an Older Book—MLA

Hurston, Zora Neale. <u>Their Eyes Were Watching God</u>. 1937.
    Urbana: U of Illinois P, 1978.

Republishing information can be found on the copyright page. Give the date of the original version before the publication information for the version you are citing.

19 Book in a Series—MLA

McClave, Heather. <u>Women Writers of the Short Story</u>.
    Twentieth Century Views Ser. Englewood Cliffs:
    Prentice, 1980.

20 Book with a Title Within a Title—MLA

Lumiansky, Robert M., and Herschel Baker, eds. <u>Critical
    Approaches to Six Major English Works</u>: Beowulf
    <u>Through</u> Paradise Lost. Philadelphia: U of
    Pennsylvania P, 1968.

21 Government Publication—MLA

United States. Cong. House Committee on the Judiciary.
    <u>Immigration and Nationality with Amendments and Notes
    on Related Laws</u>. 7th ed. Washington: GPO, 1980.

For government publications that name no author, start with the name of the government or governmental body. Then name the government agency. *GPO* is a standard abbreviation for *Government Printing Office,* the publisher of most U.S. government publications.

22 Published Proceedings of a Conference—MLA

Harris, Diana, and Laurie Nelson-Heern, eds. <u>Proceedings
    of NECC 1981</u>: <u>National Education Computing
    Conference</u>. 17–19 June 1981. Iowa City: Weeg
    Computing Center, U of Iowa, 1981.

23 Article from a Daily Newspaper—MLA

Dullea, Georgia. "Literary Folk Look for Solid Comfort."
    <u>New York Times</u> 16 Apr. 1986: C14.

"Fire Delays School Election." <u>Patriot Ledger</u> [Quincy, MA]
    14 June 1994: A1.

Omit *A* or *The* as the first word in a newspaper title. If the city of publication is not part of the title, put it in square brackets after the title, not underlined. Give the day, month, and year of the issue. If sections are designated, give the section letter as well as the page number. If an article runs on nonconsecutive pages, give the starting page number followed by a plus sign (for example, *23+* for an article that starts on 23 and continues on 42).

24 Editorial, Letter to the Editor, Review—MLA

"Facing Space, After the Cold War." Editorial. New York
    Times 1 May 1989: A16.

Childress, Glenda Teal. Letter. Newsweek 9 June 1986: 10.

Linebaugh, Peter. "In the Flight Path of Perry Anderson."
    Rev. of In the Tracks of Historical Materialism,
    by Perry Anderson. History Workshop 21 (1986):
    141—46.

25 Unsigned Article from a Daily Newspaper—MLA

"Hospitals, Competing for Scarce Patients, Turn to
    Advertising." New York Times 20 Apr. 1986: 47.

26 Article from a Weekly or Biweekly Magazine or Newspaper—MLA

Toufexis, Anastasia. "Dining with Invisible Danger." Time
    27 Mar. 1989: 28.

27 Article in a Monthly or Bimonthly Periodical—MLA

Roosevelt, Anna. "Lost Civilizations of the Lower Amazon."
    Natural History Feb. 1989: 74—83.

28 Unsigned Article from a Weekly or Monthly Periodical—MLA

"A Salute to Everyday Heroes." Time 10 July 1989: 46+.

29 Article from a Collection of Reprinted Articles—MLA

Curver, Phillip C. "Lighting in the 21st Century."
    Futurist Jan./Feb. 1989: 29—34. Ed. Eleanor
    Goldstein. Vol. 4. Boca Raton: SIRS, 1990.
    Art. 84.

Give the citation for the original publication first, followed by the citation for the collection.

30 Article in a Journal with Continuous Pagination—MLA

Cochran, D. D., W. Daniel Hale, and Christine P.
    Hissam. "Personal Space Requirements in Indoor
    versus Outdoor Locations." Journal of Psychology
    117 (1984): 132—33.

(If the first issue of a journal with continuous pagination ends on page 228, the second issue starts with page 229.) Give only the volume number before the year. Use arabic numerals for all numbers.

31 Article in a Journal That Pages Each Issue Separately—MLA

Hashimoto, Irvin. "Pain and Suffering: Apostrophes and
Academic Life." <u>Journal of Basic Writing</u> 7.2 (1988):
91–98.

When each issue begins with page 1, give both the volume number
(here, 7) and the issue number (here, 2), separated by a period.

32 Published and Unpublished Letters—MLA

Lapidus, Jackie. Letter to her mother. 12 Nov. 1975.
<u>Between Ourselves: Letters Between Mothers &</u>
<u>Daughters</u>. Ed. Karen Payne. Boston: Houghton, 1983.
323–26.

Brown, Theodore. Letter to the author. 13 June 1988.

33 Map, Chart—MLA

<u>The Caribbean & South America</u>. Map. Falls Church: AAA,
1992.

Nonprint Sources

34 Interview—MLA

Friedman, Randi. Telephone interview. 30 June 1997.

For a face-to-face interview, use *Personal interview* in place of *Telephone interview*.

35 Lecture, Speech, Address—MLA

Kennedy, John Fitzgerald. Address. Greater Houston
Ministerial Association. Houston. 12 Sept. 1960.

36 Film, Videotape—MLA

<u>Erendira</u>. By Gabriel García Marquez. Dir. Ruy Guerra. With
Irene Pappas. Miramax, 1984.

Give the title first and include the director, the distributor, and the
year. Other information (writer, producer, major actors) is optional
but helpful. Put first names first.

37 Recording—MLA

Smetana, Bedrich. <u>My Country</u>. Cond. Karel Anserl. Czech
Philharmonic Orch. LP. Vanguard, 1975.

Springsteen, Bruce. "Local Hero." <u>Lucky Town</u>. Columbia,
1992.

Put first the name most relevant to what you discuss in your paper
(performer, conductor, the work performed, etc.). Include the record-

ing's title, the medium for any recording other than a CD (e.g., LP, Audiocassette), name of the issuer (e.g., Vanguard), and the year.

38 Live Performance—MLA

The Real Thing. By Tom Stoppard. Dir. Mike Nichols. Perf. Jeremy Irons and Glenn Close. Plymouth Theatre, New York. 3 June 1984.

Put first the information most relevant to your paper.

39 Work of Art or Musical Composition—MLA

Cassatt, Mary. La Toilette. Art Institute of Chicago, Chicago.

Schubert, Franz. Symphony no. 8 in B minor.

Schubert, Franz. Unfinished Symphony.

Do not underline or put in quotation marks music identified only by form, number, and key, but do underline any work that has a title, such as an opera or ballet or the title name of a symphony.

40 Radio or Television Program—MLA

The Little Sister. Writ. and dir. Jan Egleson. Perf. Tracy Pollan and John Savage. Prod. Rebecca Eaton. American Playhouse. PBS. WGBH, Boston. 7 Apr. 1986.

Include at least the title of the program (underlined), the network, the local station and its city, and the date of the broadcast. For a series, also supply the title of the specific episode (in quotation marks) before the title of the program (underlined) and the title of the series (neither underlined nor in quotation marks).

41 Microfiche Collection of Articles—MLA

Wenzell, Ron. "Businesses Prepare for a More Diverse Work Force." St. Louis Post Dispatch 3 Feb. 1990. Newsbank: Employment 27 (1990): fiche 2, grid D12.

Electronic Sources

According to the 1995 edition of the *MLA Handbook for Writers of Research*, the following basic blocks of information are used to document an electronic source in MLA style. A period ends each block.

1. Documentation information about the print version, if any. (Many sources accessed electronically also exist in published, print versions. Others exist only in electronic form.) Follow the models in directory items 1–33 above for print sources. You may not find all the details about a print version in an

electronic version, but provide as much information as you can. Information about a print version usually is given at the beginning or the end of an electronic document.

2 Author (if any) and title (underlined) of the electronic source or database. If there is no print version, start your Works Cited entry with this information.

3 Electronic medium, such as CD-ROM, Diskette, Magnetic tape, Online (capitalized as shown here).

4 Name of the producer (for "portable" sources such as CD-ROMs and diskettes) or computer network or service (for online sources).

5 Publication date (for portable sources) or date of access (for online sources).

Compare items 42 and 43, which show Works Cited entries for the same abstract from *Psychological Abstracts* (a source with a print version). Item 42 documents the abstract accessed via a CD-ROM database named PsycLIT, and item 43 documents access via an online database named PsycINFO.

42 CD-ROM Database: Abstract with a Print Version—MLA

```
Marcus, Hazel R., and Shinobu Kitayamo. "Culture
     and the Self: Implications for Cognition, Emotion,
     and Motivation." Psychological Abstracts 78
     (1991): item 23878. PsycLIT. CD-ROM. SilverPlatter.
     Sept. 1991.
```

All the information through item 23878 is for the print version of this source. The volume number is 78, and the abstract's number is 23878. All the information from PsycLIT to the end of the entry is for the electronic version of the source. PsycLIT is the name of the CD-ROM database, and SilverPlatter is the name of the producer of the CD-ROM. The CD-ROM was issued in September 1991.

43 Online Database: Abstract with a Print Version—MLA

```
Marcus, Hazel R., and Shinobu Kitayamo. "Culture and the
     Self: Implications for Cognition, Emotion, and
     Motivation." Psychological Abstracts 78 (1991): item
     23878. PsycINFO. Online. Dialog. 10 Oct. 1991.
```

This entry is for the same abstract from *Psychological Abstracts* shown in item 42 but accessed online. This model notes PsycINFO, the name of the online database, where item 42 notes PsycLIT, the name of the CD-ROM database; it notes Online where item 42 notes CD-ROM; and it notes Dialog, the computer service through which PsycINFO was accessed, where item 42 notes the CD-ROM producer SilverPlatter. The last information unit—10 Oct. 1991—is the access date.

44 CD-ROM: Article from a Periodical with a Print Version—MLA

"The Price Is Right." <u>Time</u>. 20 Jan. 1992: 38. <u>Time</u>
<u>Man of the Year</u>. CD-ROM. Compact Publishing, Inc.
1993.

Information for the print version ends with the article's page number, 38. The title of the CD-ROM is *Time Man of the Year*, its producer is Compact Publishing, Inc., and its copyright year is 1993. Both the title of the print publication and the title of the CD-ROM are underlined.

45 CD-ROM: Selection from a Book with a Print Version—MLA

"Prehistoric Humans: Earliest Homo Sapiens." <u>The Guinness</u>
<u>Book of Records 1994</u>. Guinness Publishing, Ltd.,
1994.

<u>The Guinness Multimedia Disk of Records</u>, 1994 Edition.
Version 2.0. CD-ROM. Grolier Electronic Publishing.
1994.

Version 2.0 signals that this CD-ROM is updated periodically; the producer changes version numbers rather than giving update dates.

46 CD-ROM: Material with No Print Version—MLA

Wick, James, and Dave Jackson. <u>Wayzata World Factbook</u>,
1993 Edition. CD-ROM. Wayzata Technology, 1992.

"Spanish Dance." <u>Encarta 1994</u>. CD-ROM. Redmond, WA:
Microsoft, 1993.

Encarta is a CD-ROM encyclopedia with no print version. "Spanish Dance" is the title of an article in *Encarta 1994*.

47 Work in More Than One Publication Medium—MLA

Clarke, David James. <u>Novell's CNE Study Guide</u>. Book.
<u>Network Support Encyclopedia</u>. CD-ROM. Alameda: Sybex,
1994.

This book and CD-ROM come together. Each has its own title, but the publication information—Alameda: Sybex, 1994—applies to both.

48 Online: Article from a Periodical with a Print Version—MLA

Kapor, Mitchell, and Jerry Berman. "A Superhighway Through
the Wasteland?" <u>New York Times</u>. 24 Nov. 1993: Op-ed
page. <u>New York Times Online</u>. Online. AOL. 5 May
1995.

Information applying to the print version of this article in the *New York Times* ends with Op-ed page, and information about the electronic version starts with the title of the database, New York Times Online. Online is the publication medium, AOL stands for America Online, the computer service through which the database was accessed, and 5 May 1995 is the access date.

```
"Homeowners Insurance." Consumer Reports. October 1993: n.
     pag. Online. CompuServe. 5 May 1995.
```

When an online source does not show page numbers even though a source has a print version, put *n. pag.* (meaning "no pagination") at the end of the information about the print version. This abbreviation in a Works Cited entry explains why there are no page references to this source in a paper.

49 Online: Material with No Print Version—MLA

```
"Microsoft Licenses OSM Technology from Henter-Joyce."
     WinNews Electronic Newsletter. 2:6 (1 May 1995): n.
     pag. Online. CompuServe. 15 May 1995.
```

The designation *2:6* indicates volume 2, number 6 of this electronic newsletter.

50 Online: An Electronic Text—MLA—New

```
"Athenian-Spartan Rivalry." Academic American Encyclopedia.
     Online. CompuServe 3 Feb. 1995.
Heredotus. The History of Heredotus. Trans. George
     Rawlinson. The InternetClassics Archive. Ed. Daniel
     C. Stevenson. 11 Jan. 1998. Massachusetts Institute
     of Technology. 17 Jan. 1998
     <http://classics.mit.edu/Heredotus/history.sum.html>.
```

The model above for the electronic text The History of Heredotus shows the new style MLA authorizes for documenting online sources with URLs (Universal Resource Locators, or direct Internet "addresses"). These new guidelines from MLA cover sources you find on the World Wide Web, at gopher and ftp sites, in listservs and discussion groups. For such sources, provide as much of the following information as you can:

1. Author's name.
2. In quotation marks, title of a short work (poem, short story, essay, article, posted message).
3. Underlined, title of a book.
4. If relevant, name of an editor, translator, or compiler introduced by Ed., Trans., or Comp.
5. Publication for a print version, if any.
6. Underlined, title of the database, periodical, project, or site. (If the site has no title, describe it: for example, Home page.)
7. After Ed., the name of the editor of a scholarly project or database.

8. For a journal, the volume number, issue number, or other number referring to its date. For other sources, a version number, if any (unless it has already been given as part of the title).

9. Date of electronic publication, posting, or the most recent update.

10. Name of a listserv or discussion group.

11. Inclusive or total page, paragraph, or section numbers, if any: for example, pp. 2-4, 3 pp., 15 pars.

12. Name of any sponsoring institution or organization.

13. Date you accessed the material.

14. URL in angle brackets. Put a period after the closing bracket.

51 Online: A Public Message--MLA

Be cautious about using online postings as sources. Some of them contain cutting-edge information from experts, and some of them contain trash. Unfortunately, there is no way to know that people online are who they claim to be. To cite an online message, give the author name (if any), the title of the message in quotation marks, and then Online posting. Then give the access date, and, in angle brackets, the address.

52 Other Online Sources

For more models of online sources in the newly authorized MLA style, go to page 358. You might also want to check out the MLA Web site periodically for coverage of MLA documentation and style matters: http://www.mla.org/main_stl.htm#sources

M3 A Student's MLA Research Paper

Preparing your research paper using MLA format guidelines   **M3.a**

Check whether your instructor has special instructions for you to use when you prepare the final draft of your research paper. If there are no special instructions, you can use the MLA guidelines here. The student paper in **M3.b** was prepared according to MLA guidelines.

General Instructions—MLA

Use 8-1/2-inch by 11-inch white paper. Double-space throughout, whether the paper is typed or prepared on a computer. Set a 1-inch margin on the left and leave no less than 1 inch on the right and at the bottom. If you are using a computer, do not justify the type.

Drop down 1/2 inch from the top edge of the paper to the name-and-page-number line described below. Then, drop down another 1/2 inch to the first line, whether that is a heading, a title, or a line of the text of your paper.

If you are typing, paragraph indents and indents in Notes and Works Cited are 5 characters. The indent for a set-off quotation, described on the next page, is 10 characters. If you are preparing your paper on a computer, paragraph indents and indents in Notes and Works Cited are 1/2 inch, and the indent for a set-off quotation is 1 inch.

Order of Parts—MLA

Use this order for the parts of your paper: body of the paper; endnotes, if any; Works Cited list; attachments, if any (such as questionnaires, data sheets, or any other material your instructor tells you to include). Number all pages consecutively.

Name-and-Page-Number Line for All Pages—MLA

Use a name-and-page-number line on every page of your paper. Drop down 1/2 inch from the top edge of the sheet of paper. Type your last name, then a 1-character space and the page number. Align the typed line about 1 inch in from the right edge of the paper.

First Page—MLA

Use a name-and-page-number line. If your instructor does not require a cover sheet, use a four-line heading at the top of the first page. Drop down 1 inch from the top edge of the paper. Starting each line at the left margin, include the following information:

> Your name [first line]
>
> Your instructor's name [second line]
>
> Your course name and section [third line]
>
> The date you hand in your paper [fourth line]

For the submission date, MLA style uses day-month-year form: *26 November 1998*, for example.

On the line below this heading, center the title of your paper. Do not underline the title or enclose it in quotation marks. On the line below the title, start your paper.

! **Capitalization Alert:**   Use a capital letter for the first word of your title and the first word of a subtitle, if you use one. Start all NOUNS, PRONOUNS, VERBS, ADVERBS, ADJECTIVES, and SUBORDINATING CONJUNCTIONS with a capital letter. Capitalize the last word of your title, no matter what part of speech it is. In a hyphenated compound word (two or more words used together to express one idea), capitalize the word after a hyphen: Father-In-Law.

Do not capitalize an article (*an, an, the*) unless one of the preceding capitalization rules applies to it. Do not capitalize PREPOSITIONS, no matter how many letters they contain. Do not capitalize COORDINATING CONJUNCTIONS. Do not capitalize the word *to* used in an INFINITIVE.

Set-Off Quotations—MLA

Set quotations of more than four lines off from your words. Start a new line for the quoted words, indenting each line of the (double-spaced) quotation 10 spaces (or 1 inch) from the left margin. Do not enclose the quoted words in quotation marks.

If you are quoting part of a paragraph or one complete paragraph, do not indent the first line of quoted words more than 10 spaces. But if you quote more than one paragraph, indent the first line of each paragraph after the first an additional 3 spaces (13 spaces in all).

When the quotation is finished, leave a space after the sentence-ending punctuation, and then give the parenthetical citation. Begin a new line to resume your own words. For examples of set-off quotations in MLA style, see **P7.a** and Carlos Velez's paper in **M3.b**.

Notes—MLA

If you use a note in your paper (see **M1.c**), try to arrange the sentence so that the note number falls at the end. The ideal place for a note number is after the sentence-ending punctuation. Leave one space before the number, and raise the number slightly above the line of words, if possible. Also leave one space after the note number.

Put your notes on a separate page after the last page of the body of your paper and before the Works Cited list. Use a name-and-page-number line, then drop down 1 inch from the top edge of the paper and center the word *Notes*; do not underline it or put it in quotation marks.

On the next line, start your first note. Indent 5 characters (or 1/2 inch). Raise the note number slightly, if possible. After the number, type one space, and then start the words of your note. Do not indent any lines except the first. Use double-spacing for each note and between notes.

Number the notes consecutively throughout the paper, except for notes referring to tables or figures.

Place table or figure notes below the table or illustration. Instead of note numbers, use lowercase letters (a, b, c).

Works Cited List—MLA

Starting a new page, type a name-and-page-number line. Then, 1 inch below the top edge of the paper, type the words *Works Cited*. Do not underline them or put in quotation marks.

On the next line, start the first entry in your Works Cited list at the left margin. If an entry takes more than one line, indent each line after the first 5 characters (or 1/2 inch). Use double-spacing for each entry and between entries.

M3.b Reading a sample research paper that uses MLA documentation

A first-year college student, Carlos Velez, wrote the following research paper in MLA documentation style in response to this assignment: Write a research paper on an unconscious process in humans. Be sure to narrow the subject to a topic you can present well in 1,800–2,000 words.

Velez 1

DOUBLE-SPACED
THROUGHOUT

Carlos Velez

Professor Didier

English 101, Section B4

18 November 19XX

Biological Clocks:

The Body's Internal Timepieces

INTRODUCTORY
PARAGRAPH

    Life in modern, technological societies is built around timepieces. People set clocks on radios, microwave ovens, VCRs, and electric coffee makers. Students respond to bells that start and end the school day as well as dividing it into blocks of time. Almost everyone relies on clocks to manage time well. While carefully managing the minutes and hours each day, people are often encouraged or forced by current styles of family and work life to violate another kind of time: their body's time. Biological

THESIS
STATEMENT

clocks, which are also known as circadian cycles, are a significant feature of human design that greatly affect personal and professional lifestyles.

    The term "circadian," which is Latin for "about a day," describes the rhythms of people's internal biological clocks. Circadian cycles are in tune with

BODY
PARAGRAPH:
KEY TERM
"CIRCADIAN"
EXPLAINED

external time cycles such as the 24-hour period of the earth's daily rotation as signaled by the rising and setting of the sun. Usually, humans set their biological clocks by seeing these cycles of daylight and darkness. Studies conducted in caves or similar environments that allowed researchers to control light and darkness have shown that most people create cycles slightly over 24 hours when they are not exposed to

Continued next page

Velez 2

natural cycles of day and night (Allis and Haederle 52; Enright 14). Human perception of the external day-night cycle affects the production and release of a brain hormone, melatonin, which is important in initiating and regulating the sleep-wake cycle, as Alfred Lewy and other scientists at the National Institute of Health in Bethesda, Maryland, have found (Winfree 49).

An individual's lifestyle reflects that person's own circadian cycle. Scientists group people as "larks" or "owls" based on whether individuals are more efficient in the morning or at night. The idea behind the labels is that "in nature certain animals are diurnal, active during the light period; others are nocturnal, active at night. The 'morning lark' and 'night owl' connotations typically are used to categorize the human extremes" ("Are You" 11).

> BODY PARAGRAPH: ABOUT "LARKS" AND "OWLS"

"Larks" who must stay up late at night and "owls" who must awaken early in the morning experience mild versions of the disturbances, called "jet lag," that time-zone travelers often encounter. Bonner explains that jet lag, a condition characterized by fatigue and irregular sleep patterns, results from disruption of circadian rhythms, a common problem among people who travel great distances by jet airplane to different time zones:

> BODY PARAGRAPH: ABOUT JET LAG

> Jet lag syndrome is the inability of the internal body rhythm to rapidly resynchronize after sudden shifts in the timing. For a variety of reasons, the system attempts to maintain stability and resist temporal change. Consequently, complete adjustment can often be delayed for several days--sometimes for a week--after arrival at one's destination. (72)

Interestingly, research shows that the number of flying hours is not the cause of jet lag. Rather, as Coleman reports in <u>Wide Awake at 3 a.m.: By Choice or by Chance?</u>, "the number, rate, and direction of time-

> BODY PARAGRAPH: MORE ABOUT JET LAG

Continued next page

Velez 3

zone changes are the critical factors in determining
the extent and degree of jet lag symptoms" (67-68).
Eastbound travelers find it harder than westbound
travelers to adjust, because traveling east forces
people to go to bed before their biological clocks are
ready for them to do so (Coleman 69).

BODY PARAGRAPH: ABOUT ERRATIC WORK SCHEDULES

Another group that suffers greatly from
biological clock disruptions consists of people whose
livelihoods depend on erratic schedules. This situation
affects 20- to 30-million U.S. workers whose work
schedules differ from the usual morning starting time
and afternoon or early evening ending time (Weiss 37).
Charles Czeisler, director of the Center for Circadian
and Sleep Disorders at Brigham and Woman's Hospital in
Boston, reports that 27 percent of the U.S. workforce
does shift work (Binkley 211). Shift work can mean,
for example, working from 7:00 a.m. to 3:00 p.m. for
six weeks, from 3:00 p.m. to 11:00 p.m. for six weeks,
and from 11:00 p.m. to 7:00 a.m. for six weeks. Many
shift workers endure stomach and intestinal-tract
disorders, and, on average, they have a three times
higher risk of heart disease than non-shift workers
(The Time of Our Lives). In a 1989 report to the
American Association for the Advancement of Science,
Czeisler states that "police officers, [medical]
interns, and many others who work nights perform
poorly and are involved in more on-the-job accidents
than their daytime counterparts" (qtd. in Chollar 26).

BODY PARAGRAPH: MORE ABOUT ERRATIC WORK SCHEDULES

Other researchers confirm that safety is at risk
during late-shift hours (Chollar 26). In a study by
Czeisler of 28 medical interns observed during late
night shifts over a one-year period, 25 percent
admitted to falling asleep while talking on the phone,
and 34 percent had at least one accident or near-
accident during that period (Weiss 37).

Investigations into the Challenger Shuttle
explosion and the nuclear-reactor disasters at Three-

Continued next page

Velez 4

Mile Island and Chernobyl reveal critical errors made
by people undergoing stresses of lack of sleep and
unusual work schedules (Toufexis 66).

One especially negative effect of an upset
biological clock is a syndrome increasingly recognized
as a medical problem: the disorder known as Seasonal
Affective Disorder (SAD). Table 1 lists some of the
major symptoms of SAD.

BODY
PARAGRAPH:
ABOUT
SEASONAL
AFFECTIVE
DISORDER (SAD)

Table 1

Common Symptoms of Seasonal Affective Disorder

Sadness	Later waking
Anxiety	Increased sleep time
Decreased physical activity	Interrupted, unrefreshing sleep
Irritability	Daytime drowsiness
Increased appetite	Decreased sexual drive
Craving for carbohydrates	Menstrual problems
Weight gain	Work problems
Earlier onset of sleep	Interpersonal problems

Source: Discussion in Binkley 204

SAD appears to be related to the short daylight
(photoperiod) of winter in the temperate zones of the
northern and southern hemispheres. The phenomenon of
SAD not only illustrates the important role of
circadian rhythms, but also dramatically proves that
an understanding of circadian principles can help
scientists to improve the lives of people who
experience disruptions of their biological clocks.
Binkley claims that exposure to bright light for
periods of up to two hours a day during the short
photoperiod days of winter reduces SAD-related
"depression in 87 percent of patients . . . within a
few days; relapses followed" (203-04) when light
treatment ended.

BODY
PARAGRAPH:
MORE
ABOUT SAD

Continued next page

Velez 5

BODY
PARAGRAPH:
ABOUT SAFETY
HAZARDS

Exposure to long periods of bright light is not, however, an appropriate solution for people whose safety is at risk because of continual assaults on their circadian cycles by shift schedules at work. Establishing work schedules more sensitive to biological clocks could reduce certain safety hazards. A group of police officers in Philadelphia were studied while on modified schedules (Locitzer 66; Toufexis 67). These officers changed between day shifts and night shifts less frequently than they had on former shift schedules; they rotated forward rather than backward in time; and they worked four rather than six consecutive days. Officers reported 40 percent fewer patrol-car accidents and decreased use of drugs or alcohol to get to sleep. Overall, the police officers preferred the modified shift schedules. Emphasizing the importance of these results of Charles Czeisler's research, Binkley summarizes: "When schedules are introduced that take into account the properties of the human circadian system, subjective estimates of work schedule satisfaction and health improve, personnel turnover decreases, and worker productivity increases" (213).

CONCLUDING
PARAGRAPH

Scientists like Charles Czeisler are beginning to help individuals live harmoniously with their biological clocks. Growing awareness of the effects of such situations as shift work and travel across time zones is one significant step toward control. The use of light to manipulate the body's sense of time is another. As more people become aware of how circadian rhythms affect lifestyles, the day might soon come when we can fully control our biological clocks instead of their controlling us.

Continued next page

Works Cited

Allis, Tim, and Michael Haederle. "Ace in the Hole:
    Stefania Follini Never Caved In." People 12 June
    1989: 52.

"Are You a Day or Night Person?" USA Today Magazine
    Mar. 1989: 11.

Binkley, Sue. The Clockwork Sparrow. Englewood Cliffs,
    NJ: Prentice, 1990.

Bonner, Phillip. "Travel Rhythms." Sky Magazine July
    1991: 72+.

Chollar, Susan. "Safe Solutions for Night Work."
    Psychology Today Nov. 1989: 26.

Coleman, Richard. Wide Awake at 3:00 a.m.: By Choice
    or by Chance? New York: Freeman, 1986.

Enright, J. T. The Timing of Sleep and Wakefulness.
    Berlin: Springer-Verlag, 1980.

Locitzer, Kay. "Are You Out of Sync with Each Other?"
    Psychology Today July/Aug. 1989: 66.

The Time of Our Lives. Writ. and dir. Robert Bingham.
    Prod. Commercial Television of Southern
    California. PBS. 7 Apr. 1989.

Toufexis, Anastasia. "The Times of Your Life." Time 5
    June 1989: 66-67.

Weiss, R. "Safety Gets Short Shrift on Long Night
    Shift." Science News 21 Jan. 1989: 37.

Winfree, Arthur. The Timing of Biological Clocks. New
    York: Freeman, 1987.

APA, CM, and CBE Documentation

A APA, CM, AND CBE DOCUMENTATION

A1 APA In-Text Citations

The American Psychological Association (APA) has developed a documentation style used often in the social sciences and in other disciplines as well. APA in-text citations, described in this chapter, alert readers to material used from outside sources. These citations function with an alphabetical References list at the end of the paper containing information that enables readers to retrieve the sources that were quoted from (see **R3.c**), paraphrased (see **R3.d**), or summarized (see **R3.e**); see **A2** for detailed information about the References list.

| Understanding details about APA style | A1.a |

In-text citations identify a source by a name (usually an author name) and a year (for print sources, usually the copyright year). You can often incorporate the relevant name, and sometimes the year, into your sentence. Otherwise, put this information in parentheses, placing the parenthetical reference close by so that a reader knows exactly what it refers to.

The APA *Publication Manual*, Fourth Edition, published in 1994, recommends that if you refer to a work more than once in a paragraph, you give the author name and date at the first mention and then give only the name after that. There is one exception: If you are citing two or more works by the same author or if two or more of your sources have the same name, each citation must include the date so that a reader knows which work is being cited.

APA style requires page numbers for direct quotations and recommends them for paraphrases. Some instructors expect page references for any use of a source, so find out your instructor's preference.

Put page numbers in parentheses, using the abbreviation *p.* before a single page number and *pp.* when the material you are citing falls on more than one page. For a direct quotation from an electronic source that numbers paragraphs, give a paragraph number (or numbers). Handle paragraph numbers as you do page numbers, but omit *p.* or *pp.*

Citations of paraphrases

People from the Mediterranean prefer an elbow-to-shoulder distance from each other (Morris, 1977). [Name and date cited in parentheses.]

Desmond Morris notes that people from the Mediterranean prefer an elbow-to-shoulder distance from each other (1977, p. 131). [Name cited in text, date and page cited in parentheses.]

Citations of quotations	A recent report of reductions in SAD-related "depression in 87 percent of patients" (Binkley, 1990, p. 203) reverses the findings of earlier studies. [Name, date, and page reference in parentheses immediately following the quotation.]
	Binkley reports reductions in SAD-related "depression in 87 percent of patients" (1990, p. 203). [Name incorporated into the words introducing the quotation, and date and page number in parentheses immediately following the quotation.]

Formatting Quotations

Incorporate a direct quotation of fewer than 40 words into your own sentence(s) and enclose it in quotation marks. Place the parenthetical citation after the closing quotation mark and, if the quotation falls at the end of the sentence, before the sentence-ending punctuation.

When you use a quotation of 40 words or longer, set it off from your words by starting it on a new line and indenting each line of the quotation five to seven spaces from the left margin. Do not enclose it in quotation marks. Place the parenthetical citation two spaces after the end punctuation of the last sentence. Start a new line for your own words following the quotation.

Displayed Quotation

Jet lag, with its characteristic fatigue and irregular sleep patterns, is a common problem among those who travel great distances by jet airplane to different time zones:

> Jet lag syndrome is the inability of the internal body rhythm to rapidly resynchronize after sudden shifts in the timing. For a variety of reasons, the system attempts to maintain stability and resist temporal change. Consequently, complete adjustment can often be delayed for several days--sometimes for a week--after arrival at one's destination. (Bonner, 1991, p. 72)

Interestingly, this research shows that the number of flying hours is not the cause of jet lag.

A1.b Citing specific kinds of sources in APA style

The following examples illustrate parenthetical citations for various types of sources. Remember, though, that you often can introduce source names, including titles when necessary, and sometimes even years, in your own sentences rather than in parenthetical citations.

One Author—APA
All the examples in section **A1.a** show citations of works by one author. Notice that in a parenthetical reference, a comma and a space separate a name from a year and a year from a page reference.

Two or More Authors—APA
If a work has two authors, give both names in each citation.

- One report describes 2,123 occurrences (Worchel & Cooper, 1994).
- The results Worchel and Cooper (1994) report would not support the conclusions Davis and Shebilskie draw in their review of the literature (1992).

For three, four, or five authors, use all the authors' last names in the first reference; in all subsequent references, use only the first author's last name followed by *et al.*

First Reference
- In one anthology, 35 percent of the selections had not been anthologized before (Elliott, Kerber, Litz, & Martin, 1992).

Subsequent Reference
- Elliott et al. (1992) include 17 authors whose work has never been anthologized.

For six or more authors, use the name of the first author followed by *et al.* for all references, including the first.

For any work by more than one author, use an ampersand (&) between the (last) two names in a parenthetical citation. But if you work the information into your own sentence, use the word *and*.

Author(s) with Two or More Works in the Same Year—APA
If you use more than one source written in the same year by the same author(s), alphabetize the works by their titles for the References list, and assign letters in alphabetical order to the years: *(1996a)*, *(1996b)*, *(1996c)*. Use this year-letter combination in in-text citations. Note that if two or more of such works are listed in the same citation, the years appear in alphabetical order: *1996a, 1996b*.

- Most recently, Jones (1996c) draws new conclusions from the results of 17 sets of experiments (1996a, 1996b).

Two or More Authors with the Same Last Name—APA

Use first- and middle-name initials for every in-text citation of authors who share a last name.

- R. A. Smith (1997) and C. Smith (1989) both confirm these results.

- These results have been confirmed independently (C. Smith, 1989; R. A. Smith, 1997).

Group or Corporate Author—APA

For a source in which the "author" is the name of a corporation, agency, or group, an in-text citation gives that name as author. Use the full name in each citation unless an abbreviated version of the name is likely to be familiar to your audience. In that case, use the full name and give its abbreviation at the first citation; then use the abbreviation for subsequent citations.

First Citation

- This exploration will continue into the 21st century (National Aeronautics and Space Administration [NASA], 1996).

Second Citation

- Many more questions need answers (NASA, 1996).

Works Cited by Title—APA

If no author is named, use a shortened form of the title in citations. Ignoring *A, An,* or *The,* make the first word the one by which you alphabetize the title in References. The following citation is to an article fully titled "Are You a Day or Night Person?"

- The morning lark and night owl connotations typically are used to categorize the human extremes ("Are You," 1989).

Reference to More Than One Source—APA

If more than one source has contributed to an idea or opinion in your paper, cite the sources alphabetically in a single reference; separate each block of information with a semicolon.

- Conceptions of personal space vary among cultures (Morris, 1977; Worchel & Cooper, 1983).

Citing Graphics and Table Data—APA

If you use a graphic from another source or you create a table using data from another source, give a note in the text at the bottom of the table or graphic crediting the original author and the copyright holder.

Here are examples of two source lines, one for a graphic from an article, the other for a graphic from a book.

Graphic from an Article—APA

- Note. From "Bridge over troubled waters? Connecting research and pedagogy in composition and business/technical communication" by J. Allen, 1992, *Technical Communication Quarterly, 1*(4), p. 9. Copyright 1992 by the Association of Teachers of Technical Writing.

Graphic from a Book—APA

- Note. From *How to lower your fat thermostat: The no-diet reprogramming plan for lifelong weight control* (p. 74), by D. Remington, M.D., A. G. Fisher, Ph.D., and E. Parent, Ph.D., 1983, Provo: Vitality House International. Copyright 1983 by Vitality House International.

Writing an abstract for an APA-style paper   A1.c

You may be asked to include an abstract at the start of a paper you prepare in APA style. As the APA *Publication Manual* explains, "an abstract is a brief, comprehensive summary" (p. 8) of a longer piece of writing. Make a summary accurate, objective, and exact. You may be familiar with effective abstracts, for many disciplines have online abstracts of longer sources.

Here is an abstract prepared for a paper on biological clocks.

- Circadian rhythms, which greatly affect human lives, often suffer disruptions in technological societies, resulting in such disorders as jet lag syndrome and seasonal affective disorder (SAD). With growing scientific awareness both of natural circadian cycles and the effects of disturbances of these cycles, individuals are learning how to control some negative effects.

See **A1.e** for formatting the Abstract page.

Using content notes in an APA-style paper   A1.d

Content notes can be used in APA-style papers for additional relevant information that cannot be worked effectively into a text discussion. Use consecutive arabic numerals for note numbers, both within your paper and on a separate page following the last text page of your paper. See **A1.e** for formatting the Notes page.

A1.e Preparing your research paper using APA format guidelines

Ask if your instructor has instructions for preparing a final draft. If not, you can use the APA guidelines here.

General Instructions—APA

Use 8-1/2-inch by 11-inch white bond paper. Double-space throughout, whether the paper is typed or prepared on a computer (the APA *Publication Manual* recommends double-spacing a final manuscript like a research paper, but suggests that heading, titles, captions, and quotations longer than 40 words may be easier to read if they are single-spaced). Set at least a 1-inch margin on the left (1-1/2 inches if you submit your paper in a binder) and leave no less than 1 inch on the right and at the bottom.

Drop down 1/2 inch from the top edge of the paper to the title-and-page-number line, described below. Then drop down 1 inch from the top edge of the paper to the next line on the page, whether that is a heading (like "Abstract" or "Notes") or a line of your paper.

If you are typing, use five- to seven-character indents where indents are called for (see below). If you are preparing your paper on a computer, use 1/2-inch indents. Indent the first line of paragraphs five to seven characters (1/2 inch) except in an abstract, where the first line is not indented. Do not justify the right margin.

Order of Parts—APA

Use this order for the parts of your paper: title page, Abstract (if required), body of the paper; References; Notes, if any; attachments, if any (such as questionnaires, data sheets, or any other material your instructor tells you to include). Number all pages consecutively.

Title-and-Page-Number Line for All Pages—APA

Use a title-and-page-number line on all pages of your paper. Drop down 1/2 inch from the top edge of the paper. Type the title (use a shortened version if necessary), leave a five-character space, and then type the page number. End the title-and-page-number line 1 inch from the right edge of the paper. Ask if your instructor wants you to include your last name in this title-and-page-number line.

Title Page—APA

Use a separate title page. On it, begin with the title-and-page-number line described above, using the numeral 1 for this first page. Then center the complete title vertically and horizontally on the page. Use two or more double-spaced lines if the title is long. Do not underline the title or enclose it in quotation marks. On the next line center your name, and below that center the course title and section.

Capitalization Alert: Use the guidelines here for capitalizing the title of your own paper and for capitalizing titles you mention in the body of your paper. *But* see **QA Box 57** (page 233) for the rules for capitalizing titles in a References list, where different rules apply.

Use a capital letter for the first word of your title and the first word of a subtitle, if you use one. Start all NOUNS, PRONOUNS, VERBS, ADVERBS, and ADJECTIVES with a capital letter. Capitalize each word in a hyphenated compound word (two or more words used together to express one idea): *Father-in-Law*. Capitalize the word after a colon or a dash.

Do not capitalize articles (*a, an, the*) unless one of the preceding capitalization rules applies to it. Do not capitalize PREPOSITIONS and CONJUNCTIONS unless they are four or more letters long. Do not capitalize the word *to* used in an INFINITIVE.

Abstract—APA

See **A1.c** for advice about what to include in an abstract of your paper. Type the abstract on a separate page, using the numeral 2 in the title-and-page-number line. Drop down 1 inch from the top of the paper and center the word *Abstract*. Double-space twice below this title, and then start your abstract, double-spacing it. Do not indent the first line.

Set-Off Quotations—APA

Set quotations of 40 words or more off from your words. Start a new line for the quoted words, indenting each line of the (double-spaced) quotation five spaces from the left margin. Do not enclose the quoted words in quotation marks.

If you are quoting part of a paragraph or one complete paragraph, do not indent the first line of quoted words more than five spaces. But if you quote two or more paragraphs, indent the first line of the second and subsequent paragraphs 10 spaces.

When the quotation is finished, leave a space after the sentence-ending punctuation, and then give the parenthetical citation. Begin a new line to resume your own words.

References List—APA

Start a new page for your References list immediately after the end of the body of your paper. Use a title-and-page-number line. Drop down 1 inch from the top of the paper and center the word *References*. Do not underline it or put it in quotation marks. Double-space below it.

Indent the first line of each entry in your References list five to seven characters from the left margin. If an entry takes more than one line, do not indent any line after the first. Double-space within each entry and between entries.

Alert: Ask if your instructor prefers "hanging indent" style for a References list. If so, start the first line of each entry at the left margin, and indent any subsequent lines five to seven characters (or 1/2 inch).

Notes—APA

If you use a content note in your paper (see **A1.d**), try to arrange the sentence so that the note number falls at the end. The ideal place for a note number is after the sentence-ending punctuation. Use a numeral raised slightly above the line of words and immediately after the sentence-ending punctuation mark.

Put your notes on a separate page after the last page of your References list. Use a title-and-page-number line. Then, drop down 1 inch from the top of the paper and center the word *Notes*; do not underline it or put it in quotation marks.

On the next line, start your first note, indent five to seven characters (or 1/2 inch). Raise the note number slightly, and then start the words of your note, double-spacing throughout. If the note uses more than one typed line, do not indent any lines except the first.

A2 APA Documentation for a References List

The References list provides information for readers who may want to access the sources you cite in your paper.

A2.a Understanding details about the References list

Include in References all sources that you quote from (see **R3.c**), paraphrase (see **R3.d**), or summarize (see **R3.e**) in your paper that any other person could access with reasonable effort. Do not include any source not generally available to others; see, for example, item 34 about personal interviews. Major points about APA style for a References list are outlined in **QA Box 57**, below.

**QA
Box
57**

COMPILING A REFERENCES LIST IN APA STYLE

TITLE
References

PLACEMENT OF LIST
Start a new page numbered sequentially with the rest of the paper, after Notes pages, if any.

CONTENTS AND FORMAT
Include all quoted, paraphrased, or summarized sources in your paper that your readers could access. Start each entry on a new line. See **A1.e** for formatting guidelines.

Continued on next page

➤ *QA Box 57, continued from previous page*

SPACING AFTER PUNCTUATION
Use one space after a colon, comma, semicolon, or sentence-ending punctuation. Put one space after a period at the end of an abbreviation when the information unit continues (as in p. 96) but no space after a period within an abbreviation (a.m.). Put no space after a colon in a ratio (2:1).

ARRANGEMENT OF ENTRIES
Alphabetize by author's last name. If no author is named, alphabetize by the title's first significant word (not *A, An,* or *The*).

AUTHORS' NAMES
Use last names, first-name initials, and middle initials, if any, and use an ampersand (&) between the second-to-last and last authors (Mills, J. F., & Holahan, R. H.). List the authors in the order used on the title page. Place a comma between the first author's last name and first initial, and after each complete author name except the last. After the last name, use a period.

DATE
Put date information after name information, enclosing it in parentheses, followed by a period and a space.

For books, articles in journals that have volume numbers, and many other print and nonprint sources, the year of publication or production is the date to use. For articles from most magazines and newspapers, use the year followed by a comma and the month, and sometimes the day-date. Individual entries later in this chapter show how much information to give for various sources.

CAPITALIZATION OF TITLES
For titles of books and articles, capitalize the first word, the first word after a colon, and any proper nouns. For other titles, follow the rules in the Capitalization Alert in **A1.e**.

SPECIAL TREATMENT OF TITLES
Use no special treatment for titles of shorter works (poems, short stories, essays, articles). Underline titles of longer works (books, names of newspapers or journals containing cited articles), using an unbroken line if possible. Underline a journal's volume number with the same unbroken line used for the journal's name. See the model below. Do not drop *A, An,* or *The* from a newspaper, magazine, or journal title.

PUBLISHER
Use shortened names of publishers as long as they are identifiable. Drop *Co., Inc., Publishers,* and the like, but do not drop the word *Press: Dover Press, University of Chicago Press*.

PUBLICATION MONTH ABBREVIATIONS
Do not abbreviate publication months.

INCLUSIVE PAGE NUMBERS
Use the full second number. Use *p.* and *pp.* before numerals.

Continued on next page

➤ *QA Box 57, continued from previous page*

DISCONTINUOUS PAGES

List all pages, with discontinuous numbers set off by commas: 32, 44–45, 47–49, 53.

REFERENCES ENTRIES: BOOKS

Citations for books have four main parts: author, date, title, and publication information (place of publication and publisher). Each part ends in a period followed by a space. The models in this handbook use the APA's "copy manuscript" style of indenting the first line of each entry five spaces and not indenting any other lines of an entry.

AUTHOR	DATE	BOOK TITLE

Didion, J. (1977). A book of common prayer.

PUBLICATION INFORMATION

New York: Simon & Schuster.

REFERENCES ENTRIES: ARTICLES

Citations for periodical articles contain four major parts: author, date, title of article, and publication information (usually the periodical title, volume number, and page numbers).

AUTHOR	DATE	ARTICLE TITLE

Shuter, R. (1977). A field study of nonverbal

communication in Germany, Italy, and the United States.

PERIODICAL TITLE	VOLUME NUMBER	PAGE NUMBERS

Communication Monographs, 44, 298–305.

A2.b Using sample References models in APA style

The directory below is a numbered list corresponding to the examples that follow the directory. Not every possible documentation model is here. You may find that you have to combine features of models to document a particular source. You will also find more information in the *Publication Manual* of the American Psychological Association, Fourth Edition.

DIRECTORY—APA STYLE

Print Sources

1 Book by One Author—APA

2 Book by Two Authors—APA

Electronic Sources

Print Sources

1 Book by One Author—APA

Welty, E. (1984). <u>One writer's beginnings.</u> Cambridge: Harvard University Press.

2 Book by Two Authors—APA

Leghorn, L., & Parker, K. (1981). <u>Woman's worth.</u> Boston: Routledge & Kegan Paul.

3 Book by Three or More Authors—APA

Moore, M. H., Estrich, S., McGillis, D., & Spelman, W. (1984). <u>Dangerous offenders: The elusive target of justice.</u> Cambridge: Harvard University Press.

4 Two or More Books by the Same Author(s)—APA

Morris, D., Ed. (1967). <u>Primate ethology.</u> London: Wiedenfeld.

Morris, D. (1977). <u>Manwatching: A field guide to human behavior.</u> New York: Henry N. Abrams.

References by the same author are arranged chronologically, with the earlier date of publication listed first.

5 Book by Group or Corporate Author—APA

The Boston Women's Health Collective. (1986). <u>Our bodies, ourselves.</u> New York: Simon & Schuster.

American Psychological Association. (1994). <u>Publication manual of the American Psychological Association</u> (4th ed.). Washington, DC: Author.

Cite the full name of the corporate author first. If the author is also the publisher, use the word *Author* as the name of the publisher.

6 Book with No Author Named—APA

<u>The Chicago manual of style</u> (14th ed.). (1993). Chicago: University of Chicago Press.

7 Book with an Author and an Editor—APA

Brontë, E. (1985). <u>Wuthering heights</u> (D. Daiches, Ed.).
London: Penguin.

8 Translation—APA

Freire, P. (1970). <u>Pedagogy of the oppressed</u> (M. B.
Ramos, Trans.). New York: Seabury Press.

9 Work in Several Volumes or Parts—APA

Randall, J. H., Jr. (1962). <u>The career of philosophy</u>
(Vols. 1–2). New York: Columbia University Press.

10 One Selection from an Anthology or an Edited Book—APA

Galarza, E. (1972). The roots of migration. In
L. Valdez & S. Steiner (Eds.), <u>Aztlan: An anthology
of Mexican American literature</u> (pp. 127–132). New York:
Alfred A. Knopf.

Give the author of the selection first. The word *In* introduces the larger work from which the selection is taken.

11 Two Selections from One Anthology or an Edited Book—APA

Gilbert, S., & Gubar, S. (Eds.). (1985). <u>The Norton
anthology of literature by women.</u> New York: W. W. Norton.

Kingston, M. H. (1985). No name woman. In S. Gilbert &
S. Gubar (Eds.), <u>The Norton anthology of literature by women.</u>
New York: W. W. Norton.

Provide full reference information for each selection cited from an anthology (or collection), using *In* to show the larger work from which the selection is taken.

12 Signed Article in a Reference Book—APA

Holt, R. R. Freud, Sigmund. In D. L. Sills (Ed.),
<u>International encyclopedia of the social sciences</u> (pp. 1–11).
New York: Macmillan.

Use *In* before the title of the larger work from which the selection is taken.

13 Unsigned Article in a Reference Book—APA

Ireland. (1974). In <u>Encyclopedia Britannica.</u>

14 Edition—APA

Mandell, M. I. (1984). <u>Advertising</u> (4th ed.). Englewood
Cliffs, NJ: Prentice Hall.

When a book is not the first edition, the edition number appears on the title page. Place this information after the title and in parentheses. Use the year of the edition you are citing.

15 Anthology or Edited Book—APA

> Valdez, L., & Steiner, S. (Eds.). (1972). <u>Aztlan: An anthology of Mexican American literature.</u> New York: Alfred A. Knopf.

16 Introduction, Preface, Foreword, or Afterword—APA

> Boas, F. (1959). Introduction. In R. Benedict, <u>Patterns of culture.</u> Boston: Houghton Mifflin. (Original work published 1934)

If you are citing an introduction, preface, foreword, or afterword, give its author's name first. After the year, give the name of the part cited. If the writer of the material you are citing is not the author of the book, use the word *In* and the author's name before the title of the book.

17 Unpublished Dissertation or Essay—APA

> Geissinger, S. B. (1984). <u>Openness versus secrecy in adoptive parenthood.</u> Unpublished dissertation, University of North Carolina at Greensboro.

18 Reprint of an Older Book—APA

> Hurston, Z. N. (1978). <u>Their eyes were watching God.</u> Urbana: University of Illinois Press. (Original work published 1937)

Republishing information appears on the copyright page.

19 Book in a Series—APA

> McClave, H. (1980). <u>Women writers of the short story.</u> Englewood Cliffs, NJ: Prentice Hall.

Give the title of the book, but not of the whole series.

20 Book with a Title Within a Title—APA

> Lumiansky, R. M., & Baker, H. (Eds.). (1968). <u>Critical approaches to six major English works:</u> Beowulf <u>through</u> Paradise Lost. Philadelphia: University of Pennsylvania Press.

Do not underline an incorporated title even if it would be underlined by itself.

21 Government Publication—APA

United States Congressional House Committee on the Judiciary. (1980). <u>Immigration and nationality with amendments and notes on related laws</u> (7th ed.). Washington, DC: U.S. Government Printing Office.

Use the complete name of a government agency as author when no specific person is named.

22 Published Proceedings of a Conference—APA

Harris, D., & Nelson-Heern, L. (Eds.). (1981). <u>Proceedings of NECC 1981: National Education Computing Conference.</u> Iowa City: Weeg Computing Center, University of Iowa.

23 Article from a Daily Newspaper—APA

Dullea, G. (1986, April 16). Literary folk look for solid comfort. <u>New York Times,</u> p. C14.

24 Editorial, Letter to the Editor, Review—APA

Facing space, after the Cold War [Editorial]. (1989, May 1). <u>New York Times,</u> p. A16.

Childress, G. T. [Letter to the editor]. (1986, June 9). <u>Newsweek,</u> p. 10.

Linebaugh, P. (1986). In the flight path of Perry Anderson [Review of the book <u>In the tracks of historical materialism</u>]. <u>History Workshop, 21,</u> 141–146.

25 Unsigned Article from a Daily Newspaper—APA

Hospitals, competing for scarce patients, turn to advertising. (1986, April 20). <u>New York Times,</u> p. 47.

26 Article from a Weekly or Biweekly Magazine or Newspaper—APA

Toufexis, A. (1989, March 27). Dining with invisible danger. <u>Time,</u> 28.

Use the abbreviation *p.* (or *pp.* for more than one page) for newspapers. Do not use this abbreviation for magazines or journals. Give year, month, and day-date for a periodical published every week or every two weeks.

27 Article in a Monthly or Bimonthly Periodical—APA

Roosevelt, A. (1989, February). Lost civilizations of the lower Amazon. <u>Natural History,</u> 74–83.

Give the year and month(s) for a periodical published every month or every other month.

28 Unsigned Article from a Weekly or Monthly Periodical—APA

A salute to everyday heroes. (1989, July 10). <u>Time,</u> 46–51, 54–56, 58–60, 63–64, 66.

29 Article from a Collection of Reprinted Articles—APA

Curver, P. C. (1990). Lighting in the 21st century. In <u>Social issues resources series. Energy</u> (Vol. 4, Article 84). Boca Raton, FL: Social Issues Resources.

When citing an article in a collection of reprinted articles, you do not have to cite the original source of publication. Cite only the reprinted publication.

30 Article in a Journal with Continuous Pagination—APA

Cochran, D. D., Hale, W. D., & Hissam, C. P. (1984). Personal space requirements in indoor versus outdoor locations. <u>Journal of Psychology, 117,</u> 132–133.

Give only the volume number after the journal title, and underline the volume number.

31 Article in a Journal That Pages Each Issue Separately—APA

Hashimoto, I. (1988). Pain and suffering: Apostrophes and academic life. <u>Journal of Basic Writing,</u> <u>7</u>(2), 91–98.

Give the volume number, underlined with the journal title. Give the issue number in parentheses; do not underline it.

32 Published and Unpublished Letters—APA

Lapidus, J. (1983). Letter to her mother. In K. Payne (Ed.), <u>Between ourselves: Letters between mothers and</u> <u>daughters</u> (pp. 323–326). Boston: Houghton Mifflin.

In the APA system, unpublished letters are considered personal communication inaccessible to general readers, so they do not appear in References. Personal communications do not provide recoverable data and so are cited only in the body of the paper, as shown in item 34, Interview.

33 Map, Chart—APA

<u>The Caribbean and South America</u> [Map]. (1992). Falls Church, VA: American Automobile Association.

Nonprint Sources

34 Interview—APA

In APA style, a personal interview is considered personal correspondence and is not included in References. Cite the interview in the text with a parenthetical notation that it is a personal communication:

> Randi Friedman (personal communication, June 30, 1992)
> endorses this view.

35 Lecture, Speech, Address—APA

> Kennedy, J. F. (1960, September 12). Address. Speech
> presented to the Greater Houston Ministerial Association,
> Houston.

36 Film, Videotape—APA

> Garcia Marquez, G. (Writer), & Guerra, R. (Director).
> (1984). Erendira [Film]. New York: Miramax.

37 Recording—APA

> Smetana, B. (1975). My country. [With K. Anserl
> conducting the Czech Philharmonic Orch.]. [Record].
> London: Vanguard Records.
>
> Springsteen, B. (Performer). (1992). Local hero.
> On Lucky town [CD]. New York: Columbia Records.

38 Live Performance—APA

> Stoppard, T. (Author), Nichols, M. (Director), Irons,
> J., & Close, G. (Performers). (1984, June 3). The real thing
> [Live performance]. New York: Plymouth Theatre.

39 Work of Art or Musical Composition—APA

> Cassatt, M. La toilette [Artwork]. Chicago: Art
> Institute of Chicago.
>
> Handel, G. F. Water music [Musical composition].

40 Radio or Television Program—APA

> Egleson, J. (Writer and Director), Pollan, T.
> (Performer), Savage, J. (Performer), & Eaton, R. (Producer).
> (1986, April 7). The little sister [Television program].
> Boston: WGBH, PBS American Playhouse.

Electronic Sources

Information from online sources that your readers probably cannot retrieve for themselves—many e-mail messages and bulletin board

board communications, for example--should be treated as personal communications. Identify the material in your paper, but do not include it in your References list. To cite an e-mail sent to you, for example, do this:

> John LeBlanc (personal communication, June 6, 1998) expects the experiment "to run for 18 months to 2 years."

Also see item 34, above.

APA has a website titled "How to Cite Information from the World Wide Web." The URL for this APA website it:

http://www.apa.org/journals/webref.html

Items 41, 42, 43, and 44, below, give models for documenting electronic sources as described in the APA Publication Manual. For documentation models of World Wide Web, gopher, and ftp sources in the newly authorized APA style, go to page 359.

41 Electronic Documents—APA

> Wallach, D. S. (1993, September 22). FAQ: Typing injuries (2/5): General Info. [Online]. Available FTP: rtfm.mit.edu Directory: pub/usenet/news.answers File: typing-injury-faq/general.Z

Keep capitalization exactly the same as found in the source. Punctuation in the availability statement, directory statement, and file statement should be used sparingly because any extra punctuation could be mistaken for part of the address. In the example, ending punctuation has been omitted for clarity.

42 Computer Software—APA

> Microsoft word. Vers. 5.0 [Computer software]. (1989). Microsoft. MS-DOS 2.0 or higher or OS/2 1.0. 512K, disk.

Do not underline the title of the software. Add any other important information, such as the computer on which the software can be used, number of kilobytes or units of memory required, the operating system required, and the form of the program (cartridge, disk, or CD).

43 Information Services: ERIC and NewsBank—APA

> Breland, H. M. (1987). <u>Assessing writing skill.</u> (ERIC Document Reproduction Service No. ED 286 920).

If the material in ERIC (Educational Resources Information Center) or any other information service was previously published, give the publishing information before the ERIC number.

Wenzell, R. (1990). <u>Businesses prepare for a more diverse work force.</u> (NewsBank Document Reproduction Service No. EMP 27:D12).

44 Abstract on CD-ROM—APA

Marcus, H. F., & Kitayamo, S. (1991). Culture and the self: Implications for group dynamics. [CD-ROM]. <u>Psychological Review, 88</u>(2), 224, 253. Abstract from: SilverPlatter File: PsycLIT Item: 78-23878

A3 CM-Style Documentation

The University of Chicago Press endorses two styles of documentation. One is a name-date style similar to that of the MLA and APA systems of in-text information that directs readers to a bibliographic list. The other, described in this chapter, is a note system often used in the disciplines of English, humanities, and history.

Understanding details about CM documentation with bibliographic notes

A3.a

The CM (for *Chicago Manual*) note system gives complete bibliographic information within a footnote or endnote the first time a source is cited.

If the source is cited again, the note gives less information. A separate bibliography is unnecessary because each first-citation note contains all the information a reader needs to identify the source. (As *The Chicago Manual of Style* points out, a separate bibliography is a convenience for readers of long works citing many sources.)

In CM style, the notes are either at the end of a paper (endnotes) or at the foot of the page on which a citation falls (footnotes).

Text   Welty also makes this point.[3]

Note   3. Eudora Welty, <u>One Writer's Beginnings</u> (Cambridge: Harvard University Press, 1984).

Endnotes may be easier for you to format than footnotes, especially if you are hand-writing or typing your paper. Most word-processing programs facilitate either system.

QA Box 58

Guidelines for CM-style notes

TITLE

For endnotes, *Notes,* on a new page numbered sequentially with the rest of the paper, after the last text page of the paper. (Footnotes appear at the bottom of the page where the relevant citation occurs.)

CONTENTS AND FORMAT

Include a note for every use you make of a source. Place endnotes after the text of your paper, on a separate page entitled *Notes.* Center the word *Notes* about an inch from the top of the page, and double-space after it. Single-space the notes themselves. Indent each note's first line three characters (or one tab space in your word-processing program), but do not indent a note's subsequent lines.

In the body of your paper, use raised (superscript) arabic numerals for the note numbers. Position note numbers after any punctuation marks except the dash, preferably at the end of a sentence. On the Notes page, make note numbers the same type size as the notes, and position them on, not above, the line, followed by a period. (Not all word-processing programs allow you to observe these guidelines. Adapt these guidelines if necessary, using a consistent style throughout your paper.)

SPACING AFTER PUNCTUATION

No specific requirements.

ARRANGEMENT

Use sequential numerical order throughout the paper. Even if you use footnotes, do not start with 1 on each page.

AUTHORS' NAMES

Give the name in standard (first name first) order, with names and initials as given in the original source. Use the word *and* between (the last) two authors.

CAPITALIZATION OF TITLES

Capitalize the first word and all major words.

SPECIAL TREATMENT OF TITLES

Underline the titles of long works, and use quotation marks around the titles of shorter works.

Continued on next page

▶ *QA Box 58, continued from previous page*

Omit *A*, *An*, and *The* from the titles of newspapers and periodicals. In parentheses, give the city (and state, if the city is not well known) for an unfamiliar newspaper title: (*Newark, N.J.*) *Star-Ledger*, for example.

PUBLICATION INFORMATION

Enclose in parentheses. Use a colon and one space after the city of publication. Give complete publishers' names or abbreviate them according to standard abbreviations in *Books in Print*. Omit *Co.*, *Inc.*, and the like. You can use *Univ.* for *University*; spell out *Press*. Do not abbreviate publication months. Note that CM Style uses state name abbreviations different from the two-letter postal abbreviations. See Section 14.17 in the 14th edition of the *Chicago Manual* for a list.

PAGE NUMBERS

In inclusive page numbers, give the full second number for 2 through 99. For 100 and beyond, give the full second number only if a shortened version is ambiguous: *243–47, 202–6, 300–304.*

List all discontinuous page numbers; see the model at "First Citation: Book," below.

Use a comma to separate parenthetical publication information from the page numbers that follow it.

Use the abbreviations *p.* and *pp.* with page numbers for material from journals that do not use volume numbers.

CONTENT NOTES

Try to avoid using content notes. If you must use them, make footnotes, and use symbols rather than numbers: an asterisk (*) for the first note on a page and a dagger (†) for a second note on that page.

FIRST CITATION: BOOK

Citations for books include the author, title, publication information, and page numbers if applicable.

   1. Eudora Welty, <u>One Writer's Beginnings</u> (Cambridge: Harvard University Press, 1984), 25–26, 30, 43–51, 208.

FIRST CITATION: ARTICLE

Citations for articles include the author, article title, journal title, volume number, year, and page numbers.

   35. D. D. Cochran, W. Daniel Hale, and Christine P. Hissam, "Personal Space Requirements in Indoor versus Outdoor Locations," <u>Journal of Psychology</u> 117 (1984): 132–33.

Using sample note forms in CM style

The directory below is a numbered list corresponding to the sample bibliographic notes forms that follow it. Not every possible documentation model is here. *The Chicago Manual of Style*, 14th edition, gives note and reference-list forms for every imaginable source. If you cannot find the information you need in this section, consult the *Chicago Manual.*

DIRECTORY—CM STYLE

1 Book by One Author—CM

1. Eudora Welty, <u>One Writer's Beginnings</u> (Cambridge: Harvard University Press, 1984).

CM style can combine notes with a bibliography; see **A3.a**. Here is the bibliographic entry for note 1.

Welty, Eudora. <u>One Writer's Beginnings</u>. Cambridge: Harvard University Press, 1984.

2 Book by Two or Three Authors—CM

2. Lisa Leghorn and Katherine Parker, <u>Woman's Worth</u> (Boston: Routledge, 1981).

3. Alfred H. Kelly, Winfred A. Harbison, and Herman Belz, <u>The American Constitution: Its Origins and Development</u> (New York: Norton, 1983).

If you are using a bibliography as well as notes, invert only the first name listed.

Kelly, Alfred H., Winfred A. Harbison, and Herman Belz. <u>The American Constitution: Its Origins and Development</u>. New York: Norton, 1983.

3 Book by More Than Three Authors—CM

4. Mark H. Moore et al., <u>Dangerous Offenders: The Elusive Target of Justice</u> (Cambridge: Harvard University Press, 1984).

Give the name of the author listed first on the title page, and then put either *et al.* or *and others*, using no punctuation after the author's name.

4 Multiple Citation of a Single Source—CM

For subsequent references to a work you have already cited, give the last name of the author followed by a comma and the page number. Note 5 shows the form for a subsequent reference to the work fully described in note 1.

5. Welty, 25.

If you cite more than one work by the same author, give the title between the name and the page number. If the title is long, you may shorten it.

6. Welty, <u>One Writer's Beginnings</u>, 25.

If you cite two or more authors with the same last name, include first names or initials in each note.

```
7. Eudora Welty, 25.
```

If you cite the same source as the source immediately preceding, you may use *Ibid.* followed by a comma and the page number rather than repeating the author's name.

```
8. Ibid., 25.
```

5 Book by a Group or Corporate Author—CM

```
9. The Boston Women's Health Collective, Our Bodies,
Ourselves (New York: Simon, 1986).
10. American Psychological Association, Publication
Manual of the American Psychological Association, 4th ed.
(Washington, D.C.: American Psychological Association,
1994).
```

If a work issued by an organization has no author listed on the title page, cite the name of the organization as the author of the work. The organization may also be the publisher of the work.

6 Book with No Author Named—CM

```
11. The Chicago Manual of Style, 14th ed. (Chicago:
University of Chicago Press, 1993).
```

Begin the citation with the name of the book.

7 Book with an Author and an Editor—CM

```
12. Emily Brontë, Wuthering Heights, ed. David Daiches
(London: Penguin, 1985).
```

In this position, the abbreviation *ed.* stands for *edited by*, not *editor*. Therefore, *ed.* is correct whether a work has one or more than one editor. (Also see items 14 and 15.)

8 Translation—CM

```
13. Paulo Freire, Pedagogy of the Oppressed, trans. Myra
Bergman Ramos (New York: Seabury Press, 1970).
```

The abbreviation *trans.* stands for *translated by*, not *translator*, and so is correct whether a work has one or more than one translators.

9 Work in Several Volumes or Parts—CM

The two notes numbered 14 show ways to give bibliographic information for a specific place in *one* volume of a multivolume work. Use whichever you prefer, being consistent throughout a paper. If you are writing about the volume as a whole (as opposed to citing specific pages), end the note with the publication information.

14. Ernest Jones, <u>The Last Phase</u>, vol. 3 of <u>The Life and Work of Sigmund Freud</u> (New York: Basic, 1957), 97.

14. Ernest Jones, <u>The Life and Works of Sigmund Freud</u>, vol. 3, <u>The Last Phase</u> (New York: Basic, 1957), 97.

If you are citing an entire in two or more volumes, use the form shown in note 15.

15. John Herman Randall, Jr., <u>The Career of Philosophy</u>, 2 vols. (New York: Columbia University Press, 1962).

10 One Selection from an Anthology or an Edited Book—CM

16. Ernest Galarza, "The Roots of Migration," in <u>Aztlan: An Anthology of Mexican Literature</u>, ed. Luis Valdez and Stan Steiner (New York: Alfred A. Knopf, 1972), 127–32.

Give page numbers for the cited work.

11 Two Selections from an Anthology or an Edited Book—CM

If you cite selections from an anthology or edited book, give complete bibliographical information in each citation.

12 Signed Article in a Reference Book—CM

17. Robert R. Holt, "Freud, Sigmund," in <u>International Encyclopedia of the Social Sciences</u>, ed. David L. Sills (New York: Macmillan, 1968), 1–11.

13 Unsigned Article in a Reference Book—CM

18. <u>Encyclopaedia Britannica</u>, 10th ed., s.v. "Ireland."

The abbreviation *s.v.* stands for *sub verbo,* meaning "under the word." Capitalize the heading of the entry only if it is a proper noun. Omit publication information except for the edition number.

14 Edition—CM

19. Maurice I. Mandell, <u>Advertising</u>, 4th ed. (Englewood Cliffs, N.J.: Prentice Hall, 1984).

Here the abbreviation *ed.* stands for *edition,* not *edited by* (see item 7). Give the copyright date for the edition that you are citing.

15 Anthology or Edited Book—CM

20. Luis Valdez and Stan Steiner, ed., <u>Aztlan: An Anthology of Mexican American Literature</u> (New York: Knopf, 1972).

16 Introduction, Preface, Foreword, or Afterword—CM

21. Franz Boas, introduction to <u>Patterns of Culture</u>, by Ruth Benedict (Boston: Houghton Mifflin, 1959).

If the author of the book is different from the author of the cited part, give the name of the book's author after the title of the book.

17 Unpublished Dissertation or Essay—CM

22. Shirley Burry Geissinger, "Openness versus Secrecy in Adoptive Parenthood" (Ph.D. diss., University of North Carolina at Greensboro, 1984), 45–56.

State the author's name first, the title in quotation marks (not underlined), then a descriptive label (such as *Ph.D. diss.* or *master's thesis*), then the degree-granting institution, the date, and finally the page numbers.

23. Kimberli M. Stafford, "Trapped in Death and Enchantment: The Liminal Space of Women in Three Classical Ballets" (paper presented at the annual meeting of the American Comparative Literature Association Graduate Student Conference, Riverside, Calif., April 1993).

To cite a paper read at a meeting, give the name of the meeting in parentheses, along with the location and the date.

18 Reprint of an Older Book—CM

24. Zora Neale Hurston, <u>Their Eyes Are Watching God</u> (1937; reprint, Urbana: University of Illinois Press, 1978).

Republishing information is located on the copyright page. List the original date of publication first, followed by the publication information for the reprint.

19 Book in a Series—CM

25. Heather McClave, <u>Women Writers of the Short Story</u>, Twentieth Century Views Series (Englewood Cliffs, N.J.: Prentice Hall, 1980).

If the series numbers its volumes and the volume number is not part of the title, include the volume number after the series title. Separate the volume number from the title with a comma.

20 Book with a Title Within a Title—CM

26. Robert M. Lumiansky and Herschel Baker, eds., <u>Critical Approaches to Six Major English Works: "Beowulf" Through "Paradise Lost"</u> (Philadelphia: University of Pennsylvania Press, 1968).

If the name of a work that is usually underlined appears in a title, add quotation marks around it. If the name of a work that is usually in quotations appears in a title, keep it in quotation marks and underline it. Use the abbreviation *ed.* or *eds.* depending on whether there is one or more than one editor.

21 Government Publication—CM

27. House Committee on the Judiciary, <u>Immigration and Nationality with Amendments and Notes on Related Laws</u>, 7th ed. (Washington D.C.: GPO, 1980).

If a government department, bureau, agency, or committee produces a document, cite that group as the author. The initials *GPO* stand for *Government Printing Office*, which publishes many federal publications.

22 Published Proceedings of a Conference—CM

28. Arnold Eskin, "Some Properties of the System Controlling the Circadian Activity Rhythm of Sparrows," in <u>Biochronometry</u>, ed. Michael Menaker (Washington, D.C.: National Academy of Sciences, 1971), 55–80.

Treat published conference proceedings as you would a chapter in a book.

23 Article from a Daily Newspaper—CM

29. Georgia Dullea, "Literary Folk Look for Solid Comfort," <u>New York Times</u> 16 April 1986, sec. C, p. 14.

If a large paper prints more than one edition a day (such as a morning edition and a final edition), identify the specific edition, make this the last information in the entry, preceded by a comma. For a paper that specifies sections, use *sec.* before the page number. If a paper gives column numbers, use *col.* after the page number. Separate all items with commas.

24 Editorial, Letter to the Editor, Review—CM

30. "Facing Space: After the Cold War," editorial, <u>New York Times</u>, 1 May 1989, sec. A, p. 16.

31. Glenda Teal Childress, letter, <u>Newsweek</u>, 9 June 1986, 10.

32. Peter Linebaugh, "In the Flight Path of Perry Anderson," review of <u>In the Tracks of Historical Materialism</u>, by Perry Anderson, <u>History Workshop</u> 21 (May 1986): 141–46.

Before page numbers, use a comma for popular magazines and a colon for journals.

25 Unsigned Article from a Daily Newspaper—CM

33. "Hospitals, Competing for Scarce Patients, Turn to Advertising," <u>New York Times</u>, 20 April 1986, p. 47.

26 Article from a Weekly or Biweekly Magazine or Newspaper—CM

34. Anastasia Toufexis, "Dining with Invisible Danger," <u>Time</u>, 27 March 1989, 28.

For popular weekly or biweekly magazines or newspapers, give the day-date, month, and year of publication. Separate page numbers from the year with a comma.

27 Article from a Monthly or Bimonthly Magazine—CM

35. Anna Roosevelt, "Lost Civilizations of the Lower Amazon," <u>Natural History</u>, February 1989, 74–83.

For popular monthly or bimonthly magazines, give the month and year of publication. Separate page numbers from the year with a comma.

28 Unsigned Article from a Weekly or Monthly Magazine—CM

36. "A Salute to Everyday Heroes," <u>Time</u>, 10 July 1989, 46–51, 54–56, 58–60, 63–64, 66.

If the article is printed on discontinuous pages, give all pages in the note.

29 Article from a Collection of Reprinted Articles—CM

37. Phillip C. Curver, "Lighting in the 21st Century," <u>Energy</u>, Social Issues Resources Series, vol. 4 (Boca Raton, Fla.: Social Issues Resources, 1990).

Cite only the publication actually consulted, not the original source. If you use a bibliography, in it cite both the reprinted publication you consulted and the publication where the article first appeared.

30 Article in a Journal with Continuous Pagination—CM

38. D. D. Cochran, W. Daniel Hale, and Christine P. Hissam, "Personal Space Requirements in Indoor versus Outdoor Locations," <u>Journal of Psychology</u> 117 (1984): 132–33.

31 Article in a Journal That Pages Each Issue Separately—CM

39. Irvin Hashimoto, "Pain and Suffering: Apostrophes and Academic Life," <u>Journal of Basic Writing</u> 7, no. 6 (1988): 91–98.

The issue number of a journal is required only if each issue of the journal starts with page 1. In this example, the volume number is 7 and the issue number, abbreviated as *no.*, is 6.

32 Personal Interview—CM

> 40. Randi Friedman, interview by author, Ames, Iowa, 30 June 1992.

For an unpublished interview, give the name of the interviewee and the interviewer, the location of the interview, and the date of the interview.

33 Published and Unpublished Letters—CM

> 41. Jackie Lapidus to her mother, 12 November 1975, <u>Between Ourselves: Letters Between Mothers and Daughters</u>, ed. Karen Payne (Boston: Houghton, 1983), 323–26.

> 42. Theodore Brown, letter to author, 13 June 1988.

For an unpublished letter, give the name of the author, the name of the recipient, and the date the letter was written.

34 Film or Videotape—CM

> 43. Gabriel Garcia Marquez, <u>Erendira</u> (New York: Miramax, 1984), filmstrip.

For a videotape, use the word *videocassette* in place of the word *filmstrip*.

35 Recording—CM

> 44. Bedrich Smetana, <u>My Country</u>, Czech Philharmonic, Karel Anserl, Vanguard SV-9/10.

Bedrich Smetana is the composer and Karel Anserl is the conductor.

> 45. Bruce Springsteen, "Local Hero," on <u>Lucky Town</u>, Columbia, CK 53001.

36 Computer Software—CM

> 46. Microsoft Word Ver. 5.0, Microsoft, Seattle, Wash.

Place the version or release number, abbreviated *Ver.* or *Rel.*, directly after the name of the software. Then list the company that owns the rights to the software, followed by that company's location.

37 ERIC Information Service—CM

> 47. Hunter M. Breland, <u>Assessing Writing Skills</u> (New York: College Entrance Examination Board, 1987), ERIC ED 286920.

ERIC stands for Educational Resources Information Center.

38 Electronic Documents—CM

The Chicago Manual of Style, 14th edition, describes electronic sources as an "extremely complex, fluid, and rapidly expanding field of source material" (634). The *Manual* shows several samples of acceptable documentation of electronic sources. Sample footnote 48 below shows you CM style for documenting a USENET newsgroup posting. CM style for electronic sources is based on the International Standards Organization (ISO) documentation system. If you are using CM style and do not find enough information in sample footnote 48 in this book to document your electronic sources, consult the ISO guidelines. Your college library should have a copy of ISO recommendations.

```
48. Dan S. Wallach, "FAQ: Typing Injuries (2/5): General
Info.," in typing-injury-faq/general.Z [USENET newsgroup],
1993- [cited 14 November 1993]; available from mail-server @
rtfm.mit.edu; INTERNET.
```

39 Secondary Source—CM

```
49. Mary Wollstonecraft, A Vindication of the Rights
of Woman (1792), 90, quoted in Caroline Shrodes,
Harry Finestone, and Michael Shugrue, The Conscious
Reader, 4th ed. (New York: Macmillan Publishing Company,
1988), 282.
```

When you quote one person's words, having found them in another person's work, give information as fully as you can about both sources. Note 49 shows the form when the point of your citation is Mary Wollstonecraft's words. If your point is what Shrodes, Finestone, and Shugrue have to say about Wollstonecraft's words, handle the information as in note 50.

```
50. Caroline Shrodes, Harry Finestone, and Michael
Shugrue, The Conscious Reader, 4th ed. (New York:
Macmillan Publishing Company, 1988), 282, quoting Mary
Wollstonecraft, A Vindication of the Rights of Woman
(1792), 90.
```

Using and Citing Graphics—CM

Place the credit line for a table or illustration from another source next to the reproduced material. (If you intend to publish your paper, you must receive permission to reprint copyrighted material from a source.) Spell out the terms *map, plate,* and *table,* but abbreviate *figure* as *fig.*

```
Reprinted, by permission, from Dennis Remington, M.D.,
A. Garth Fisher, Ph.D., and Edward Parent, Ph.D., How to
Lower Your Fat Thermostat: The No-Diet Reprogramming Plan
for Lifelong Weight Control (Provo, Utah: Vitality House
International, 1983), 74, fig. A2-1
```

A4 CBE-Style Documentation

In its 1994 style manual, *Scientific Style and Format,* the Council of Biology Editors (CBE) endorses two documentation systems widely used in mathematics and the physical and life sciences.

Understanding details about CBE documentation A4.a

The first system endorsed by CBE uses name-year parenthetical citations in the text of a paper, together with an alphabetically arranged References list that gives full bibliographic information for each source. A second system uses numbers to mark citations in the text of a paper that correlate with a numerically arranged References list. This chapter focuses on this numbered reference system. Here is the way it works:

1 The first time you cite each source in your paper, assign it a number in sequence, starting with 1.

2 Mark each subsequent reference to that source with the assigned number.

3 For your Reference list, list and number each entry in that order of its appearance in your paper, starting with 1.

CBE recommends using superscript numbers for marking source citations in your paper, although numbers in parentheses are also acceptable. Here is a brief example showing two sources cited in a paper and a References list arranged in citation sequence.

In-text citations	Sybesma[1] insists that this behavior occurs periodically, but Crowder[2] claims never to have observed it.
References list	1. Sybesma C. An introduction to biophysics. New York: Academic Press; 1977. 648 p.
	2. Crowder W. Seashore life between the tides. New York: Dodd, Mead & Co.; 1931. New York: Dover Publications Reprint; 1975. 372p.

Throughout this paper, each citation of Sybesma's *Introduction to Biophysics* is followed by a superscript 1, and each citation of Crowder's *Seashore Life* is followed by superscript 2.

QA Box 59

Guidelines for a CBE References List

TITLE

References *or* Cited References

PLACEMENT OF LIST

Start a new page numbered sequentially with the rest of the paper.

CONTENTS AND FORMAT

Include all sources quoted from, paraphrased, or summarized in your paper.

Center the title about 1 inch from the top of the page. Start each entry on a new line. Put the number, followed by a space at the regular left margin. If an entry takes more than one line, indent the second and all other lines. Double-space each entry and between entries.

SPACING AFTER PUNCTUATION

Follow the spacing in the models.

ARRANGEMENT OF ENTRIES

Arrange the entries in the sequence in which each is first cited in the text.

AUTHORS' NAMES

Invert all author names, giving the last name first. You can give first names or use only initials of first and middle names. If you use initials, do not use a period or a space between first and middle initials, and separate the names of multiple authors with a comma. If you use full first names, separate the names of multiple authors with a semicolon. With multiple authors, do not use & or *and*. Place a period after the last author's name.

TREATMENT OF TITLES

Capitalize a newspaper title's major words, dropping a first word of *A*, *An*, or *The*. Capitalize the titles of academic journals. If a journal title is one word, give it in full; otherwise, abbreviate it according to *American National Standard for Abbreviations of Titles of Periodicals* recommendations. Do not underline titles or enclose them in quotation marks.

PLACE OF PUBLICATION

Use a colon after the city of publication. Add a state postal abbreviation, in parentheses, or a country name to a city whose name by itself might be ambiguous or unfamiliar (see the example in item 3).

PUBLISHER

Give publishers' names, omitting *Co.*, *Press*, *Ltd.*, and so on. Place a semicolon after the publisher's name.

PUBLICATION MONTH ABBREVIATIONS

Abbreviate publication months to their first three letters. Do not use a period at the end.

Continued on next page

➤ QA Box 59, continued from previous page

INCLUSIVE PAGE NUMBERS

Shorten the second number as much as possible while keeping the number unambiguous (*233-4* for 233 to 234, *233–44* for 233 to 244; *233–304*). Where *p* is used, do not follow it with a period unless it is the last item in the entry. Follow the guidelines in the models.

DISCONTINOUS PAGE NUMBERS

List all discontinuous pages, shortening inclusive page number.

TOTAL PAGE NUMBERS

When citing an entire book, for the last information unit give the total pages followed by the abbreviation *p* and a period to end the information unit.

REFERENCES ENTRY: BOOK

Citations for books usually have four main parts: author(s), title, publication information, and pages (either total pages for citing an entire book or inclusive pages for citing part of a book). A period ends each information unit.

```
1. Stacy RW, Williams DT, Worden RE, McMorris RO.
   Essentials of biological and medical sciences. New
   York: McGraw-Hill; 1955. 727 p.
```

REFERENCES ENTRY: ARTICLE

Citations for articles usually have four main parts: author(s), article title, journal name, and publication information. The first two sections end with a period. In the example below, *Sci Am* is the abbreviated form of *Scientific American*. Note there is no space between elements after the year. The volume number is 269, and the issue number is (3).

```
1. Weissmann IL, Cooper MD. How the immune system
   develops. Sci Am 1993 Mar;269(3):65–71.
```

Using sample References forms in CBE style

A4.b

The directory below is a numbered list corresponding to the sample references that follow it. Not every possible documentation model is here. For guidance in citing sources other than the ones modeled here, consult CBE's *Scientific Style and Format*, Sixth Edition (1994) or a journal in the discipline for which you are writing.

DIRECTORY—CBE STYLE

1 Book by One Author—CBE

1. Hawking SW. Black holes and baby universes and other essays. New York: Bantam Books; 1993. 320 p.

Use one space but no punctuation between an author's last name and the initial of the first name. Do not put punctuation or a space between a first and middle initial. Do, however, keep the hyphen in a hyphenated first and middle name. See model 2, below, where *Gille J-C* represents *Jean-Claude Gille*.

2 Book by More Than One Author—CBE

1. Wegzyn S, Gille J-C, Vidal P. Developmental systems: at the crossroads of system theory, computer science, and genetic engineering. New York: Springer-Verlag; 1990. 595 p.

3 Book by Group or Corporate Author—CBE

1. Chemical Rubber Company. Handbook of laboratory safety. 3rd ed. Boca Raton (FL): CRC Press; 1990.

4 Anthology or Edited Book—CBE

1. Heerman B, Hummel S., editors. Ancient DNA: recovery and analysis of genetic material from paleontological, archeological, museum, medical, and forensic specimens. New York: Springer-Verlag; 1994. 1029 p.

5 One Selection or Chapter from an Anthology or Edited Book—CBE

1. Basov NG, Feoktistov LP, Senatsky YV. Laser driver for inertial confinement fusion. In: Brueckner KA, editor. Research trends in physics: inertial confinement fusion. New York: American Institute of Physics; 1992: p 24—37.

6 Translation—CBE

1. Magris C. A different sea. Spurr MS, translator. London: Harvill; 1993. 194 p. Translation of: Un mare differente.

7 Reprint of an Older Book—CBE

1. Carson R. The sea around us. New York: Oxford University Press; 1951. New York: Limited Editions Club Reprint; 1980. 220 p.

8 All Volumes of a Multivolume Work—CBE

1. Crane FL, Moore DJ, Low HE, editors. Oxidoreduction at the plasma membrane: relation to growth and transport. Boca Raton (FL): Chemical Rubber Company Press; 1991. 2 vol.

9 Unpublished Dissertation or Thesis—CBE

1. Baykul MC. Using ballistic electron emission microscopy to investigate the metal-vacuum interface [dissertation]. Orem (UT): Polytechnic University; 1993. 111 p.

10 Published Article from Conference Proceedings—CBE

1. Tsang CP, Bellgard MI. Sequence generation using a network of Boltzmann machines. In: Tsang CP, editor. Proceedings of the 4th Australian Joint Conference on Artificial Intelligence; 1990 Nov 8—11; Perth, Australia. Singapore: World Scientific; 1990. p 224—33.

11 Signed Newspaper Article—CBE

1. Hoke F. Gene therapy: clinical gains yield a wealth of research opportunities. Scientist 1993 Oct 4;Sect A:1, 5, 7.

Sect stands for *Section.*

12 Unsigned Newspaper Article—CBE

1. [Anonymous]. Irish urge postgame caution. USA Today 1993
   Nov 12;Sect C:2.

13 Article in a Journal with Continuous Pagination—CBE

1. Scott ML, Fredrickson RJ, Moorhead BB. Characteristics
   of old-growth forests associated with northern spotted
   owls in Olympic National Park. J Wildlf Mgt
   1993;57:315—21.

Give only the volume number, not an issue number, before the page
numbers.

14 Article in a Journal That Pages Each Issue Separately—CBE

1. Weissman IL, Cooper MD. How the immune system develops.
   Sci Am 1993 Mar;269(3):65—71.

Give both the volume number and the issue number (here, *269* is the
volume number and *3* is the issue number).

15 Journal Article on Discontinuous Pages—CBE

1. Richards FM. The protein folding problem. Sci Am 1991
   Nov;246(1):54—7, 60—6.

16 Article with Author Affiliation—CBE

1. DeMoll E, Auffenberg T (Dept. of Microbiology, Univ. of
   Kentucky). Purine metabolism in Methanococcus vannielii. J
   Bacteriol 1993;175:5754—61.

17 Entire Issue of a Journal—CBE

1. Whales in a modern world: a symposium held in London,
   November 1988. Mamm Rev 1990 Jan;20(9).

November 1988, the date of the symposium, is part of the title of this
issue.

18 Article with No Identifiable Author—CBE

1. [Anonymous]. Cruelty to animals linked to murders of
   humans. AWI Q 1993 Aug;42(3):16.

19 Map—CBE

1. Russia and Post-Soviet Republics [political map].
   Moscow: Mapping Production Association; 1992. Conical
   equidistant projection; 40 x 48 in.; colored, scale
   1:8,000,000.

20 Unpublished Letter—CBE

1. Darwin C. [Letter to Mr. Clerke, 1861]. Located at: University of Iowa Library, Iowa City, IA.

21 Filmstrip—CBE

1. Volcano: the eruption and healing of Mount St. Helens [filmstrip]. Westminster (MD): Random House: 1988. 114 frames: color; 35 mm. Accompanied by: cassettetape; 22 min.

After the title and description of the filmstrip, give the author, producer, and year. Then give other descriptive information.

22 Videorecording—CBE

1. The discovery of the pulsar: the ultimate ignorance [videocassette]. London: BBC; 1983. 1 cassette: 48 min, sound, color.

23 Slide Set—CBE

1. Human parasitology [slides]. Chicago (IL): American Society of Clinical Pathologists Press; 1990. Color. Accompanied by: guide.

24 Electronic Sources—CBE

In general, the CBE Manual advises that you cite electronic sources by starting with a statement of the type of document, and then giving the information you would give for a print version. Next, give information that would help a reader to locate the electronic source. End with a date: your access date for online sources or the date of the update you used for CD-ROM databases that are updated periodically.

Focus on ESL

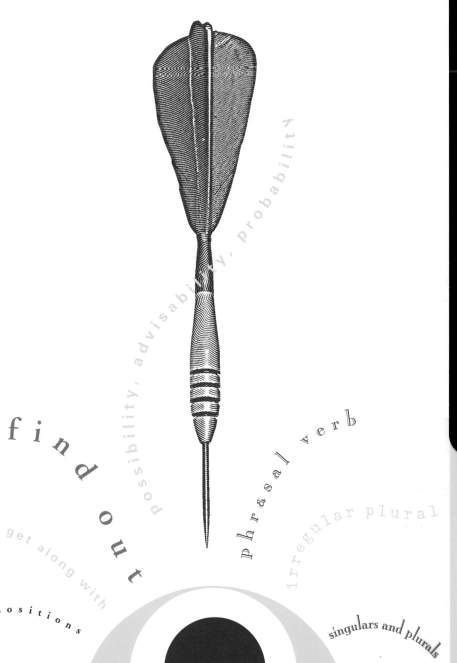

find out

get along with

possibility, advisability, probability

phrasal verb

irregular plural

epositions

singulars and plurals

gular plural

F FOCUS ON ESL

F1 Singulars and Plurals

Understanding count and noncount nouns   F1.a

Count nouns name items that can be counted: *radio, street, fingernail, idea.* **Noncount nouns** name things that cannot be counted: *knowledge, rain, traffic.*

UNCOUNTABLE ITEMS   QA
                                                              Box
                                                              60

- Groups of similar items making up "wholes": *clothing, equipment, furniture, luggage, mail, money*
- Abstractions: *equality, fun, health, ignorance, knowledge, peace, respect*
- Liquids: *blood, coffee, gasoline, water*
- Gases: *air, helium, oxygen, smog, smoke, steam*
- Materials: *aluminum, cloth, cotton, ice, wood*
- Food: *beef, bread, butter, macaroni, meat, cheese*
- Particles or grains: *dirt, dust, hair, rice, salt, wheat*
- Sports, games, activities: *chess, reading, sailing, soccer*
- Languages: *Arabic, Chinese, Japanese, Spanish*
- Fields of study: *biology, computer science, history, literature, math*
- Events in nature: *electricity, heat, moonlight, sunshine, thunder*

Count nouns can be SINGULAR (*radio, street*) or PLURAL (*radios, streets*), and so they may use singular or plural VERBS. Noncount nouns are used in singular form only, and so they use only singular verbs.

Alert: If you are not sure whether a noun is count or noncount, look it up in a dictionary such as the *Longman Dictionary of American English.* **!**

Some nouns can be countable or uncountable depending on their meaning in a sentence. Most of these nouns name things that can be meant either individually or as "wholes" made up of individual parts.

Count	The rains were late last year. [individual, countable occurrences of rain]
Noncount	The rain is soaking the garden. [all the drops of rain considered together]

When you are EDITING your writing, be sure that you have not added a plural *s* to any noncount nouns, which are always singular in form.

! **Alert:** Be sure to use a singular verb with any noncount noun that functions as a SUBJECT in a CLAUSE.

F1.b Knowing which determiners to use with singular and plural nouns

Determiners, also called expressions of quantity, are used to tell "how much" or "how many" about NOUNS. Choosing the right determiner with a noun can depend on whether the noun is NONCOUNT or COUNT. For count nouns, you must also decide whether the noun is SINGULAR or PLURAL. **QA Box 61**, below, lists many determiners and the kinds of nouns that they can accompany.

QA Box 61

USING DETERMINERS WITH COUNT AND NONCOUNT NOUNS

GROUP 1: DETERMINERS FOR SINGULAR COUNT NOUNS

With every singular count noun, always use one of the determiners listed in Group 1.

- We live in ^an^ apartment in ^that^ large, white house.

- ■ *a, an, the*
  - **a** house
  - **an** egg
  - **the** car

- ■ *one, any, some, every, each, either, neither, another, the other*
  - **any** house
  - **each** egg
  - **another** car

- ■ *my, our, your, his, her, its, their*, nouns with 's or s'
  - **your** house
  - **its** egg
  - **Connie's** car

- ■ *this, that*
  - **this** house
  - **that** egg
  - **this** car

- ■ *one, no, the first, the second*, etc.
  - **one** house
  - **no** egg
  - **the fifth** car

GROUP 2: DETERMINERS FOR PLURAL COUNT NOUNS

All the determiners listed in Group 2 can be used with plural count nouns. Plural count nouns can also be used without determiners, as discussed in **F2.b**.

- ~~The~~ ^T^ tomatoes are tasty in salad. Be sure that ^all the^ tomatoes you select are ripe.

- ■ *the*
  - **the** bicycles
  - **the** rooms
  - **the** ideas

- ■ *some, any, both, many, more, most, few, fewer, the fewest, a number of, other, several, all, all the, a lot of*
  - **some** bicycles
  - **many** rooms
  - **all** ideas

Continued on next page

▸ *QA Box 61, continued from previous page*

- *my, our, your, his, her, its, their, nouns with 's or s'*
  - **our** bicycles
  - **her** rooms
  - **students'** ideas
- *these, those*
  - **these** bicycles
  - **those** rooms
  - **these** ideas
- *no, two, three, four, etc., the first, the second, the third, etc.*
  - **no** bicycles
  - **four** rooms
  - **the first** ideas

GROUP 3: DETERMINERS FOR NONCOUNT NOUNS

All the determiners listed in Group 3 can be used with noncount nouns (always singular). Noncount nouns can also be used without determiners, as discussed in **F2.b**.

- You have ~~the~~ curly hair. I have *Some* hair on my sleeve.
  ^

- *the*
  - **the** rice
  - **the** rain
  - **the** pride
- *some, any, much, more, most, other, the other, little, less, the least, enough, all, all the, a lot of*
  - **enough** rice
  - **a lot of** rain
  - **more** pride
- *my, our, your, his, her, its, their, nouns with 's or s'*
  - **their** rice
  - **India's** rain
  - **your** pride
- *this, that*
  - **this** rice
  - **that** rain
  - **this** pride
- *no, the first, the second, the third, etc.*
  - **no** rice
  - **the first** rain
  - **no** pride

Alert: (1) The phrases *a few* and *a little* convey the meaning "some": *I have **a few** rare books* means "I have some rare books." *They are worth **a little** money* means "They are worth some money." Without the word *a, few* and *little* convey the meaning "almost none": *I have **few** [or very few] books* means "I have almost no books." *They are worth **little** money* means "They are worth almost no money." !

(2) *One of the* constructions always have a plural noun as the OBJECT of the PREPOSITION *of*. The verb agrees with *one*, not with the plural noun, so it is always singular: *One of the most important inventions of the twentieth century is* [not *are*] *television*. For verb agreement in *one of the . . . who* constructions, see **G4.a**.

▌ Using correct forms for nouns used as adjectives   F1.c

Some words that function as NOUNS can also function as ADJECTIVES. Adjectives in English do not have plural forms. If you use a noun as an adjective, do not add *s* (or *es*) to the adjective even when the noun or PRONOUN it modifies is PLURAL.

- Many Americans students are basketball fans.

- My nephew likes to look at pictures books.

F2 Articles

The words *a*, *an*, and *the* are **articles**. Articles are one type of DETERMINER. They signal that a NOUN will follow and that any MODIFIERS between the article and the noun refer to that noun.

- **a** chair
- **a** cold, metal chair
- **the** computer
- **the** lightning-fast computer

F2.a Understanding how to use *a*, *an*, or *the* ▌with singular count nouns

Every time you use a singular COUNT NOUN (a common noun that names one countable item), the noun requires some kind of DETERMINER; see Group 1 in **QA Box 61** for a list. To choose between *a* or *an* and *the*, you need to determine whether the noun is specific or nonspecific. A noun is considered specific when anyone who reads your writing can understand from the context of your message exactly and specifically to what the noun is referring.

For nonspecific singular count nouns, use *a* (or *an*). When the singular noun is specific, use *the* or some other determiner. **QA Box 62**, on the next page, can help you decide when a singular count noun is specific and therefore requires *the*.

! **Alert:** *An* is used before words that begin with a vowel sound; *a* is used before words that begin with a consonant sound. Words that begin with *h* or *u* can have either a vowel or a consonant sound. Make the choice based on the sound of the first word after the article, even if that word is not the noun.

- an idea
- an umbrella
- an honor
- a good idea
- a useless umbrella
- a history book

USING *THE* WITH SINGULAR COUNT NOUNS

RULE 1

A noun is specific and requires *the* when it names something unique or generally known.

- **The** sun has risen above **the** horizon. [Because *sun* and *horizon* are generally known nouns, they are specific nouns in the context of this sentence.]

RULE 2

A noun is specific and requires *the* when it names something used in a representative or abstract sense.

- Benjamin Franklin favored **the** turkey as **the** national bird of the United States. [Because *turkey* and *national bird* are representative references rather than references to a particular turkey or bird, they are specific nouns in the context of this sentence.]

RULE 3

A noun is specific and requires *the* when it names something defined elsewhere in the same sentence or in an earlier sentence.

- **The** ship *Savannah* was the first steam vessel to cross the Atlantic Ocean. [*Savannah* names a specific ship.]
- **The** carpet in my bedroom is new. [*In my bedroom* defines exactly which carpet is meant, so *carpet* is a specific noun in this context.]
- I have a computer in my office. **The** computer is often broken. [*Computer* is not specific in the first sentence, so it uses *a*. In the second sentence, *computer* has been made specific by the first sentence, so it uses *the*.]

RULE 4

A noun is specific and requires *the* when it names something that can be inferred from the context.

- I need an expert to fix **the** problem. [If you read this sentence after reading the two sentences about a computer in Rule 3, above, you understand that *problem* refers to the broken computer; *problem* is specific in this context.]

Alert: One common exception affects Rule 3 in **QA Box 62**. A noun may still require *a* (or *an*) after the first use if one or more descriptive adjectives come between the article and the noun: *I bought a sweater today. It was a* [not *the*] **red** *sweater.*

F2.b Understanding how to use articles with plural count nouns and with noncount nouns ▌

PLURAL COUNT NOUNS and NONCOUNT NOUNS with specific meanings usually use *the* according to the rules in **QA Box 62** on page 267. However, a plural count noun or a noncount noun with a general meaning usually does not use *the*.

Plural Count Nouns

- Geraldo planted tulips this year. **The** tulips will bloom in April.

The plural count noun *tulips* is used in a general sense in the first sentence, without *the*. Because the first sentence makes tulips specific, *the tulips* is correct in the second sentence. This example is related to Rule 3 in **QA Box 62** (page 267).

Noncount Nouns

- Kalinda served rice to us. She flavored **the** rice with curry.

Rice is a noncount noun. By the second sentence, *rice* has become specific, so *the* is used. This example is related to Rule 3 in **QA Box 62** (page 267).

Generalizations with Plural or Noncount Nouns

Omit *the* in generalizations using plural or noncount nouns.

- ~~The~~ ^T^ tulips are ~~the~~ flowers that grow from ~~the~~ bulbs.

F2.c Understanding how to use *the* with proper nouns ▌

Proper nouns name specific people, places, or things. Most proper nouns do not require ARTICLES: *We visited Lake Mead* [not *the Lake Mead*] *with Asha and Larry*. However, certain types of proper nouns do require *the*.

- ■ Nouns with the pattern of *the . . . of . . .* : *the United States of America, the President of Mexico*
- ■ Plural proper nouns: *the Johnsons, the Chicago Bulls, the United Arab Emirates*
- ■ Collective proper nouns (nouns that name a group): *the Society of Friends, the AFL-CIO.*
- ■ Some, but not all, geographical features: *the Amazon, the Gobi Desert, the Indian Ocean*

F3 Word Order

Understanding standard and inverted word order in sentences

Standard word order, the most common pattern for DECLARATIVE SENTENCES in English, has the SUBJECT coming before the VERB: *That book* [subject] *was* [verb] *heavy*.

Inverted word order, with a verb coming before the subject, is common for direct questions in English: *Was* [verb] *that book* [subject] *heavy? Were* [verb] *you* [subject] *close to it when it fell?*

A very common way to form questions with MAIN VERBS other than *be* and *have* is to use inverted order with a form of the verb *do* as an AUXILIARY VERB before the subject, and the SIMPLE FORM of the main verb after the subject: ***Do you want** me to put the book away?*

Also use inverted order when a question begins with a question-forming word such as *what, why, when, where,* or *how:* ***Where does** the book belong?*

When a question has more than one auxiliary verb, put the subject after the first auxiliary verb: ***Would you** have replaced the book?*

Alert: Do not use inverted word order with indirect questions: *She asked why I dropped the book* [not *She asked why did I drop the book*]. **!**

Verb-subject word order rules also apply to emphatic exclamations: ***Was** that **book** heavy! **Did she** enjoy that book!* For advice about inverted word order to create emphasis in declarative sentences, see **E3.e.**

Understanding the placement of adjectives

In English, an ADJECTIVE ordinarily comes directly before the NOUN it modifies. **QA Box 63,** below, shows the most common order for positioning several adjectives that modify the same noun.

WORD ORDER FOR ADJECTIVES

1 Determiners, if any: *a, an, the, my, your, Jan's, these,* etc.

2 Expressions of order, including ordinal numbers, if any: *first, second, next, last, final,* etc.

3 Expressions of quantity, including cardinal numbers, if any: *one, two, few, each, every, some,* etc.

4 Adjectives of judgment or opinion, if any: *smart, happy, interesting, sad, boring,* etc.

Continued on next page

> → *QA Box 63, continued from previous page*

> **5** Adjectives of size and/or shape, if any: *big, small, short, round, rectangular*, etc.
>
> **6** Adjectives of age and/or condition, if any: *new, young, broken, dirty, shiny*, etc.
>
> **7** Adjectives of color, if any: *red, green, beige, turquoise*, etc.
>
> **8** Adjectives that can also be used as nouns, if any: *French, metal, Protestant, cotton*, etc.
>
> **9** The noun
>
> | 1 | 2 | 3 | 4 | 5 | 6 | 7 | 8 | 9 |
> |---|---|---|---|---|---|---|---|---|
> | A | | few | | tiny | | red | | ants |
> | The | last | six | | | | | Thai | carvings |
> | My | | | fine | | old | | oak | table |

F3.c Understanding the placement of adverbs ▐

Adverbs and adverbial PHRASES modify VERBS, ADJECTIVES, other adverbs, or whole sentences. They can go in three different places in a CLAUSE: first, middle, or last.

QA Box 64

TYPES AND POSITIONS OF ADVERBS

- Adverbs of manner describe how something is done and usually go in middle or last position.
  - Nick **carefully** groomed the dog. Nick groomed the dog **carefully**.

- Adverbs of time describe when or how long about an event and usually go in first or last position.
  - **First**, he shampooed the dog. He shampooed the dog **first**.

- Adverbs of place describe where an event takes place and usually go in last position.
  - He lifted the dog **into the tub**.

- Adverbs of frequency describe how often an event takes place and go in the middle position to modify a verb or in the first position to modify an entire sentence.
  - Nick has **never** been bitten by a dog.
  - **Occasionally**, he is scratched while shampooing a cat.

- Adverbs of degree or emphasis describe how much or to what extent about other modifiers and come directly before the word they modify. They include *only*, which is easy to misposition; see **C4.a.**
  - Nick is **rather** quiet around animals.

Continued on next page

➤ QA Box 64, continued from previous page

> ■ Sentence adverbs modify an entire sentence. They include
> transitional words and expressions as well as *maybe, probably,*
> *possibly, fortunately, incredibly,* and others. They go in the first
> position.
>
> • **Incredibly,** he once had to groom a squirrel.

F4 Prepositions

Prepositions, along with their OBJECTS, form prepositional PHRASES,
which often describe relationships in time or space. Prepositions,
when combined with certain verbs, often have idiomatic meanings in
American English. A dictionary such as the *Longman Dictionary of
Contemporary English* or the *Oxford Advanced Learner's Dictionary* can
be especially helpful when you need to find the correct preposition for
these idiomatic uses.

Understanding the use of *in, at,* and *on* to show time and place
F4.a

Time

- *in* a year or a month (*during* is also correct but less common): *in 1999, in May*
- *in* a period of time: *in a few months* (*seconds, days, years*)
- *in* a period of a day: *in the morning (afternoon, evening), in the daytime (morning, evening)* BUT: *at night*
- *on* a specific day: *on Friday, on my birthday*
- *at* a specific time or periods of time: *at noon, at 2:00, at dawn, at nightfall, at takeoff* [the time a plane leaves], *at breakfast* [the time a specific meal takes place]

Place

- *in* a location surrounded by something else: *in the province of Alberta, in Utah, in downtown Bombay, in the kitchen, in my apartment, in the bathtub*
- *at* a specific location: *at your house, at the bank, at the corner of Third Avenue and Main Street*

F4.b Understanding the use of prepositions in phrasal verbs

Phrasal verbs are verbs that combine with PREPOSITIONS to deliver their meaning. The meaning of many phrasal verbs is idiomatic, not literal; *pick on*, for example, means "annoy" or "tease" rather than anything associated with either *pick* or *on*. Also, many phrasal verbs are informal and more appropriate for conversation than for academic writing. For a research paper, for example, *propose* or *suggest* would usually be better choices than *come up with*.

In some phrasal verbs, the verb and the preposition should not be separated by other words: **Look at** *the moon* [not **Look** *the moon* **at**].

In other phrasal verbs, called *separable phrasal verbs*, words can separate the verb and the preposition without interfering with meaning: *I* **threw** *my homework* **away** [or *I* **threw away** *my homework*.] When a separable phrasal verb has a PRONOUN OBJECT, that object should be positioned between the verb and the preposition: *I* **threw** *it* **away** [not *I* **threw away** *it*]. Object PHRASES or CLAUSES with more than four or five words should usually be positioned after the preposition: *I threw away* **the homework that was assigned last week**.

Here is a list of some common phrasal verbs. The ones that cannot be separated are marked with an asterisk (*).

LIST OF SELECTED PHRASAL VERBS

ask out	find out	look into*
break down	get along with*	look out for*
bring about	get back	look over
call back	get off*	make up
call off	go over*	run across*
call up	hand in	speak to*
drop off	keep up with*	speak with*
figure out	leave out	throw away
fill out	look after*	throw out
fill up	look around*	turn down

F4.c Using prepositions in common expressions

In many common expressions, different PREPOSITIONS convey great differences in meaning. For example, check a dictionary to see that four prepositions can be used with the VERB *agree* to create different meanings: *agree to, agree about, agree on,* and *agree with*.

You can find entire books filled with English expressions containing prepositions, and comprehensive dictionaries often give meanings for verb–preposition combinations as part of the entry for the verb.

F5 Gerunds and Infinitives

GERUNDS and INFINITIVES are types of verbals. **Verbals** are VERB forms that function as NOUNS or MODIFIERS. Like all nouns, gerunds and infinitives can be DIRECT OBJECTS. Some verbs call for gerund objects to follow them, and other verbs must be followed by infinitive objects. Still other verbs can be followed by either gerund or infinitive objects. A few verbs change meaning depending on whether a gerund object or an infinitive object is used.

Recognizing verbs that use a gerund, not an infinitive, object   F5.a

Certain VERBS cannot be followed by INFINITIVES as DIRECT OBJECTS; they require GERUNDS: *Yuri considered* **calling** [not *to call*] *the mayor.*

VERBS THAT USE GERUND OBJECTS

acknowledge	discuss	mind
admit	dislike	object to
advise	dream about	postpone
anticipate	enjoy	practice
appreciate	escape	put off
avoid	evade	quit
cannot help	favor	recall
complain about	finish	recommend
consider	give up	resent
consist of	have trouble	resist
contemplate	imagine	risk
defer from	include	suggest
delay	insist on	talk about
deny	keep (on)	tolerate
detest	mention	understand

Using a Gerund After *go*

Although *go* is usually followed by an infinitive object (*We can go to see* [not *go seeing*] *a movie*), *go* is followed by a gerund in such phrases as *go swimming, go fishing, go shopping,* and *go driving*: *I will go swimming* [not *go to swim*] *tomorrow.*

Using Gerunds After *be* + Complement + Preposition

LIST OF SELECTED *BE* + COMPLEMENT + PREPOSITION EXPRESSIONS

be (get) accustomed to	be interested in
be angry about	be prepared for
be bored with	be responsible for
be capable of	be tired of
be committed to	be (get) used to
be excited about	be worried about

- We are excited about voting [*not* to vote] in the election.
- They were interested in hearing [*not* to hear] the candidates' debate.

! **Alert:** Always use a gerund, not an infinitive, as the object of a preposition. Be especially careful when the word *to* is functioning as a preposition in a phrasal verb (see **F4.b**): *We are committed to changing the rules* [not *committed to change*].

F5.b Recognizing verbs that use an infinitive, not a gerund, object

Certain VERBS cannot be followed by GERUNDS as DIRECT OBJECTS; they use INFINITIVES: *Three people decided to question* [not *decided questioning*] *the speaker.*

VERBS THAT USE INFINITIVE OBJECTS

afford	demand	plan
agree	deserve	prepare
aim	expect	pretend
appear	fail	promise
arrange	give permission	refuse
ask	hesitate	seem
attempt	hope	struggle
be able (unable)	intend	tend
be left	know how	threaten
beg	learn	try
care (not care)	like	volunteer
claim	manage	wait
consent	mean	want
decide	offer	would like
decline		

Using Infinitives After *be* + Complement

- We are eager **to go** [*not* going] to the mountains.
- I am ready **to sleep** [*not* sleeping] in a tent.

Using Unmarked Infinitive Objects

An unmarked infinitive uses a verb's SIMPLE FORM but not the word *to*.
Some common verbs followed by unmarked infinitive objects are *feel, have, hear, let, listen to, look at, make* (meaning "compel"), *notice, see,* and *watch.*

- Please **let** me **take** [not *to take*] you to lunch. [*Take* is an unmarked infinitive used after *let*.]
- I want **to take** you to lunch. [*To take* is a marked infinitive used after *want*.]

The verb *help* can be followed by either a marked or an unmarked infinitive: *Help me put* [or *Help me to put*] *these groceries away.*

Alert: Be careful about parallel structure when you use two or more verbals as objects after one verb. Put the verbals into the same form. !

- We went sailing and ~~to scuba dive~~. *diving.*

- We heard the wind blow and the waves crashing~~,~~.

But if you are using verbal objects in a COMPOUND PREDICATE, be sure to use the kind of verbal that each verb requires.

- We enjoyed scuba diving but do not want ~~sailing~~ again. *to sail*

  [*Enjoyed* requires a gerund object and *want* requires an infinitive object.]

| **Understanding how meaning changes depending on whether gerund or infinitive objects follow *stop*, *remember*, and *forget*** | **F5.c** |

Followed by a GERUND, *stop* means "finish, quit": *We stopped eating* means "We finished our meal." Followed by an INFINITIVE, *stop* means "stop or interrupt one activity to begin another": *We stopped to eat* means "We stopped doing something [such as driving or painting the house] to eat."

Followed by an infinitive, *remember* means "not to forget to do something": *I must remember to talk with Isa.* Followed by a gerund, *remember* means "recall a memory": *I remember talking to you last night.*

Followed by an infinitive, *forget* means "to not do something": *If you forget to put a stamp on that letter, it will be returned.* Followed by a gerund, *forget* means "to do something and not recall it": *I forget having put my keys in the refrigerator.*

F5.d Understanding that certain sense verbs use gerund and infinitive objects without changing meaning

Sense VERBS such as *see, notice, hear, observe, watch, feel, listen to,* and *look at* usually do not change meaning whether a GERUND or an INFINITIVE is used as an OBJECT. *I saw the water rising* and *I saw the water rise* (unmarked infinitive—see **F5.b**) both deliver the same message.

F5.e Choosing between *-ing* forms and *-ed* forms for adjectives

Deciding whether to use the *-ing* form (PRESENT PARTICIPLE) or the *-ed* form (PAST PARTICIPLE of a REGULAR VERB) as an ADJECTIVE in a specific sentence can be difficult. For example, *I am amused* and *I am amusing* are both correct in English, but their meanings are very different. To make the right choice, decide whether the modified NOUN or PRONOUN is causing or experiencing what the participle describes.

Use a present participle (*-ing*) to modify a noun or pronoun that is the agent or the cause of the action.

- Mica explained your interesting plan.   [The noun *plan* causes what its modifier describes—interest; so *interesting* is correct.]
- I find your plan exciting.   [The noun *plan* causes what its modifier describes—excitement; so *exciting* is correct.]

Use a part participle (*-ed* in regular verbs) to modify a noun or pronoun that experiences or receives whatever the modifier describes.

- An interested committee wants to hear your plan.   [The noun *committee* experiences what its modifier describes—interest; so *interested* is correct.]
- Excited by your plan, I called a board meeting.   [The noun *I* experiences what its modifier describes—excitement; so *excited* is correct.]

Here is a list of some frequently used participles that require your close attention when you use them as adjectives. To choose the right form, decide whether the noun or pronoun experiences or it causes what the participle describes.

amused, amusing   appalled, appalling
annoyed, annoying   bored, boring

confused, confusing	offended, offending
depressed, depressing	overwhelmed, overwhelming
disgusted, disgusting	pleased, pleasing
fascinated, fascinating	reassured, reassuring
frightened, frightening	satisfied, satisfying
insulted, insulting	shocked, shocking

F6 Modal Auxiliary Verbs

Modal auxiliary verbs include *can, could, may, might, should, had better, must, will, would,* and others. Like the auxiliary verbs *be, do,* and *have,* modal auxiliary verbs help main verbs convey more information. Modal auxiliary verbs convey meaning about ability, necessity, advice, possibility, and other conditions.

Modal auxiliary verbs differ from *be, do,* and *have* in two important ways.

- Modal auxiliary verbs are always followed by the simple form of a main verb: *I might go tomorrow.*
- One-word modal auxiliary verbs usually do not have an *s* ending in third-person singular: *She **could** go with me, you **could** go with me,* and *they **could** go with me.* Exceptions include modals such as *have to* and *need to,* which make the third-person singular changes that *have* and *need* ordinarily do (for example, *I **have** to stay, she **has** to stay; you **need** to smile, he **needs** to smile*).

F6.a Using modal auxiliary verbs to convey ability, necessity, advisability, and probability

Conveying Ability

Can conveys ability in the present. *Could* conveys ability in the past. These words deliver the meaning of "able to."

- You **can work** late tonight. I **could work** late last night.

Adding *not* between a MODAL AUXILIARY VERB and the MAIN VERB makes the sentence negative: *I could not work late last night.*

! **Alert:** Negative forms of modal auxiliary verbs are often turned into contractions: *can't, couldn't, won't, wouldn't,* and so on. Because contractions can be considered informal usage, you will never be wrong to avoid them in academic writing.

Conveying Necessity

Must, have to, and *need to* convey the message of a need to do something. *Must* implies future action. *Have to* and *need to* are used in all verb tenses.

- You **must leave** before midnight. She **has to leave** when I leave. We **needed to be** with you tonight.

Conveying Advisability or the Notion of a Good Idea

Should and *ought to* convey that doing the action of the MAIN VERB in the present or future is a good idea. The PAST-TENSE forms are *should have* and *ought to have*; they are followed by the PAST PARTICIPLE.

- You **should go** to class tomorrow morning. I **ought to have called** my sister last week.

The modal *had better* delivers the meaning of good advice or warning or threat.

- You **had better see** a doctor before your cough gets worse.

Conveying Probability

May, might, could, and *must* can convey the idea of probability, possibility, or likelihood.

- We **may become** hungry before long. We **could eat** lunch now.

The past-tense forms for *may, might, could,* and *must* add *have* and the main verb's past participle to the modals.

- I **must have neglected** to eat breakfast.

Using modal auxiliary verbs to convey preference, plan, and past habit   F6.b

Conveying Preferences

Would rather (present tense) and *would rather have* (past tense) express a preference. In the past tense, the modal is also followed by a past participle.

- We **would rather see** a comedy than a mystery. We **would rather have seen** a movie last night.

Conveying Plan or Obligation

A form of *be* followed by *supposed to* and the SIMPLE FORM of a MAIN VERB, in both present and past tense, delivers a meaning of something planned or of an obligation.

- I **was supposed to meet** them at the bus stop.

Conveying Past Habit

Used to and *would* deliver a meaning that something happened repeatedly in a time that has passed.

- I **used to hate** getting a flu shot. I **would dread** the injection for weeks beforehand.

Alert: Both *used to* and *would* can be used for repeated actions in the past, but *would* cannot be used for a situation that lasted for a duration of time in the past.

- I ~~would~~ live in Arizona.

    used to

Usage Glossary

This usage glossary presents the customary manner of using particular words and phrases. "Customary manner," however, is not as firm in practice as the term implies. Usage standards change. If you think a word's usage might differ from what you read here, consult a dictionary published more recently than this book.

As used here, *informal* indicates that the word or phrase occurs commonly in speech but should be avoided in academic writing. *Nonstandard* indicates that the word or phrase should not be used in either standard spoken English or writing.

Some commonly confused words appear in this Usage Glossary; for an extensive list see **QA Box 42** on pages 157–161. Parts of speech, sentence structures, and other grammatical terms mentioned in this Usage Glossary are all defined in the Grammatical Terms Glossary, which starts on page 299.

a, an   Use *a* before words beginning with consonants (*a dog, a grade, a hole*) or consonant sounds (*a one-day sale, a European*). American English uses *a*, not *an*, with words starting with a pronounced *h*: *a* [not *an*] *historical event.*

accept, except   *Accept* means "agree to; receive." As a verb, *except* means "exclude, leave out"; as a preposition, *except* means "leaving out":

- **Except** [preposition] for one detail, the workers were ready to **accept** [verb] management's offer: They wanted the no-smoking rule **excepted** [verb] from the contract.

advice, advise   *Advice*, a noun, means "recommendation"; *advise*, a verb, means "recommend; give advice":

- I **advise** [verb] you to follow your car mechanic's **advice** [noun].

affect, effect   As a verb, *affect* means "cause a change in; influence" (*affect* also functions as a noun in the discipline of psychology). As a noun, *effect* means "result or conclusion"; as a verb, it means "bring about":

- Many groups **effected** [verb] amplification changes at their concerts after discovering that high decibel levels **affected**

[verb] their hearing. Many fans still choose to ignore the harmful **effects** [noun] of sound.

aggravate, irritate   *Aggravate* is used colloquially to mean "irritate." Use *aggravate* to mean "intensify; make worse." Use *irritate* to mean "annoy; make impatient."

- The coach was **irritated** by her assistant's impatience, for it **aggravated** the team's inability to concentrate.

ain't   Nonstandard contraction for *am not, is not,* and *are not.*

all ready, already   *Already* means "before; by this time"; *all ready* means "completely prepared":

- The ball players were **all ready**, and the manager had **already** given the lineup card to the umpire.

all right   Two words, never one (not *alright*).

all together, altogether   *All together* means "in a group, in unison"; *altogether* means "entirely, thoroughly":

- The judge decided it was **altogether** absurd to expect the jurors to stay **all together** in one hotel room.

allude, elude   *Allude* means "refer to indirectly or casually"; *elude* means "escape notice":

- They were **alluding** to budget cuts when they said that "constraints beyond our control enabled the suspect to **elude** us."

allusion, illusion   An *allusion* is an indirect reference to something; an *illusion* is a false impression or idea.

a lot   Informal for *a great deal* or *a great many*; avoid it in academic writing.

a.m., p.m.   Also A.M., P.M. Use only with numbers, not as substitutes for the words *morning, afternoon,* or *evening*:

- We will arrive **in the afternoon** [*not* in the p.m.], and we have to leave no later than **8:00 a.m.**

among, between   Use *among* for three or more items and *between* for two items:

- My roommates and I discussed **among** ourselves the choice **between** staying in school and getting full-time jobs.

amount, number   Use *amount* for uncountable things (*wealth, work, corn, happiness*); use *number* for countable items:

- The **amount** of rice to cook depends on the **number** of dinner guests.

and/or   Appropriate in business and legal writing when either or both items it connects can apply: *This process is quicker if you have a modem and/or a fax machine.* In the humanities, usually express alternatives in words: *This process is quicker if you have a modem, a fax machine, or both.*

anymore   Use *anymore* with the meaning "now, any longer" in negations or questions only:

- No one knits **anymore**.

For positive statements, use an adverb such as *now*:

- Summers are so hot **now** [*not* anymore] that holding yarn is unbearable.

anyplace   Informal for *any place* or *anywhere*.

anyways, anywheres   Nonstandard for *anyway, anywhere*.

apt, likely, liable   *Apt* and *likely* are used interchangeably. Strictly, *apt* indicates a tendency or inclination. *Likely* indicates a reasonable expectation or greater certainty than *apt*. *Liable* denotes legal responsibility or implies unpleasant consequences.

- Alan is **apt** to leave early on Friday. I will **likely** go with him to the party. Maggy and Gabriel are **liable** to be angry if we do not show up.

as, like, as if, as though   Use *as*, not *like*, as a subordinating conjunction introducing a clause:

- This hamburger tastes good, **as** [*not* like] a hamburger should.

Use *as if* (or *as though*), not *like*, to introduce a subjunctive or other conditional clause:

- That hamburger tastes **as if** [*not* like] it had been grilled all day.

As and *like* can both function as prepositions in comparisons. Use *like* to suggest a point of similarity or an area of resemblance, but not complete likeness, between nouns or pronouns:

- Mexico, **like** [*not* as] Argentina, belongs to the United Nations.

Use *as* to show equivalence:

- Beryl acted **as** [*not* like] the moderator of our panel.

Also, if the items are in prepositional phrases, use *as* even if you are suggesting only one point of similarity:

- In Mexico, **as** [*not* like] in Argentina, Spanish is the main language.

assure, ensure, insure   *Assure* means "promise, convince"; *ensure* means "make certain or secure"; *insure* means "indemnify or guarantee against loss" and is reserved for financial or legal certainty, as in insurance:

- The agent **assured** me that he could **insure** my roller blades but that only I could **ensure** that my elbows and knees would outlast the skates.

as to   Avoid as a substitute for *about*:

- They answered questions **about** [*not* as to] their safety record.

awful, awfully   The adjective *awful* means "causing fear." Avoid it as a substitute for intensifiers such as *very* or *extremely*. In academic writing, also avoid the informal usage *awfully* for *very* or *extremely*.

a while, awhile   As two words, *a while* is an article and a noun that can function as a subject or object. As one word, *awhile* is an adverb; it modifies verbs. In a prepositional phrase, the correct form is *a while*: *for a while, in a while, after a while.*

bad, badly   *Bad* is an adjective; use it after linking verbs. (Remember that verbs like *feel* and *smell* can function as either linking verbs or action verbs.) *Badly* is an adverb and is nonstandard after linking verbs (see **G8.c**):

- Farmers feel **bad** because a bad drought has **badly** damaged the crops.

been, being   *Been* is the past participle of the verb *be; being* is the present participle of *be*. As main verbs, *being* and *been* must be used with auxiliary verbs:

- You **are being** [*not* being] silly if you think I believe you **have been** [*not* been] to Sumatra.

being as, being that   Nonstandard for *because* or *since*:

- We forfeited the game **because** [*not* being as *or* being that] our goalie has appendicitis.

beside, besides   *Beside* is a preposition meaning "next to, by the side of":

- She stood **beside** the new car, insisting that she would drive.

As a preposition, *besides* means "other than, in addition to":

- No one **besides her** had a driver's license.

As an adverb, *besides* means "also, moreover":

- **Besides**, she owned the car.

better, had better   Used in place of *had better, better* is informal:

- We **had better** [*not* We better] be careful.

breath, breathe   *Breath* is a noun; *breathe* is a verb.

- Don't take a **breath** [noun] because you will **breathe** [verb] diesel fumes.

bring, take Use *bring* for movement from a distant place to a near place or to the speaker; use *take* for movement from a near place or from the speaker to a distant place:

- If you **bring** a leash when you come to my house, you can **take** Vicious to the vet.

but, however, yet Use *but*, *however*, or *yet* alone, not in combination with each other:

- The economy is strong, **but** [*not* but yet *or* but however] unemployment is high.

calculate, figure, reckon Informal or regional for *estimate*, *imagine*, *expect*, *think*, and similar words.

can, may *Can* signifies ability or capacity; *may* requests or grants permission. In negations, however, *can* is acceptable in place of *may*:

- You **cannot** [*or* **may not**] leave yet.

can't hardly, can't scarcely Nonstandard; double negatives (see **G8.b**).

censor, censure The verb *to censor* means "to delete objectionable material; to judge"; the verb *to censure* means "to condemn or to reprimand officially."

- The town council **censured** the mayor for trying to **censor** information in the annual spending report.

chairman, chairperson, chair Many writers and speakers prefer the gender-neutral terms *chairperson* and *chair* to *chairman*; *chair* is more common than *chairperson*.

choose, chose *Choose* is the simple form of the verb; *chose* is the past-tense form:

- I **chose** the movie last week, so you **choose** it tonight.

cloth, clothe *Cloth* is a noun meaning "fabric"; *clothe* is a verb meaning "cover with garments or fabric; dress."

complement, compliment *Complement* means "bring to perfection, go well with; complete"; *compliment* means "praise; flatter":

- They **complimented** us on the design of our experiment, saying that it **complemented** work done twenty years ago.

conscience, conscious The noun *conscience* means "a sense of right and wrong", the adjective *conscious* means "being aware or awake."

consensus of opinion Redundant; use *consensus* only.

continual(ly), continuous(ly) *Continual* means "occurring repeatedly"; *continuous* means "going on without interruption":

- Intravenous fluids were given **continuously** for three days after surgery; nurses were **continually** hooking up new bottles of saline.

couple, a couple of Nonstandard for *a few* or *several*:

- Rest for **a few** [*not* a couple *or* a couple of] minutes.

data Plural of *datum*, a rarely used word. Informally, *data* is commonly used as a singular noun requiring a singular verb. In the sciences, *data* is used with a plural verb.

different from, different than *Different from* is preferred for formal writing; *different than* is common in speech.

disinterested, uninterested *Disinterested* means "impartial, unbiased" in its preferred usage and is also used to mean "uninterested, indifferent." Some authorities object to this second usage, so you may want to reserve *disinterested* to convey "impartial" and *uninterested* to convey "indifferent."

don't A contraction for *do not*, but not for *does not* (*doesn't*):

- She **doesn't** [*not* don't] like crowds.

emigrate (from), immigrate (to) *Immigrate* means "enter a country to live there"; *emigrate* means "leave one country to live in another."

enthused   Nonstandard substituting for the adjective *enthusiastic*:

- Are you **enthusiastic** [*not* enthused] about seeing a movie?

etc.   Abbreviation for the Latin *et cetera,* meaning "and the rest." For writing in the humanities, avoid in-text use of *etc.;* acceptable substitutes are *and the like, and so on, and so forth.*

everyday, every day   The adjective *everyday* means "daily" and modifies nouns; *every day* is an adjective-noun combination, which can function as a subject or object:

- Being late for work has become an **everyday** occurrence. **Every day** that I am late brings me closer to being fired.

everywheres   Nonstandard for *everywhere.*

explicit, implicit   *Explicit* means "directly stated or expressed"; *implicit* means "implied, suggested":

- The warning on cigarette packs is **explicit**: "Smoking is dangerous to health." The **implicit** message is "Don't smoke."

farther, further   Although many writers reserve *farther* for geographical distances and *further* for all other cases, current usage treats them as interchangeable.

fewer, less   Use *fewer* for anything that can be counted (with count nouns): *fewer dollars, fewer fleas, fewer haircuts.* Use *less* with collective or other noncount nouns: *less money, less scratching, less hair.*

fine, find   *Fine* can be a noun or an adjective:

- She risked a $100 **fine** [noun] for parking in a reserved space when she ran into Sears to buy a **fine** [adjective] electric drill.

Find is the simple form of the verb:

- We **find** new evidence each day.

former, latter   When two items are referred to, *former* signifies the first one and *latter* signifies the second. Do not use *former* and *latter* for references to more than two items.

- Brazil and Ecuador are South American countries. Portuguese is the most common language in the **former**, and Spanish is the most common language in the **latter**.

go, say   *Go* is nonstandard for *say, says,* or *said*:

- After he stepped on my hand, he **said** [*not* he goes], "Your hand was in my way."

gone, went   *Gone* is the past participle of *go; went* is the past tense of *go*:

- They **went** [*not* gone] to the concert after Ira **had gone** [*not* had went] home.

good and   Nonstandard intensifier:

- They were **exhausted** [*not* good and tired].

good, well   *Good* is an adjective (*good idea*). Using it as an adverb is nonstandard. *Well* is the equivalent adverb: *run well* [not *run good*].

got, have   *Got* is nonstandard in place of *have*:

- What do we **have** [*not* got] for supper?

have, of   Use *have,* not *of,* after such verbs as *could, should, would, might, must*:

- You **should have** [*not* should of] called first.

have got, have, have got to   Avoid using *have got* when *have* alone delivers your meaning:

- I **have** [*not* have got] two more sources to read.

Avoid *have got to* for *must*:

- I must [*not* have got to] finish this assignment today.

*I **have to** finish this assignment is informal.*

hopefully An adverb meaning "with hope, in a hopeful manner," *hopefully* can modify a verb, an adjective, or another adverb: *They waited hopefully for the plane to land. Hopefully* is commonly used as a sentence modifier with the meaning "I hope," but you should avoid this usage in academic writing:

- **I hope** [*not* Hopefully] the plane will land safely.

if, whether Use either *if* or *whether* at the start of a noun clause:

- I don't know **if** [*or* **whether**] I want to dance with you.

In conditional clauses, use *whether* (or *whether or not*) when alternatives are expressed or implied:

- I will dance with you **whether or not** I like the music.
  I will dance with you **whether** the next song is fast **or** slow.

Use *if* in a conditional clause that does not express or imply alternatives:

- **If** you promise not to step on my feet, I will dance with you.

imply, infer *Imply* means "hint at or suggest without stating outright"; *infer* means "draw a conclusion from what is being expressed." A writer or speaker implies; a reader or listener infers:

- When the governor **implied** that she would not seek reelection, reporters **inferred** that she was planning to run for Vice President.

incredible, incredulous *Incredible* means "extraordinary; not believable"; *incredulous* means "unable or unwilling to believe." A person would be incredulous in response to finding something incredible:

- Listeners were **incredulous** as the freed hostages described the **incredible** hardships they had experienced.

inside of, outside of Nonstandard for *inside* or *outside*:

- She waited **outside** [*not* outside of] the dormitory.

Also, *inside of* meaning "in less than" in time references is an Americanism inappropriate for academic writing:

- I changed clothes **in less than** [*not* inside of] ten minutes.

irregardless   Nonstandard for *regardless*.

is when, is where   Avoid these constructions in giving definitions:

- Defensive driving **involves** [*not* is when] drivers' staying alert to avoid accidents that other drivers might cause.

its, it's   *Its* is a personal pronoun in the possessive case:

- The dog buried **its** bone.

It's is a contraction of *it is* or *it has*:

- **It's** a hot day; **it's** seemed hotter than usual this summer.

kind, sort   Use *this* or *that* with these singular nouns; use *these* or *those* with the plural nouns *kinds* and *sorts*. Also, do not use *a* or *an* after *kind of* or *sort of*:

- Drink **these kinds of** fluids [*not* this kind of fluids] on **this sort of** [*not* this sort of a] day.

kind of, sort of   Informal as adverbs meaning "in a way; somewhat":

- The hikers were **somewhat** [*not* kind of] dehydrated by the time they got back to camp.

later, latter   *Later* means "after some time; subsequently"; *latter* refers to the second of two:

- The college library stays open **later** than the town library; also, the **latter** is closed on weekends.

lay, lie   *Lay, (laid, laid, laying)* means "place or put something, usually on something else" and needs a direct object; *lie (lay,* *lain, lying*), meaning "recline," does not take a direct object (see **G3.c**). Substituting *lay* for *lie* is nonstandard:

- **Lay** [*not* lie] the blanket down, and then **lay** the babies on it so they can **lie** [*not* lay] in the shade.

leave, let   *Leave* means "depart"; *let* means "allow, permit." *Leave* is nonstandard for *let*:

- **Let** [*not* Leave] me use your car tonight.

lots, lots of, a lot of   Informal for *many, much, a great deal*:

- **Many** [*not* A lot of] bees were in the hive.

may be, maybe   *May be* is a verb phrase; *maybe* is an adverb:

- Our team **may be** [verb phrase] tired, but **maybe** [adverb] we can win anyway.

media   Plural of *medium*, but common usage pairs it with a singular verb. In most cases, a more specific word is preferable:

- **Television reporters offend** [*not* The media offends] me by shouting personal questions at grief-stricken people.

morale, moral   *Morale* is a noun meaning "a mental state relating to courage, confidence, or enthusiasm." As a noun, *moral* means "ethical lesson implied or taught by a story or event"; as an adjective, *moral* means "ethical":

- One **moral** to draw from corporate down-sizings is that overstressed employees suffer from low **morale**. Under such stress, sometimes even employees with otherwise high **moral** standards steal time, supplies, or products from their employers.

most   Nonstandard for *almost*: *Almost* [not *most*] *all the dancers agree*. *Most* is correct as the superlative form of an adjective (*some, more, most*): *Most dancers agree*. It also makes the superlative form of adverbs and some adjectives: *most suddenly, most important*.

Ms.   A women's title free of reference to marital status, equivalent to *Mr.* for men.

nowheres   Nonstandard for *nowhere*.

off of   Nonstandard for *off*:

- Don't fall **off** [*not* off of] the piano.

OK, O.K., okay   All three forms are acceptable in informal writing. In academic writing, try to express meaning more specifically:

- The weather was **satisfactory** [*not* okay] for the race.

on account of   Wordy; use *because* or *because of*:

- **Because of** [*not* On account of] the high humidity, paper jams in the photocopier.

percent, percentage   Use *percent* with specific numbers: *two percent, 95 percent*. Use *percentage* when descriptive words accompany amounts that have been expressed as percentages:

- About **47 percent** of the eligible U.S. population votes regularly; but when presidential elections are excluded, the **percentage** [*not* percent] of voters in the population drops sharply.

plus   Nonstandard as a substitute for *and*:

- The band will do three concerts in Hungary, **and** [*not* plus] it will tour Poland for a month.

Nonstandard as well as a substitute for *also, in addition, moreover*:

- **Also** [*not* Plus], it may be booked to do one concert in Vienna.

precede, proceed   *Precede* means "go before"; *proceed* means "advance, go on, undertake, carry on":

- **Preceded** by elephants and tigers, the clowns **proceeded** into the tent.

pretty Informal qualifying word; use *rather, quite, somewhat,* or *very* in academic writing:

- The flu epidemic was **quite** [*not* pretty] severe.

principal, principle *Principle* means "a basic truth or rule." As a noun, *principal* means "chief person; main or original amount"; as an adjective, *principal* means "most important":

- During assembly, the **principal** said, "A **principal** value in this society is the **principle** of free speech."

raise, rise *Raise* (*raised, raised, raising*) needs a direct object; *rise* (*rose, risen, rising*) does not take a direct object. Using these verbs interchangeably is nonstandard:

- What if the mob **rises** [*not* raises] up and runs amok?

rarely ever Informal; in academic writing, use *rarely* or *hardly ever*:

- The groups **rarely** [*not* rarely ever] meet, so they **hardly ever** interact.

real, really Nonstandard intensifiers.

reason is because Redundant; use *reason is that*:

- One **reason** we moved away **is that** [*not* is because] we changed jobs.

reason why Redundant; use either *reason* or *why*:

- I still do not know the **reason that** [or **I still do not know why,** *not* the reason why] they left home.

regarding, concerning, in regard to, with regard to Too stiff or wordy for most writing purposes; use *about, concerning,* or *for*:

- What should I do **about** [*not* with regard to] dropping this course?

respective, respectively The adjective *respective* relates the noun it modifies to two or more individual persons or things; the adverb *respectively* refers to a second set of items in a sequence established by a preceding set of items:

- After the fire drill, Dr. Pan and Dr. Moll returned to their **respective** offices [that is, each to his or her office] on the second and third floors, **respectively**. [Dr. Pan has an office on the second floor; Dr. Moll has an office on the third floor.]

Do not confuse *respective* and *respectively* with *respectful* and *respectfully*, which refer to showing regard for or honor to something or someone.

right Colloquial intensifier; use *quite, very, extremely,* or a similar word for most purposes:

- You did **very** [*not* right] well on the quiz.

seen Past participle of *see* (*see, saw, seen, seeing*), *seen* is a nonstandard substitute for the past-tense form, *saw*. As a verb, *seen* must be used with an auxiliary verb:

- Last night, I **saw** [*not* seen] the show that you **had seen** in Florida.

set, sit *Set* (*set, set, setting*) means "put in place, position, put down" and must have a direct object. *Sit* (*sat, sat, sitting*) means "be seated." *Set* is nonstandard as a substitute for *sit*:

- Susan **set** [*not* sat] the sandwiches beside the salad, made Spot **sit** [*not* set] down, and then **sat** [*not* set] on the sofa.

shall, will *Shall* was once used with *I* or *we* for future-tense verbs, and *will* was used with all other persons (*We **shall** leave Monday, and he **will** leave Thursday*); but *will* is commonly used for all persons now.

  Similarly, distinctions were once made between *shall* and *should*. *Should* is much more common with all persons now, although *shall* is used about as often as *should* in questions asking what to do: **Shall** [or **Should**] I get your jacket?

should, would Use *should* to express condition or obligation:

- If you **should** [condition] see them, tell them that they **should** [obligation] practice what they preach.

Use *would* to express wishes, conditions, or habitual actions:

- If you **would** buy a VCR for me, I **would** tape all the football games for you.

sometime, sometimes, some time   The adverb *sometime* means "at an unspecified time"; the adverb *sometimes* means "now and then"; *some time* is as adjective-noun combination meaning "an amount or span of time":

- **Sometime** next year we have to take qualifying exams. I **sometimes** worry about finding **some time** to study for them.

stationary, stationery   *Stationary* means "not moving"; *stationery* refers to paper and related writing products.

such   Informal intensifier; avoid it in academic writing unless it precedes a noun introducing a *that* clause:

- The play got **terrible** [*not* such bad] reviews. It was **such** a dull drama **that** it closed after one performance.

supposed to, used to   The final *d* is essential:

- We were **supposed to** [*not* suppose to] leave early. I **used to** [*not* use to] wake up as soon as the alarm rang.

sure   Nonstandard for *surely* or *certainly*:

- I was **certainly** [*not* sure] surprised at the results.

than, then   *Than* indicates comparison:

- One is smaller **than** [*not* then] two.

Then relates to time:

- I tripped and **then** fell.

that there, them there, this here, these here   Nonstandard for *that, them, this,* and *these,* respectively.

that, which   Use *that* with restrictive (essential) clauses only. *Which* can be used with both restrictive and nonrestrictive clauses; many writers, however, use *which* for nonrestrictive clauses only, using *that* for all restrictive clauses.

- The house **that** [*or* **which**] Jack built is on Beanstalk Street, **which** [*not* that] runs past the reservoir.

their, there, they're   *Their* is a possessive; *there* means "in that place" or is part of an expletive construction; *they're* is a contraction of *they are*:

- **They're** going to **their** accounting class in the building **there** behind the library. **There** are twelve sections of Accounting 101.

theirself, theirselves, themself   Nonstandard for *themselves*.

them   Use as an object pronoun only. Nonstandard for the adjectives *these* or *those*:

- Buy **those** [*not* them] strawberries.

thusly   Nonstandard for *thus*.

till, until   Both are acceptable; except in expressive writing, avoid the contracted form *'til* in academic writing.

to, too, two   *To* is a preposition; *too* is an adverb meaning "also; more than enough"; *two* is the number:

- When you go **to** Chicago, visit the Art Institute. Go **to** Harry Caray's for dinner, **too**. It won't be **too** expensive because **two** people can share an entrée.

toward, towards   Both are acceptable; *toward* is somewhat more common.

try and, sure and   Nonstandard for *try to* and *sure to*:

- If you **try to** [*not* try and] find a summer job, be **sure to** [*not* sure and] list on your résumé all the software programs you can use.

type   Nonstandard for *type of*:

- Use that **type of** [*not* type] glue on plastic.

unique An absolute adjective; do not combine it with *more, most,* or other qualifiers. You might want to use a different adjective:

- Solar heating is **uncommon** [*not* somewhat unique] in the northeast. A **unique** [*not* very unique] heating system in one Vermont home uses hydrogen for fuel.

wait on Informal for *wait for*; appropriate in the context of persons giving service to others:

- I had to **wait** a half hour **for** that clerk to **wait on** me.

where Nonstandard for *that* as a subordinating conjunction:

- I read **that** [*not* where] Michael Jordan is the greatest basketball player ever.

where . . . at Redundant; drop *at*:

- **Where** is your house [*not* house at]?

-wise The suffix *-wise* means "in a manner, direction, or position." Be careful not to attach *-wise* indiscriminately to create new words rather than using good words that already exist. When in doubt, check your dictionary to be sure that a *-wise* word you want to use is acceptable.

your, you're *Your* is a possessive; *you're* is the contraction of *you are*:

- **You're** generous to share **your** Internet time with us.

Terms Glossary

This glossary defines important terms used in your *Quick Access Reference for Writers*. Terms printed throughout the book in SMALL CAPITAL LETTERS are defined here. Many of these glossary entries include parenthetical references to the handbook section(s) where the specific term is most fully discussed.

absolute phrase   A phrase containing a subject and a participle that modifies an entire sentence: *The semester* [subject] *being* [present participle of *be*] *over, the campus looks deserted.* (**G2.d**)

abstract noun   A noun that names things not knowable through the five senses: *idea, respect.* (**G1.a**)

action verb   A verb that describes an action or occurrence done by or to the subject.

active voice   An attribute of verbs showing that the action or condition expressed in the verb is done by the subject, in contrast with the *passive voice*, which conveys that the action or condition of the verb is done *to* the subject. (**G3.f**)

adjective   A word that describes or limits (modifies) a noun, a pronoun, or a word group functioning as a noun: *silly, three.* (**G8, F3.b**)

adjective clause   A dependent clause also known as a *relative clause.* An adjective clause modifies a preceding noun or pronoun and begins with a relative word (such as *who, which, that,* or *where*) that relates the clause to the noun or pronoun it modifies. Also see *clause.* (**G2.e**)

adverb   A word that describes or limits (modifies) verbs, adjectives, other adverbs, phrases, or clauses: *loudly, very, nevertheless, there.* (**G8, F3.c**)

adverb clause   A dependent clause beginning with a subordinating conjunction that establishes the relationship in meaning between the adverb clause and its independent clause. An adverb clause modifies the independent clause's verb or the entire independent clause. Also see *clause, conjunction*. (**G8, QA Box 39**)

agreement   The required match of number and person between a subject and verb (**G4**) or between a pronoun and antecedent (**G5**). A pronoun that expresses gender must match its antecedent in gender also.

analogy   An explanation of the unfamiliar in terms of the familiar. Like a simile, an analogy compares things not normally associated with each other; but unlike a simile, an analogy does not use *like* or *as* in making the comparison (**E4.e**). Analogy is also a rhetorical strategy for developing paragraphs (**W4.f**).

analysis   A process of critical thinking that divides a whole into its component parts in order to understand how the parts interrelate (**T2**). Sometimes called *division*, analysis is also a rhetorical strategy for developing paragraphs (**W4.f**).

antecedent   The noun or pronoun to which a pronoun refers. (**G5–G7**)

antonym   A word opposite in meaning to another word.

APA style   Guidelines developed by the American Psychological Association (APA) for preparing and documenting papers. (**A1–A2**)

appositive   A word or group of words that renames a preceding noun or noun phrase: *my favorite month,* **October**. (**G2.c**)

argument   A rhetorical attempt to convince others to agree with a position about a topic open to debate. (**W5.b**)

articles   Also called *determiners* or *noun markers*, articles are the words *a, an,* and *the. A* and *an* are indefinite articles, and *the* is a definite article. Also see *determiner*. (**G1.e, F2**)

assertion   A statement. In the process of developing a thesis statement, an assertion is a sentence that makes a statement and expresses a point of view about a topic. (**W1.f**)

audience   The readers to whom a piece of writing is directed. (**W1.a**)

auxiliary verb   Also known as a *helping verb,* an auxiliary verb is a form of *be, do, have, can, may, will,* and others, that combines with a main verb to help it express tense, mood, and voice. Also see *modal auxiliary verb.* (**G3.b**)

base form   See *simple form.*

bibliography   A list of information about sources. (**A1.a, A2, A3.a, A4**)

brainstorming   Listing all ideas that come to mind on a topic, and then grouping the ideas by patterns that emerge. (**W1.e**)

case   The form of a noun or pronoun in a specific context that shows whether it is functioning as a subject, an object, or a possessive. In modern English, nouns change form in the possessive case only (*city* = form for subjective and objective cases; city's = possessive-case form). Also see *pronoun case.* (**G7**)

cause and effect   The relationship between outcomes (effects) and the reasons for them (causes). Cause-and-effect analysis is a rhetorical strategy for developing paragraphs. (**W4.f, T2.d, QA Box 16**)

chronological order   Also called *time order,* an arrangement of information according to time sequence; an organizing strategy for sentences, paragraphs, and longer pieces of writing. (**W.4f**)

citation   Information to identify a source referred to in a piece of writing. Also see *documentation.* (**R3, M, A**)

clause   A group of words containing a subject and a predicate. A clause that delivers full meaning is called an *independent* (or *main*) *clause.* A clause that lacks full meaning by itself is called a *dependent* (or *subordinate*) *clause.* Also see *adjective clause, adverb clause, nonrestrictive element, noun clause, restrictive element.* (**G2.e**)

cliché   An overused, worn-out phrase that has lost its capacity to communicate effectively: *flat as Kansas, ripe old age.* (**E4.f**)

climactic order   Sometimes called *emphatic order,* climactic order is an arrangement of ideas or information from least important to most important. (**W.4f**)

clustering An invention technique based on thinking about a topic and its increasingly specific subdivisions; also known as *mapping* and *webbing*. (**W1.e**)

coherence The clear progression from one idea to another using transitional expressions, pronouns, selective repetition, and/or parallelism to make connections between ideas. (**W4.e**)

collective noun A noun that names a group of people or things: *family, committee.* (**QA Box 18, G4.f, G5.d**)

comma fault See *comma splice.*

comma splice The error that occurs when only a comma connects two independent clauses. (**C2**)

common noun A noun that names a general group, place, person, or thing: *dog, house.* (**QA Box 18**)

comparative The form of a descriptive adjective or adverb that expresses a different degree of intensity between two: *bluer, less blue; more easily, less easily.* Also see *positive, superlative.* (**G8.d**)

comparison and contrast A rhetorical strategy for organizing and developing paragraphs by discussing a subject's similarities (comparison) and differences (contrast). (**W.4f**)

complement An element after a verb that completes the predicate, such as a direct object after an action verb or a noun or adjective after a linking verb. Also see *object complement, subject complement, predicate adjective, predicate nominative.* (**G2.c, QA Box 27**)

complete predicate See *predicate.*

complete subject See *subject.*

complex sentence See *sentence types.*

compound predicate See *predicate.*

compound sentence See *sentence types.*

compound subject See *subject.*

concrete noun   A noun naming things that can be seen, touched, heard, smelled, or tasted: *smoke, sidewalk*. (**QA Box 18**)

conjunction   A word that connects or otherwise establishes a relationship between two or more words, phrases, or clauses. Also see *coordinating conjunction, correlative conjunction*, and *subordinating conjunction*. (**G1.h**)

conjunctive adverb   An adverb that creates a relationship, such as of addition, contrast, comparison, result, time, or emphasis, between words. (**QA Box 22**)

connotation   Ideas implied by a word; connotations convey associations such as emotional overtones beyond a word's direct, explicit definition. (**E4.b**)

coordinate adjectives   Two or more adjectives that equally modify a noun (***big, friendly** dog*). The order of coordinate adjectives can be changed without destroying meaning. Also see *cumulative adjectives*. (**P2.d**)

coordinating conjunction   A conjunction that joins two or more grammatically equivalent structures: *and, or, for, nor, but, so, yet*. (**QA Box 23**)

coordination   The use of grammatically equivalent forms to show a balance or sequence of ideas. (**QA Box 23, E2.a**)

correlative conjunction   A pair of words that joins equivalent grammatical structures, including *both . . . and, either . . . or, neither . . . nor, not only . . . but also*. (**G1.h**)

count noun   A noun that names items that can be counted: *radio, street, idea, fingernail*. (**QA Box 18, F1, F2.a–b**)

critical response   Formally, an essay summarizing a source's central point or main idea and then presenting the writer's synthesized reactions in response. (**T3.c**)

cumulative adjectives   Adjectives that build up meaning from word to word as they get closer to the noun (***familiar rock tunes***). The order of cumulative adjectives cannot be changed without destroying meaning. Also see *coordinate adjectives*. (**P2.d**)

dangling modifier   A modifier that attaches its meaning illogically, either because it is closer to another noun or pronoun than to its true subject or because its true subject is not expressed in the sentence. (**C4.d**)

declarative sentence   A sentence that makes a statement: *Sky diving is exciting.* Also see *exclamatory sentence, imperative sentence, interrogative sentence.*

deduction   The process of reasoning from general claims to a specific instance. (**T2.e, QA Box 17**)

definite article   See *article.*

denotation   The dictionary definition of a word. (**E4.b**)

dependent clause   A clause that cannot stand alone as an independent grammatical unit; also called *subordinate clause.* Also see *adjective clause, adverb clause, noun clause.* (**G2.e**)

descriptive adjective   An adjective that describes the condition or properties of the noun it modifies and (except for a very few, such as *dead* and *unique*) has comparative and superlative forms: *flat, flatter, flattest.*

descriptive adverb   An adverb that describes the condition or properties of whatever it modifies and that has comparative and superlative forms: *happily, more happily, most happily.*

determiner   A word or word group, traditionally identified as an *adjective*, that limits a noun by telling "how much" or "how many" about it. Also called *expressions of quantity, limiting adjectives,* or *noun markers.* (**QA Box 21, F1.b, F2**)

diction   Word choice. (**E4**)

direct discourse   In writing, words that repeat speech or conversation exactly and so are enclosed in quotation marks. Also see *indirect discourse.* (**C3.d**)

direct object   A noun or pronoun or group of words functioning as a noun that receives the action (completes the meaning) of a transitive verb. (**G2.b, G3.c**)

direct question   A sentence that asks a question and ends with a question mark: *Are you going?*

direct quotation   See *quotation*.

discovery draft   See *drafting*.

documentation   The acknowledgment of someone else's words and ideas used in any piece of writing by the giving of full and accurate information about the person whose words were used and about where those words were found; for example, for a print source, documentation usually includes author name(s), title, place and date of publication, and related information. (**R2.c–e, R3, M, A**)

documentation style   Any of various systems for providing information about the source of words, information, and ideas quoted, paraphrased, or summarized from some source other than the writer. Documentation styles discussed in this handbook are MLA, APA, CM, and CBE. (**M, A**)

double negative   A nonstandard negation using two negative modifiers rather than one. (**G8.b**)

draft   See *drafting*.

drafting   A part of the writing process in which writers compose ideas in sentences and paragraphs; the documents produced by drafting are often called *drafts*. A *discovery draft* is an early, rough draft. (**W2**)

edited American English   English language use that conforms to established rules of grammar, sentence structure, punctuation, and spelling; also called *standard English*. (**E4.d**)

editing   A part of the writing process in which writers check a document for the technical correctness of its grammar, spelling, punctuation, and mechanics. (**W3.e–f, QA Box 7**)

elliptical construction   A sentence structure that deliberately omits words that are expressed elsewhere or words that can be inferred from the context.

euphemism   Language that attempts to blunt certain realities by speaking of them in "nice" or "tactful" words. **(E4.g)**

evidence   Facts, data, examples, and opinions of others used to support assertions and conclusions. **(T2.c)**

exclamation   A word or words expressing strong feeling and ending in an exclamation point.

exclamatory sentence   A sentence beginning with *What* or *How* that expresses strong feeling: *What a ridiculous statement!*

expletive   The phrase *there is (are)*, *there was (were)*, *it is*, or *it was* at the beginning of a clause, changing structure and postponing the subject: *It is Mars that we hope to reach* (compare *We hope to reach Mars*).

faulty predication   A grammatically illogical combination of subject and predicate. **(C3.3)**

first person   See *person*.

freewriting   Writing nonstop for a period of time to generate ideas by free association of thoughts. *Focused freewriting* may start with a set topic or may build on one sentence taken from earlier freewriting. **(W1.e)**

fused sentence   The error of running independent clauses together without the required punctuation that marks them as complete units. **(C2)**

future perfect progressive tense   The form of the future perfect tense that describes an action or condition ongoing until some specific future time: *I will have been talking*.

future perfect tense   The tense indicating that an action will have been completed or a condition will have ended by a specified point in the future: *I will have talked*.

future progressive tense   The form of the future tense showing that a future action will continue for some time: *I will be talking*.

future tense   The form of a verb, made with the simple form and either *shall* or *will*, expressing an action yet to be taken or a condition not yet experienced: *I will talk.*

gender   Concerning languages, the classification of words as masculine, feminine, or neuter. In English, a few pronouns show changes in gender in third-person singular: *he, him, his; she, her, hers; it, its, its.* A few nouns naming roles change form to show gender difference: *prince, princess,* for example. **(E5)**

gender-neutral language   See *sexist language.*

gerund   A present participle functioning as a noun: *Walking is good exercise.* Also see *verbal.*

gerund phrase   A gerund, along with its modifiers, and / or object(s), which functions as a subject or an object. **(G2.d)**

helping verb   See *auxiliary verb.*

homonyms   Words spelled differently that sound alike: *to, too, two.* **(S1.b)**

idiom   A word, phrase, or other construction that has a different meaning from its usual or literal meaning: *He lost his head. She hit the ceiling.*

illogical predication   See *faulty predication.*

imperative mood   The mood that expresses commands and direct requests, using the simple form of the verb and often implying but not expressing the subject, *you: Go.* **(G3.e)**

imperative sentence   A sentence that gives a command: *Go to the corner and buy me a newspaper.*

indefinite article   See *article, determiner.*

indefinite pronoun   A pronoun, such as *all, anyone, each,* and others, that refers to a nonspecific person or thing. **(G4.d, G5.c)**

independent clause   A clause that can stand alone as an independent grammatical unit. **(G2.e)**

indicative mood   The mood of verbs used for statements about real things or highly likely ones: *I think Grace is arriving today.* **(G3.e)**

indirect discourse   Reported speech or conversation that does not use the exact structure of the original and so is not enclosed in quotation marks. **(C3.d)**

indirect object   A noun or pronoun or group of words functioning as a noun that tells to whom or for whom the action expressed by a transitive verb was done. **(G2.b)**

indirect question   A sentence that reports a question and ends with a period: *I asked if you are going.*

indirect quotation   See *quotation.*

induction   The reasoning process of arriving at general principles from particular facts or instances. **(T2.e, QA Box 17)**

infinitive   A verbal made of the simple form of a verb and usually, but not always, *to,* that functions as a noun, adjective, or adverb.

infinitive phrase   An infinitive, its modifiers, and/or object, which functions as a noun, adjective, or adverb.

informal language   Word choice that creates a tone appropriate for casual writing or speaking. **(E4.d)**

informative writing   Writing that gives information and, when necessary, explains it; also known as *expository writing.*

intensive pronoun   A pronoun that ends in *-self* and that intensifies its antecedent: *Vida **himself** argued against it.* **(QA Box 19)**

interjection   An emotion-conveying word that is treated as a sentence, starting with a capital letter and ending with an exclamation point or a period: *Oh! Ouch!*

interrogative pronoun   A pronoun, such as *whose* or *what,* that implies a question: *Who called?* **(QA Box 19)**

interrogative sentence   A sentence that asks a direct question: *Did you see that?*

intransitive verb   A verb that does not take a direct object. (**G2.b, G3.c**)

invention techniques   Ways of gathering ideas for writing. (**W1.e**)

inverted word order   In contrast to standard order, the main verb or an auxiliary verb comes before the subject in inverted word order. Most questions and some exclamations use inverted word order. (**E3.e**)

irony   Using words to imply the opposite of their usual meaning. (**E4.e**)

irregular verb   A verb that forms the past tense and past participle in some way other than by adding *-ed* or *-d*. (**G3.a**)

jargon   A particular field's or group's specialized vocabulary that a general reader is unlikely to understand. (**E4.g**)

levels of formality   The degree of formality of language, reflected by word choice and sentence structure. A highly formal level is used for ceremonial and other occasions when stylistic flourishes are appropriate. A medium level, which is neither too formal nor too casual, is acceptable for most academic writing. (**E4.d**)

limiting adjective   See *determiner*.

linking verb   A main verb that links a subject with a subject complement that renames or describes the subject. Linking verbs convey a state of being, relate to the senses, or indicate a condition. (**QA Box 27, QA Box 31**)

literal meaning   What is stated by words. (**T1.b**)

logical fallacies   Flaws in reasoning that lead to illogical statements. (**T2.f**)

main clause   See *independent clause.*

main verb   A verb that expresses action, occurrence, or state of being and that shows mood, tense, voice, number, and person.

mapping   See *clustering*.

mechanics   Conventions governing matters such as the use of capital letters, italics, abbreviations, and numbers. **(S2–S6)**

metaphor   A comparison implying similarity between two things; a metaphor does not use words such as *like* or *as*, which are used in a simile and which make a comparison explicit: *a mop of hair* (compare the simile *hair like a mop*). **(E4.e)**

misplaced modifier   Describing or limiting words that are wrongly positioned in a sentence so that their message either is illogical or relates to the wrong word(s). **(C4)**

mixed construction   A sentence that unintentionally changes from one grammatical structure to another, incompatible one, thus garbling meaning. **(C3.e)**

mixed metaphors   Incongruously combined images. **(E4.e)**

MLA style   Guidelines developed by the Modern Language Association (MLA) for preparing and documenting papers. **(M)**

modal auxiliary verb   A group of auxiliary verbs that add information such as a sense of needing, wanting, or having to do something or a sense of possibility, likelihood, obligation, permission, or ability. **(F6)**

modifier, modify   A word or group of words functioning as an adjective or adverb to describe or limit (modify) another word or word group. **(G8, E3.d)**

mood   The attribute of verbs showing a speaker's or writer's attitude toward the action by the way verbs are used. English has three moods: imperative, indicative, and subjunctive. Also see *imperative mood, indicative mood, subjunctive mood*. **(G3.e)**

noncount noun   A noun that names "uncountable" things: *water, time*. **(F1, F2)**

nonessential element   See *nonrestrictive element*.

nonrestrictive element   A descriptive word, phrase, or dependent clause that provides information not essential to understanding the basic message of the element it modifies; it is therefore set off by commas. Also see *restrictive element*. (**P2.e**)

nonsexist language   See *sexist language.*

nonstandard   Language usage other than edited American English. Also see *edited American English*. (**E4.d**)

noun   A word that names a person, place, thing, or idea. Nouns function as subjects, objects, or complements. (**G1.a, G2.b–c**)

noun clause   A dependent clause that functions as a subject, object, or complement. (**G2.e**)

noun complement   See *complement.*

noun determiner   See *determiner.*

noun phrase   A noun along with its modifiers functioning as a subject, object, or complement. (**G2.d**)

number   The attribute of some words indicating whether they refer to one (singular) or more than one (plural). (**F1**)

object   A noun, pronoun, or group of words functioning as a noun or pronoun that receives the action of a verb (direct object); tells to whom or for whom something is done (indirect object); or completes the meaning of a preposition (object of a preposition). (**G2.b**)

object complement   A noun or adjective renaming or describing a direct object after certain verbs, including *call, consider, name, elect,* and *think*: *I call **joggers** [object] **fanatics** [object complement].*

objective case   The case of a noun or pronoun functioning as a direct or indirect object or object of a preposition or of a verbal. A few pronouns change form to show case (*him, her, whom*). Also see *case*. (**G7**)

paragraph   A group of sentences that work together to develop a unit of thought. (**W4**)

paragraph development   Using specific, concrete details (RENNS) to support a generalization in a paragraph; rhetorical strategies for arranging and organizing paragraphs. (**W4.d**)

parallelism   The use of equivalent grammatical forms or matching sentence structures to express equivalent ideas. (**E3.a**)

paraphrase   A restatement of someone else's ideas in language and sentence structure different from that of the original. (**R3.d**)

parenthetical documentation   See *parenthetical reference.*

parenthetical reference   Information enclosed in parentheses following quoted, paraphrased, or summarized material from another source to alert readers to the use of the material from that source. Parenthetical references and a list of bibliographic information about each source used in a paper document the writer's use of sources. (**M1.a–b** [MLA], **A1.b** [APA])

participial phrase   A phrase that contains a present participle or a past participle and any modifiers and that functions as an adjective. Also see *verbal.*

participle   A verb form. See *past participle, present participle.*

passive construction   See *passive voice.*

passive voice   The form of a verb in which the subject is acted upon; if the subject is mentioned in the sentence, it usually appears as the object of the preposition *by: I was frightened by the thunder* (compare the active-voice version *The thunder frightened me*). The passive voice emphasizes the action, in contrast to the active voice, which emphasizes the doer of the action. (**G3.f**)

past participle   The third principal part of a verb, formed in regular verbs by adding *-d,* or *-ed* to the simple form, as with the past tense. In irregular verbs, it often differs from the simple form and the past tense: *break, broke, broken.* (**G3.a, QA Box 32**)

past perfect progressive tense   The past perfect tense form that describes an ongoing condition in the past that has been ended by something stated in the sentence: (*Before the curtains caught fire,*) *I had been talking.*

past perfect tense   The tense that describes a condition or action that started in the past, continued for a while, and then ended in the past: *I had talked*.

past progressive tense   The past tense form that shows the continuing nature of a past action: *I was talking*.

past-tense form   The second principal part of a verb, in regular verbs formed by adding *-d* or *-ed* to the simple form. In irregular verbs, the past tense may change in several ways from the simple form. (**G3.a**)

perfect tenses   The three tenses—the present perfect (*I have talked*), the past perfect (*I had talked*), and the future perfect (*I will have talked*)—that help to show complex time relationships between two clauses. (**G3.d**)

person   The attribute of nouns and pronouns showing who or what acts or experiences an action. *First person* is the one speaking (*I, we*); *second person* is the one being spoken to (*you, you*); and *third person* is the person or thing spoken about (*he, she, it; they*). All nouns are third person.

personal pronoun   A pronoun that refers to people or things; *I, you, them, it*.

persuasive writing   Writing that seeks to convince the reader about a matter of opinion. (**W5.b**)

phrasal verb   A verb that combines with one or more prepositions to deliver its meaning: *ask out, look into*. (**F4.b**)

phrase   A group of related words that does not contain a subject and predicate and thus cannot stand alone as an independent grammatical unit. A phrase can function as a noun, verb, or modifier. (**G2.d**)

plagiarism   A writer's presenting another person's words or ideas without giving credit to that person. Documentation systems allow writers to give proper credit to sources in ways recognized by scholarly communities. Plagiarism is a serious offense, a form of intellectual dishonesty that can lead to course failure or expulsion. (**R3**)

planning   An early part of the writing process in which writers gather ideas. Combined with shaping, planning is sometimes called *prewriting*. (**W1**)

plural   See *number*.

positive   The form of an adjective or adverb when no comparison is being expressed: *blue, easily*. Also see *comparative, superlative*. (**G8.d**)

possessive case   The case of a noun or pronoun that shows ownership or possession. Also see *case*. (**P6.a–b**)

predicate   The part of a sentence that contains the verb and tells what the subject is doing or experiencing or what is being done to the subject. A *simple predicate* contains only the main verb and any auxiliary verb(s). A *complete predicate* contains the verb, its modifiers, objects, and other related words. A *compound predicate* contains two or more verbs and their objects and modifiers, if any. (**G2.a**)

predicate adjective   An adjective used as a subject complement: *That tree is **leafy***.

predicate nominative   A noun or pronoun used as a subject complement: *That tree is a **maple***.

preposition   A word that conveys a relationship, often of space or time, between the noun or pronoun following it and other words in the sentence. The noun or pronoun following a preposition is called its *object*. (**G1.g. F4, F5.a**)

prepositional phrase   See *phrase, preposition*.

present participle   A verb's *ing* form. Used with auxiliary verbs, present participles function as main verbs (**G3.a**). Used without auxiliary verbs, present participles function as nouns or adjectives (**G1.d**).

present perfect progressive tense   The present perfect tense form that describes something ongoing in the past that is likely to continue into the future: *I have been talking*.

present perfect tense   The tense indicating that an action or its effects, begun or perhaps completed in the past, continue into the present: *I had talked.*

present progressive tense   The present-tense form of the verb that indicates something taking place at the time it is written or spoken about: *I am talking.*

present tense   The tense that describes what is happening, what is true at the moment, and what is consistently true. It uses the simple form (*I talk*) and the *s* form in the third person singular (*he, she, it talks*). (**G3.a**)

prewriting   A term for all activities in the writing process before drafting. (**W1**)

primary sources   "First-hand" work: write-ups of experiments and observations by the researchers who conducted them; taped accounts, interviews, and newspaper accounts by direct observers; autobiographies, diaries, and journals; expressive works (poems, plays, fiction, essays); also known as *primary evidence.* Also see *secondary sources.* (**R2.a–b**)

principle parts   Verb forms. (**G3.a**)

progressive forms   Verb forms made, in all tenses with the present participle and forms of the verb *be* as an auxiliary. Progressive forms show that an action, occurrence, or state of being is ongoing. (**G3.d**)

pronoun   A word that takes the place of a noun and functions in the same ways that nouns do. Types of pronouns are demonstrative, indefinite, intensive, interrogative, personal, reciprocal, reflexive, and relative. The word (or words) a pronoun replaces is called its antecedent. (**G1.b, G5–G7**)

pronoun–antecedent agreement   The match required between a pronoun and its antecedent in number and person, and for personal pronouns, in gender as well. (**G5**)

pronoun case   The way a pronoun changes form to reflect its use as the agent of action (subjective case), the thing being acted upon (objective case), or the thing showing ownership (possessive case). (**G7**)

pronoun reference   The relationship between a pronoun and its antecedent. (**G6**)

proofreading   Reading a final draft to find and correct any spelling or mechanics mistakes, typing errors, or handwriting illegibility; the final step of the writing process. (**W3.g**)

proper adjective   An adjective formed from a proper noun: *Victorian, American.*

proper noun   A noun that names specific people, places, or things; it is always capitalized: *Rob Reiner, Buick.*

purpose   The goal or aim of a piece of writing: to express oneself, to provide information, to persuade, or to create a literary work. (**W1.a**)

quotation   Repeating or reporting another person's words. *Direct quotation* repeats another's words exactly and encloses them in quotation marks. *Indirect quotation* reports another's words without quotation marks except around any words repeated exactly from the source. Both direct and indirect quotation require documentation of the source to avoid plagiarism. Also see *indirect discourse.* (**R3, P7.a**)

reciprocal pronoun   The pronouns *each other* and *one another,* referring to individual parts of a plural antecedent: *We respect each other.*

References   In many documentation styles, including APA, the title of a list of sources cited in a research paper or other written work. (**A2, A4**)

reflexive pronoun   A pronoun that ends in *-self* and that reflects back to its antecedent: *They claim to support **themselves**.*

regular verb   A verb that forms its past tense and past participle by adding *-ed* or *-d* to the simple form. Most English verbs are regular. (**G3.a**)

relative adverb   An adverb that introduces an adjective clause: *The lot **where I usually park my car** was full.*

relative clause   See *adjective clause.*

relative pronoun   A pronoun, such as *who, which, that, who, whom, whoever,* and a few others, that introduces an adjective clause or sometimes a noun clause.

restrictive clause   A dependent clause that gives information necessary to distinguish whatever it modifies from others in the same category. In contrast to a nonrestrictive clause, a restrictive clause is not set off with commas. (**P2.e**)

restrictive element   A word, phrase, or dependent clause that provides information essential to the understanding of the element it modifies. In contrast to a nonrestrictive element, a restrictive element is not set off with commas. Also see *nonrestrictive element.* (**P2.e**)

revising, revision   A part of the writing process in which writers evaluate their rough drafts and, on the basis of their assessments, rewrite by adding, cutting, replacing, moving, and often totally recasting material. (**W3.a–d**)

rhetoric   The area of discourse that focuses on arrangement of ideas and choice of words as a reflection of the writer's purpose and sense of audience.

rhetorical strategies   In writing, various techniques for presenting ideas to deliver a writer's intended message with clarity and impact. Reflecting typical patterns of human thought, rhetorical strategies include arrangements such as chronological and climactic order; stylistic techniques such as parallelism and planned repetition; and patterns for organizing and developing writing such as description and definition. (**W4**)

run-on (run-together) sentence   See *fused sentence.*

second person See *person*.

secondary source A source that reports, analyzes, discusses, reviews, or otherwise deals with the work of someone else, as opposed to a primary source, which is someone's original work or first-hand report. A reliable secondary source should be the work of a person with appropriate credentials, should appear in a respected publication or other medium, should be current, and should be well-reasoned. (**R2**)

sentence See *sentence types*.

sentence fragment A portion of a sentence that is punctuated as though it were a complete sentence. (**C1**)

sentence types A grammatical classification of sentences by the kinds of clauses they contain. A *simple sentence* consists of one independent clause. A *complex sentence* contains one independent clause and one or more dependent clauses. A *compound-complex sentence* contains at least two independent clauses and one or more dependent clause. A *compound sentence* contains two or more independent clauses joined by a coordinating conjunction. Sentences are also classified by their grammatical function; see *declarative sentence, exclamatory sentence, imperative sentence,* and *interrogative sentence*. (**G2.f**)

sexist language Language that unfairly or unnecessarily assigns roles or characteristics to people on the basis of gender. Language that avoids gender stereotyping is called *gender-neutral* or *nonsexist language*. (**E5**)

simile A comparison, using *like* or *as*, of otherwise dissimilar things. (**E4.e**)

simple form The form of the verb that shows action, occurrence, or state of being taking place in the present. It is used in the singular for first and second person and in the plural for first, second, and third person. It is also the first principal part of a verb. The simple form is also known as the *dictionary form* or *base form*. (**G3.a**)

simple predicate See *predicate*.

simple sentence   See *sentence types*.

simple subject   See *subject*.

simple tenses   The present, past, and future tenses, which divide time into present, past, and future. (**G3.d**)

singular   See *number*.

slang   Coined words and new meanings for existing words, which quickly pass in and out of use; inappropriate for most academic writing. (**E4.d**)

source   A book, article, document, other work, or person providing information.

split infinitive   One or more words coming between the two words of an infinitive. (**C4.c**)

standard English   See *edited American English*.

standard word order   The most common order for words in English sentences: The subject comes before the predicate.

subject   The word or group of words in a sentence that acts, is acted upon, or is described by the verb. A *simple subject* includes only the noun or pronoun. A *complete subject* includes the noun or pronoun and all its modifiers. A compound subject includes two or more nouns or pronouns and their modifiers. (**G2.a**)

subject complement   A noun or adjective that follows a linking verb, renaming or describing the subject of the sentence; also called a *predicate nominative*. (**G2.c**)

subjective case   The case of the noun or pronoun functioning as subject. Also see *case*.

subject–verb agreement   The required match between a subject and verb in expressing number and person. (**G4**)

subjunctive mood   The verb mood that expresses wishes, recommendations, indirect requests, speculations, and conditional statements: *I wish you **were** here.* (**G3.e**)

subordinate clause   See *dependent clause.*

subordinating conjunction   A conjunction that introduces an adverbial clause and expresses a relationship between the idea in it and the idea in the independent clause. (**QA Box 24, E2.c**)

subordination   The use of grammatical structures to reflect the relative importance of ideas. A sentence with logically subordinated information expresses the most important information in the independent clause and less important information in dependent clauses or phrases. (**E2.c–d**)

suffix   An ending added to a basic (root) word to change function or meaning.

summary   An extraction of the main message or central point of a passage or other discourse; a critical thinking activity preceding synthesis. (**T3.a, R3.e**)

superlative   The form of an adjective or adverb that expresses comparison among three or more things: *bluest, least blue, most easily, least easily.* (**G8.d**)

synonym   A word that is close in meaning to another word. (**E4.a**)

synthesis   A component of critical thinking in which material that has been summarized, analyzed, and interpreted is connected to what is already known (one's prior knowledge). (**T3.b–c**)

tag question   An inverted verb–pronoun combination, added to the end of a sentence and creating a question, that "asks" the audience to agree with the assertion in the first part of the sentence: *You know what a tag question is,* **don't you?** A tag question is set off from the rest of the sentence with a comma. (**P2.f**)

tag sentence   See *tag question.*

tense   The time at which the action of the verb occurs: in the present, the past, or the future. (**G3.d**)

tense sequence   In sentences that have more than one clause, the accurate matching of verbs to reflect logical time relationships. (**G3.d, QA Box 33**)

thesis statement   A statement of an essay's central theme that makes clear the main idea, the writer's purpose, the focus of the topic, and perhaps the organizational pattern. (**W1.f, W3.b**)

third person   See *person*.

tone   The writer's attitude toward his or her material and reader, especially as reflected by word choice. (**E4.d**)

topic   The subject of discourse.

topic sentence   The sentence that expresses the main idea of a paragraph. (**W4.c**)

transition   The connection of one idea to another in discourse. Useful strategies for creating transitions include transitional expressions, parallelism, and planned repetition of key words and phrases. (**W4.e**)

transitional expressions   Words and phrases that signal connections among ideas and create coherence. (**W4.e, QA Box 10**)

transitive verb   A verb that must be followed by a direct object. (**G3.c**)

unity   The clear and logical relationship between the main idea of a paragraph and the evidence supporting the main idea. (**W4.b**)

usage   A customary way of using language. (**Usage Glossary**)

valid   A term applied to a deductive argument when the conclusion follows logically from the statements that create the terms of the argument. Validity describes the structure of an argument, not its truth. (**T2.e**)

verb   A class of words that show action or occurrence or that describe a state of being. Verbs change form to show time (tense), attitude (mood), and role of the subject (voice). Verbs occur in the predicate of a clause and can be in verb phrases, which may consist of a main verb, any auxiliary verbs, and any modifiers. Verbs can be described as transitive or intransitive depending on whether they take a direct object. (**G1.c, G3**)

verb phrase   A main verb, along with any auxiliary verb(s) and any modifiers.

verbal   A verb part functioning as a noun, adjective, or adverb. Verbals include infinitives, present participles (functioning as adjectives), gerunds (present participles functioning as nouns), and past participles. (**G1.d**)

verbal phrase   A group of words that contains a verbal (an infinitive, participle, or gerund) and its modifiers. (**G2.d**)

voice   An attribute of verbs showing whether the subject acts (active voice) or is acted upon (passive voice). (**G3.f**)

Works Cited   In MLA documentation style, the title of a list of all sources cited in a research paper or other written work. (**M2**)

writing process   Stages of writing in which a writer gathers and shapes ideas, organizes material, expresses those ideas in a rough draft, evaluates the draft and revises it, edits the writing for technical errors, and proofreads it for typographical accuracy and legibility. The stages often overlap. (**W**)

Index

Page numbers in ***boldface italic*** type identify Usage Glossary entries. (ESL) identifies material of special interest to speakers of English as a second language.

INDEX
page 335 INDEX

Graphics
  APA citation style for, 228–29
  CM citation style for, 254
  MLA citation style for, 211
Group authors
  APA citation style for, 228, 236
  CBE citation style for, 258
  CM citation style for, 248
  MLA citation style for, 195, 205

H

Hasty generalization, 41–42
have, of, **289**
have got, have got to, **289**
hear, here, 159
Helping verbs. *See* Auxiliary verbs
Historical periods, capitalizing, 168
hole, whole, 159
Homonyms, 307
  list of, 157–61
hopefully, **290**
human, humane, 159
Hyperbole, 121
Hyphens, 162–64
  at end of line, 162
  with prefixes, 162–63
  in spelled-out numbers, 164, 173
  with suffixes, 162–63
  in typed papers, 149

I

Ideas for writing
  brainstorming, 4
  clustering (mapping), 5
  freewriting, 4
  gathering, 3–5
  journals, 3–4
  mapping (clustering), 5
  questions, asking and answering, 4–5
  shaping, 2
Idioms, 307
ie, ei rule of spelling, 156–57
if, whether, **290**
Illogical coordination, 109–10
Illogical (faulty) predication, 99, 307
Illogical subordination, 111–12
Imperative mood, 68, 97, 307
Imperative sentences, 307
imply, infer, **290**
Incomplete sentences. *See* Sentence fragments
incredible, incredulous, **290**
Indefinite articles. *See* Articles; Determiners
Indefinite pronouns, 48, 96, 143, 307. *See also* Pronoun(s)
  as determiners, 50
  pronoun–antecedent agreement, 77
  subject–verb agreement, 72–73
Independent clauses, 10, 98, 110–11, 128–29, 135–36
  comma spliced or fused, 94–95
  defined, 307
  recognizing, 57
  semicolon between, 138–39

Online Research Basics

Computers can put you in touch with experts in any field you can think of. On the World Wide Web alone, you can find more than 15 million information sites, so online research may seem overwhelming.

In this section, you can learn some basics about finding, evaluating, and documenting source material from the Internet, especially sources you can get to through the World Wide Web. In practice, you will likely use both online and print sources for many papers that draw on outside sources. For a general picture of research, see **R** Research Writing. The information there applies to doing research—research using online sources, print sources, or both.

Finding Online Sources

If you know the general subject you are going to research, a good way to start narrowing it is to browse in a subject directory. A **subject directory** lists topics and links them to related resources. One useful subject directory is *Librarians' Index to the Internet.* (Its **URL**, or Internet address, is <http://sunsite.berkeley.edu/InternetIndex/>.)* It groups subjects by categories as well as in one alphabetical list. Clicking on a subject produces a list of titles of Internet "resources" on that subject. Each resource title is a link to that resource.

Suppose you are at the alphabetical list in *Librarians Index*, and you click on the subject *Ballooning.* One resource is listed: "Balloon Pages on the World Wide Web." Clicking on this title takes you to the "resource," a Web page listing titles of 224 Web sites about ballooning. These titles are grouped into three categories: Round the World Attempts (6 titles), New on the List (25 titles), and Published Before (193 titles). Each of these titles is also a link to its Web site. Reading through the titles, you can see that the sites range from "Unicorn Balloon Company of Arizona and Colorado" to "The European Museum of Balloons and Airships" to "Norm and Tia's Balloon Pages" to "NOAA Profiler—Wind Profiles Data Display." Visiting a few of the sites may help you to focus on an aspect of ballooning to write about.

! Alert: (1) Do not do online research by finding one site and then simply following its links. The person who created the site has chosen the links, and you have no way of knowing whether you will get complete and unbiased information on the topic by following the

*Notice the angle brackets (< >) around the URL. Angle brackets are one conventional way to distinguish a URL that is given in a sentence. They enclose the URL but are not part of it, **so leave the angle brackets out when you enter a URL to get to an Internet location.**

links. Create your own path when you do online research. (2) As a general browsing rule, ignore material with silly or personal titles ("Norm and Tia's Balloon Pages," for example). Although you are browsing, it's important to stay focused. If a source with a silly title has information valuable to your research, you will encounter it again during a key word search (described below).

Subject directories give you a way to browse subjects and start narrowing a subject. You can find addresses for subject directories at the end of this section.

Once you narrow your subject, you can use key word searches. **Key word searches** use a "search engine" to scan and list various Internet sources for the word(s) you specify. Key word searches can deliver focused information because you can frame searches to look for subtopics such as "weather balloons," "recreational ballooning," or "model balloon making hobby." A key word search on a large subject, however, yields too many items to go through. A search on *ballooning*, for example, yielded 10,229 "hits," or links to Web sites containing the one word.

One popular key word search engine, Alta Vista, can search the Web and Usenet (news groups, where group members post messages on a subject of common interest). Alta Vista (URL <http://altavista.digital.com>) permits you to tailor very specific searches based on the key words you select and the ways you connect them. Alta Vista's opening screen, like that of other search engines, shows you how to get help framing your key words for simple or advanced searches.

Other routes to Internet resources combine features of subject directories and key word searches. That is, they list a group of categories such as Business and Economy, News, or Science, any one of which you can click on and then do a key word search. Or you can do a key word search of all categories.

As you discover information that interests you during an online search, frame an assertion and keep refining it into a thesis statement (see **W1.f**), making it increasingly specific. The key words in your assertions and preliminary thesis statement(s) are likely to be good key words for searches.

Alert: As soon as you finish reading any online source that you think you may want to use, follow these steps: (1) Print it out. (2) If the URL does not print out on the document, write it **clearly and carefully** on the hard copy. Be scrupulously careful about punctuation marks, especially hyphens, underscores, and periods. (3) Staple or paper-clip the pages together. (4) If you can, "bookmark" each source so that you can get back to it easily. (5) Take down complete information so that you can document the source correctly; see **R2.c, R2.d, M2.b, A2.b, A3a.b, A4.b,** and **pages 358-59**. Because handwritten URLs are harder to read than typed ones, you may want to keep this bibliographic information about your sources in a computer file.

Here are URLs for useful and easy-to-use subject directories and search engines:

SUBJECT DIRECTORIES (general and academic)

Librarians' Index to the Internet
http://sunsite.berkeley.edu/InternetIndex/

Infomine
http://lib-www.ucr.edu

Internet Public Library
http://ipl.sils.umich.edu

SEARCH ENGINES

Alta Vista (not organized by subjects)
http://altavista.digital.com

Infoseek (organized by subject areas Arts & Entertainment, Business & Finance, Computers & Internet, Education, Government & Politics, Health & Medicine, Living, News, Reference)
http://guide.infoseek.com

Yahoo (organized by subject areas Arts, Business and Economy, Computers and Internet, Education, Entertainment, News, Recreation and Sports, Reference, Regional, Science)
http://www.yahoo.com

Evaluating Online Sources

As soon as you start online research, check whether your school has guidelines for evaluating online sources. Many schools provide checklists that can help you decide whether an online source is worth using.

Here are some questions to help you evaluate online sources. Some Internet sources, particularly those associated with educational, scientific, and cultural institutions, are well-known and widely recognized. You can evaluate them according to the guidelines in **QA Box 15** and **QA Box 50**. Others, especially personal communications such as e-mail and news group messages and personal Web pages, require special care if you are to establish them as authoritative and reliable.

GUIDELINES FOR EVALUATING ONLINE SOURCES

Evaluating Authority

1   Is an author named? Are credentials listed for the author? (Look for an academic degree, an e-mail address at an academic or

other institution, a credentials page, a list of publications. The last part of an e-mail address can be informative: .edu is an address at an educational site, .gov is an address at a government site, and .com is an address at a commercial or business site.)

2 Is the author recognized as an authority in reputable print sources?

3 Do you recognize the author as an authority from other online research into your subject? (For example, for a paper on ballooning, you might learn from your online research that Bob Martin, who is written about on the Dymocks Flyer Web page, is a ballooning authority, a fact that you might not be able to verify in print sources.)

Evaluating Reliability

4 Do you detect bias or an unbalanced presentation?

5 Why does the information exist? Who gains from it? Why was it written? Why was it put on the Internet? Are you asked to take action of any kind? (If yes, the source is likely to be an advocate for a point of view or a particular stance and thus subjective or even biased.)

6 Is the material dated? Is the date recent? When was the last update?

7 Does the author give an e-mail address for questions or comments?

8 Are the links active, authoritative, and reliable?

Evaluating Value

9 Does the material contribute anything to your knowledge about the subject?

10 Is there anything in this source material that you cannot find elsewhere? (If you're not sure what exists "elsewhere," ask a librarian, and check out these other research routes.)

Documenting Online Sources

Using online sources in your work is exactly the same as using print sources. You have the same obligation to document any use you make of others' work in your own papers; see **R3**. In **M** MLA Documentation and **A** APA Documentation, you can find models for documenting online sources as described by the Modern Language Association and the American Psychological Association. These two groups have recently endorsed forms for documenting online sources. On page 358, you can find models for such sources in MLA style. On page 359 you can find models for similar sources in APA style.

Online: E-Mail--MLA--NEW

Thompson, Jim. "Bob Martin's Address." E-mail to June
    Cain. 11 Nov. 1997.

Online: Article from a Newspaper on the Web--MLA--NEW

Lewis, Ricki. "Chronobiology Researchers Say Their Field's
    Time Has Come." Scientist 9.24 (1995): p. 14. 30
    Dec. 1997 <http://www.the-
    scientist.library.upenn.edu/yr1995/dec/chrono-
    951211.html>.

**Online: Interview from a Magazine on the Web with a Print Version--MLA--
NEW**

Kincaid, Jamaica. Interview. "Jamaica Kincaid Hates Happy
    Endings." By Marilyn Snell. Mother Jones. Sept.-
    Oct. 1997, 15 Jan. 1998 <http://www.mojones.com/
    mother_jones/SO97/snell.html>.

Online: Article from a Journal Available Only on the Web--MLA--NEW

Anderson, Virginia. "The Usual Suspects." Computers,
    Writing, Rhetoric and Literature 2.1 (1996): 25
    pars. 15 Jan. 1998
    <http://www.cwrl.utexas.edu/~cwrl/v2nl/v.anderson/an
    derson.html>.

Online: Organization Home Page--MLA--NEW

"LEARN@PZ." Project Zero. Home page. Harvard Graduate
    School of Education. 17 Jan. 1998
    <http://pzweb.harvard.edu/default.htm>.

Online: Personal Home Page--MLA--NEW

Hunter-Kilmer, Melissa. Home page. 15 Feb. 1996. 17 Jan.
    1998
    <http://www.idsonline.com/userweb/phantom/index.htm>.

Online: FTP Site--MLA--NEW

Beck, Alan. "Glass, a Fractal fig." 2 July 1994. Archive
    ftp.sunet.se. Swedish University Network SUNET. 13
    Jan. 1998
    <ftp://ftp.sunet.se/pub/pictures/fractals/>.

Online: Gopher Site--MLA--NEW

"Petshop." Transcribed by Bret Shefter 18 Mar. 1986, rev.
    Malcolm Dickinson 3 Apr. 1986. From Monty Python's
    Flying Circus and And Now for Something Completely
    Different. The Monty Python Gopher. 13 Jan. 1998
    <gopher://gopher.ocf.berkeley.edu//00.Library/Monty_
    Python/pershop%09%09%2B>.

Online: Article from a Newspaper on the Web--APA--NEW

Lewis, R. (1995, December 11). Chronobiology researchers
    say their field's time has come. The Scientist, p.
    14 [On-line newspaper]. Retrieved December 30, 1997
    from the World Wide Web: http://www.the-
    scientist.library.upenn.edu/yr1995/dec/chrono_951211
    .html

Online: Article from a Jornal or Magazine on the Web--APA--NEW

Broydo, L. (1998, January 13-18). The clean cleaner cover-
    up. Mother Jones, January/February 1998. Mother
    Jones the Mojo Wire. [Magazine, selected stories
    on-line]. Retrieved January 15, 1998 from the World
    Wide Web:
    http://www.mojones.com/mother_jones/JF98/homeplanet.
    html

Online: Announcement Posted on the Web--APA--NEW

National Institute of Mental Health. (1997, May 15).
    Mammalian clock gene closed. [Press release posted
    on the World Wide Web]. Bethesda, MD: Author.
    Retrieved December 30, 1997 from the World Wide
    Web: http://www.nimh/gov/events/prnorth.htm

Online: Material from an FTP Site--APA--NEW

Beck, A. (1994, July 2). Glass, a fractal gif. [On-line
    graphic]. Swedish University Network SUNET.
    Retrieved January 17, 1998:
    ftp://ftp.sunet.se/pub/pictures/fractals/

Online: Material from a Gopher Site--APA--New

The undertaker. (1986, May 40). [On-line script].
        Retrieved September 13, 1997:
        gopher://gopher.ocf.berkeley.edu//00.Library/Monty_
        Python/undertaker

Capsule Contents